Wiltshire Record Society

(formerly the Records Branch of the Wiltshire
Archaeological and Natural History Society)

VOLUME 51

FOR THE YEAR 1995

Impression of 500 copies

THE APPRENTICE REGISTERS OF

THE WILTSHIRE SOCIETY

1817 - 1922

EDITED BY

H.R. HENLY

TROWBRIDGE

1997

ISBN 0 901333 28 X

Produced for the Society by
Salisbury Printing Company Ltd, Salisbury
Printed in Great Britain

CONTENTS

PREFACE

The documents upon which this edition is based are the property of the Wiltshire Society, and are deposited in the Wiltshire Record Office (WRO 1475/1-4). They have been calendared by kind permission of the Chairman of the Wiltshire Society, and the Wiltshire County Archivist, Mr S.D. Hobbs.

Mr Henly, the editor of this volume, wishes to express his thanks for their co-operation and help to Mr Hobbs and the staff of the Wiltshire Record Office; Miss Jean Horsfall, the Chairman, and Governors of the Wiltshire Society; Mrs Pamela Colman, Sandell Librarian, Wiltshire Archaeological and Natural History Society; and Mr Michael Marshman and the staff of the Wiltshire Local Studies Library.

JOHN CHANDLER

ABBREVIATIONS

WA&NHS Wiltshire Archaeological and Natural History Society, Devizes
WRO Wiltshire Record Office, Trowbridge
WT Wiltshire Tracts (in WA&NHS Library)

INTRODUCTION

THE HISTORY OF THE SOCIETY

The Wiltshire Society, as its name implies, was a society of Wiltshiremen. Established at least as early as the first year of Cromwell's Protectorate, it was formally named the Wiltshire Society, but was more frequently referred to as the Wiltshire Feast, arising from the practice of holding an annual fund-raising dinner in London. Gentlemen who were natives of Wiltshire, living in London, Wiltshire and elsewhere, first attended a sermon (the Feast) preached by a Wiltshireman, and then a banquet. After their dinner they subscribed their quota towards the apprenticing of some poor Wiltshire child or another charitable cause directed at the native poor of Wiltshire. The little that is known of the history of this early society has been dealt with elsewhere.[1] It appears that it had ceased to function by the start of the nineteenth century.

The modern Wiltshire Society, with whose records this volume is concerned, was formed in May 1817 and is still carrying out its charitable work today. The records of apprenticeships, contained in two volumes covering the period from 1838 to 1958, have been deposited in the Wiltshire Record Office. The whereabouts of the corresponding records for the period 1817 to 1838 are not known; records for the period 1958 to the present day are held by the Society. The contents of the two deposited apprenticeship registers form the basis of the records contained in this volume.

The first meeting of the modern Wiltshire Society was held on 14th May 1817 at the Albion Tavern, Aldersgate Street, in the City of London. Sir Bernard Hobhouse, Bart, MP, was in the chair, and, according to a report in the *Salisbury and Winchester Journal*,[2] 'At 4.0 pm a numerous and highly respectable company sat down to dinner consisting of everything the season afforded'. This initial meeting had been preceded by several notices in the same newspaper announcing the venue. Although the *Times* newspaper carried neither a report of this inaugural meeting, nor any advertisements for it, the *Gentleman's Magazine*[3] reported the inaugural meeting thus:

> Wednesday May 14, 1817. A public meeting of Noblemen and Gentlemen of Wiltshire was held this day at the Albert Tavern, for the purpose of forming an institution, the object of which is to apprentice the children of the deserving poor belonging to the county of Wiltshire, residing in London, who might otherwise be destitute of the means of acquiring a comfortable subsistence through life. The company dined together; after which several sums were contributed, and a Committee formed to carry the resolutions of the meeting into effect.

The *Salisbury and Winchester Journal* reported the proceedings at some length, including a lengthy speech by Sir Benjamin Hobhouse, who emphasised that the aims of the new society were to be the same as those of the Somersetshire Society; namely to: 'enable the children of the poor of the county of Wilts, residing in London, to be taught habits of industry before vice has gained an ascendancy in their minds, and the means of a comfortable subsistence through life'. Other speakers at this inaugural meeting were Thomas Calley, MP for Cricklade, Philip Hurd Esq, of The Temple, Edward Frowd the Treasurer (*pro tempore*), and the Duke of Somerset, who agreed to be patron. Undoubtedly these gentlemen were among the committee formed to set up the first meeting.

The First Annual Report of the Society, under the patronage of the Duke of Somerset, was reported in the *Devizes and Wiltshire Gazette*.[4] This report contained a summary of the objects of the Society which were decided at the inaugural meeting:

> The object of the Wiltshire Society is to raise a fund by donations and by annual subscriptions, for the purpose of apprenticing the children of poor Wiltshire parents, resident in London, or within the Bills of Mortality;[5] and also for lending to such as shall be so apprenticed, if their conduct shall have been meritorious, a certain sum of money at the expiration of their apprenticeship, to establish them in business.

The Fourth Annual meeting of the Society was held on 12th May 1820 at the same venue, the Albion House Tavern. A notice in the *Devizes and Wiltshire Gazette*[6] announced the forthcoming meeting. It named Thomas G. Estcourt, MP, as the chairman, and listed the following as stewards: Ambrose Awdry, Esq; John Pearse, Esq, MP; Rev W.L. Bowles; Edward Phillips, Esq; T.C. Estcourt, Esq, MP; Charles Lewis Phipps, Esq; Richard Debary, Esq; William Salmon, Esq; Richard Hetley, Esq; Dr Stoddart; Robert Isherwood, Esq; Ernley Warriner, Esq; E.B. Kemble, Esq; William Pole Tylney Long Wellesley, Esq; Henry Merewether, Esq. Tickets for the meeting were a guinea, and could be obtained from the stewards or from John Britton, Hon. Secretary, of Burton Cottage, Burton St, Tavistock Square.

The same newspaper[7] carried a report of the meeting which opened:

> In drawing the attention of our readers to the fourth Public Meeting of this excellent Institution, the last of which took place in May 1819, we venture to predict, that as the objects of the charity become understood and duly appreciated, so will the list of subscriptions be increased, and the patrons augmented. The benevolent object of this Society is to raise a fund by donations and subscriptions, for the purpose of apprenticing the children of poor Wiltshire parents, resident in London: and in furtherance of this object, two youths have been apprenticed during the last year, and the sum of £12 10s. paid to the masters with each, in compliance with the rules of the Society, which thus becomes the foster parent to the friendless, conducting the deserving and zealous youth into a path by which he may travel to prosperity, rescuing him from the evils of idleness and vice, and affording him a fair opportunity of becoming a useful and valuable member of the community. To countenance and give effect to an Institution like this, several gentlemen, about 120 in number, met together to dine, on Friday last, at the Albion Tavern, Aldersgate Street, embracing most of the principal gentlemen resident in, or connected with, the county of Wilts.

The report goes on to detail the events of the evening which, after the meal, was taken up with a succession of speeches and toasts. The reponse by John Britton, the Hon. Secretary, to a toast to him proposed by the chairman T. G. Estcourt Esq. MP, contains a clue to the beginnings of the Society:

> The zealous Secretary then adverted to, and lamented the absence of Sir Benjamin Hobhouse, to whose excellent advice and influence was primarily indebted for its first meeting, and to whom this, as well as many other charitible institutions were under great and lasting obligations. - Though serious indisposition prevented the worthy Baronet's

presence on this occasion, Mr Britton could assure the company, that his mind would be actively awake to the proceedings of the day, and to the flattering prospects held out by this numerous and effective meeting.

The earliest surviving annual report (1823) states that:

The Committee have to report, that since the last Anniversary, four additional children have been admitted as Apprentices under this Institution; and that the petitions of other Candidates, are now under their consideration. They have been enabled by the continued support of the Friends of the Charity, to purchase a further sum of £200, 3½ per cent; so that the realized fund of the Society at present consists of 4 per cent Stock (£1029 5s.0d.); 3½ per cent do. (£300 0s.0d.); in the Banker's Hands (£27 0s.0d.).

As the Committee conceive, that the objects of the Society can only be effectually secured, by means of a permanent fund, independent of incidental contributions, they entreat the Friends of the Institution, in order to compass that end, not to relax in their efforts which have hitherto been so successfully exerted.

The yield on the above investment was of the order of £50 per annum, and it was this sum which determined the number of placements. At that date the Society had fourteen boys in the course of their apprenticeships and three further candidates listed. Only two of these boys were actually placed. At 1996 values the stated investment funds of the Society would have been approximately £54,000.[8] The list of governors and contributors numbered 269, and included many notable names from Wiltshire and the surrounding counties. From the list of apprentices it is clear that the first apprentice was actually placed in January 1819.

The president for 1823 was Sir John Dugdale Astley, Bart, MP for Wiltshire, and the committee comprised: Thomas Aston, jun, Esq; Joseph Pitt jun, Esq; William G. Hayter, Esq; Thomas Poynder jun, Esq; James Harding, Esq; Joseph Pullen, Esq; Robert Isherwood, Esq; George Reed, Esq; E.B. Kemble, Esq; Francis Newman Rogers, Esq; Edward Montagu, Esq; Robert Sutton, Esq; John Britton, Esq, FSA (Hon. Secretary); Philip Hurd, Esq (Treasurer). The laws and regulations as agreed in 1817 were also included in the prospectus for 1823, and indeed for each succeeding year of publication; these are reproduced as Appendix A.

Originally the stated aim of the Society was the apprenticing of children resident in London, but in 1859 the rules were changed to admit children resident in Wiltshire. In the Annual Report for 1860 the Committee remarked on this change in the rules:

The Committee refer with pleasure to the election, in April last, of a candidate, resident in the County of Wilts, who became eligible in consequence of the altered rule of the Society. It happens that only one County Candidate came forward, although the Committee had so arranged to elect two, having for that object increased the number of Apprentices from ten to eleven. They now feel doubly entitled to exhort the County subscribers to greater efforts in aid of the Charity, so as to augment the number of County Apprentices.

The number of apprentices to be elected was fixed each year according to the available funds. Seven apprentices were to be taken from residents in London or within the Metropolitan Board of Works, originally defined as the 'Limits of the Bills of Mortality'. The remainder were to be taken either from London or the county of Wiltshire. Applications were received by the Society in January of each year and the

Committee examined each candidate. The application was often prepared by a solicitor and supported by references from the local vicar, or the child's teacher, as to his or her suitability for an apprenticeship.

One such application has been unearthed in a Wiltshire solicitor's collection. The candidate was Frank Biggs (**665**) and the petition was made by his mother Sarah Biggs, (formerly Sarah Holder of Lacock). The parents were living in Holloway, north London, but their petition was made through the Calne solicitor Edward R. Henly.[9] The petition listed the other children in the family and the parents' total means, and it was accompanied by copies of the mother's birth and marriage certificates, and the son's birth certificate. It was a necessary condition that a candidate was born within wedlock.

Details of successful candidates, together with copies of their respective claims, were then forwarded to each governor, who could exercise one or more votes for candidates determined by his qualification. A subscription entitled a governor to one vote for each candidate to be elected. Every additional donation, subscription, or payment that a governor made entitled him to additional votes. Two of these candidate lists have survived in a parish chest, and they make interesting genealogical reading. For example the following, from the 1852 list:

> Bath, Edward (**205**); son of Thomas and Esther Bath. attained age 14 Sept 1851. Father born at Box and served his time to Mr. Tho. Shell of that place - is unable to depend on his trade in the winter months - mother who is ailing (was formerly Esther Tyler of Atworth).

and from the 1855 list:

> Dawson, Joseph William (**244**); son of Joseph and Caroline Dawson. attained age 14 Aug 1854. Parents kept a Coffee-shop in New St., Brompton, which enables them to maintain their children but not to apprentice them. Candidate conducted himself well at the National school and received awards for good conduct. Mother (formerly Caroline Beauchamp) is from West Dean.

The list of successful candidates was published in April of each year, and apprenticeship to suitable masters followed quickly after that. Payment to a master was made in two equal parts. The first moiety was paid on execution of the apprenticeship indentures; the second was paid at mid-term in the apprenticeship, after receipt by the Society of a certificate from the master to the effect that the apprentice was still in his employ, and all was proceeding according to plan. It is clear from the annotations in the apprentice registers that the Secretary, or other officers of the Society, visited apprentices at their work-place. Often an apprentice was moved to another master for a variety of reasons. For example the apprentice may have found himself in the wrong trade, as in the case of Henry Lay Smith (**364**) of Collingbourne Ducis, who was apprenticed to James Rawlings of that place, carpenter and machinist. In October 1873 he was re-apprenticed to William Carter of East Stratton (Hants), tea grocer.

Often the master was declared bankrupt or, on one or two occasions, was found unsuitable. In this latter event an order was obtained from a magistrate for the indenture to be cancelled, and the apprentice was placed elsewhere. At all times the Society acted in the best interests of the apprentice. There were several cases of apprentices absconding. Sometimes it was to seek employment before the completion of their apprenticeship whilst in others the family emigrated and the apprentice went with them. There are at least two instances where the apprentice died, one by drowning, but the circumstances were not reported.

The sum available for each apprentice was limited in 1860 to between £20 and £30, and indeed this sum had not changed significantly by 1914. Furthermore, the Society could lend up to £60 free of interest, for a maximum period of four years, to any apprentice who, on completion of his apprenticeship, wanted capital in order to set up in business. The apprenticeship term varied between one and seven years to a wide variety of trades in London and Wiltshire.

Unlike its predecessor, the Society met only once a year for a formal presentation of its accounts, the nomination of its President, and election of the Honorary Secretary and the Treasurer; and of course to enjoy an annual dinner. During the year the governors of the Society met to conduct its business, that is to elect apprentices from the applications placed before them.

By the 1880s the nature of society itself was changing and the Wiltshire Society was quick to adapt to this changing world. It was accepted that a candidate might wish to become a seaman, and a payment would be made by the Society in lieu of an apprenticeship. Some apprentices were attending night-classes at the School of Science and Art, in South Kensington. As encouragement to these students, awards of £1, £2 and £5 could be made by the committee for success in examinations. The year 1880 saw the introduction of two exhibitions (i.e., scholarships) - one for 'Town' and one for 'County' (Wiltshire) candidates - each not to exceed £40, to meet the fees for attendance full-time at the School of Science and Art at South Kensington, or other schools approved by the committee. The Annual report for 1881 contained the following:

> In April last, twenty Candidates presented themselves for election as apprentices, viz, eight from town and twelve from the county; of these seven of the former and four of the latter were elected by the Governors. The unsuccessful Candidates will be eligible for election next year.
>
> For the Town Exhibition one Candidate only presented himself, William Davis Thomas **(509)**, at present apprenticed to Messrs. Newton and Triggs, Clapham, Carpenters and Joiners. He has obtained at the night schools of Science and Art, Battersea, a second-class certificate for success in Practical Plane and Solid Geometry, and also second-class certificate for Building, Construction, and Drawing, and is about to commence study at King's College, London.
>
> For the County Exhibition three candidates presented themselves, and Emily Maud Hale, of Devizes, was elected by a large majority.

The names of only four exhibitioners have been found and are included at the end of the main apprentice list (**A1-A4**).

In 1900 the Committee permitted payments to be made to candidates for the provision of tools rather than for the apprenticeship premium.

As in most spheres of life at that time, the Great War (1914-18) caused a hiatus for the Society, as several of its committee members and the chairman were away on active service. The Annual Report for 1914 records that at the anniversary meeting of the Society on 4th November 1914 the Committee resolved that owing to the absence of the President, Lord Pembroke, on active service at the front there could not be an anniversary on the usual lines, but it would not be abandoned altogether. Colonel Calley, a former President, and Colonel Turnor consented to fill the vacancies on the Committee. The Committee also expressed their fears that the

Society's income would be curtailed by the war. However, the receipts of the Society in the year May 1914 to May 1915 show approximately a 20% increase in total income, which was balanced by a similar increase in payment of first and second apprenticeship moieties.

Many apprentices sought to have their apprenticeships held in abeyance until the end of hostilities to enable them to enlist, and a few forsook such formalities and immediately volunteered at the outbreak of war. The Society maintained a record of those on military service, their distinctions and their deaths, relying largely on letters received from the apprentices or their parents. At the end of the war many apprentices returned to their former employers, some to complete their apprenticeships. In spite of these exigencies the Society continued its work throughout the war period with many younger apprentices working in Government factories. This was summed up in the Annual report of 1920:

> 1. The Committee consider that the Governors may be interested to know that during the Period of the War up to the date of the Armistice eleven and since that date eight grants to Apprentices have been made to approved candidates. Of the former five including two girls apprenticed to Dressmakers, have completed their apprenticeship terms and one has been cancelled on a medical certificate.

> 2. About two-thirds (30) of the apprentices on the Society's books at the outbreak of the War enlisted when of military age, the remaining third being either under age unfit or in one or two cases working with firms under the War Office. Two were killed, a third as the result of wounds and several operations died two years after his discharge, and seven were wounded. Several have returned to complete their apprenticeships under the Government scheme and others have obtained good employment at high wages.

> 3. From the experience gained not only during the War but more especially since its termination the Committee are convinced of the necessity of making speedy grants to approved candidates and of their being empowered – having regard to the general rise in wages, the requirements of the Education Act, etc. – to increase the amount of the grants. With these objects and in view of the expense in the additional cost of printing and postage not only to the Society but also to the friends of candidates which a yearly election in April by voting papers issued to the Governors entails, the Committee are strongly of Opinion that by an alteration in the rules they should be empowered to continue as they have done since August 1914 to make Apprenticeship grants to approved Candidates without delay, whilst reserving the power to have an election by voting papers at any time if the Committee should think it desirable and not in the month of April only as fixed at present by the rules.

This latter change in the rules vested more power in the committee, but enabled a speedier response to be made to applicants. The savings were also significant since the cost of printing, postage etc, amounted to some 10% of the Society's expenditure.[10]

At the Annual General Meeting in 1922, held at the Trocadero restaurant in London, it was reported that the Society had agreed with Wiltshire County Council to make plans for disabled children, and to investigate placing apprentices with farmers. It should be noted here, that the records of the Society show that from its commencement in 1817 several children who were crippled or disabled in some way had been apprenticed, so this was not really an innovation.

At the Annual meeting in 1923 Judge Radcliffe spoke about the difficulties posed by the various Trades Unions who had demanded that Union wage rates be paid to apprentices. This had led to great difficulties in finding masters. Similarly the proposals by Lord Radnor and General Calley some two years earlier to apprentice boys to farmers had met with opposition from the Branch Farmer's Unions in the County, and as a result there had been no progress. Judge Radcliffe concluded by proposing an addition to the rules as an outcome of the difficulties in finding masters. He proposed that in certain cases, where a formal apprenticeship could not be concluded, the Society should make the equivalent sum available to enable the applicant to receive training at a suitable institution. This was agreed by the meeting.

The financial statement at the Anniversary meeting in 1925 reported that £6,526 was held in stock, and receipts, including donations and dividends on stock, totalled £610. Of this £528 was spent on apprenticeship payments and tool grants. At today's values the Stock Holding was worth over £200,000, a healthy improvement over the Society's position in 1823. However the cost of premiums was rising, and the average was now nearer £50.

In 1929 the main preoccupation was concern about the small numbers of apprentices who were attending evening classes. Although the Society was prepared to consider inducements, the lack of facilities was recognised as being the main obstacle in many Wiltshire towns. In that year liaison commenced with the Ministry of Labour and the Board of Education. This situation was addressed by the Wiltshire Education Committee and in 1933 the Chairman was pleased to report:

> Attendance at Evening Classes has considerably improved this year. This is due mainly to the establishment of suitable classes by the Wilts Education Committee both at Warminster and Devizes centres accessible to many of the Society's apprentices. In two cases fees and rail fares were paid by the Society to enable lads to attend the more advanced courses at Bath Municipal College. Full advantage was taken of these classes and the report on both lads was excellent.

It is apparent from the apprentice registers and the annual reports that the Society was always very deeply interested in the progress of its apprentices. An experiment in improving this contact was reported by the Secretary in 1933:

> An experiment has recently been made by the Hon. Secretary in inviting present apprentices and those recently out of their time to a tea held in towns accessible to them. About 14 young men attended at Bradford-on-Avon and about 20 at Warminster. It is hoped to hold further tea parties at Devizes, Marlborough, Chippenham and Swindon. Personal contact is thus made with the young apprentices placed by the Society and the action seems to be appreciated by them. It is pleasing to record in this connection that of the eighteen apprentices who were out of their time during the past twelve months, fifteen remained on with their employers as improvers, two found work elsewhere at their respective trades and only one failed to find work on termination of his apprenticeship.

In more recent times the Society has moved more towards grants for vocational training, with bursaries for study at universities and colleges of higher education and assistance with travel costs. Grants for the purchase of tools, books and even musical instruments are now made.

In 1952 the annual subscription and Life membership donation remained at one guinea and ten guineas respectively, unchanged since 1817.

THE RECORDS OF THE SOCIETY

In 1956 the Secretary of the Society deposited with the Wiltshire Record Office: two apprentice registers, 1830-1903 and 1903-56; a committee minute book, 1903-56; annual reports for 1850, 1882, 1913, 1925, 1929.[11]

The apprentice registers list the apprentice, the date of indenture, name and trade of master, the payment of the apprenticeship fees and a 'Remarks' column, which contains details such as apprentices who had absconded or died, and the action taken when masters were found unsuitable, or were declared bankrupt. Where the apprenticeship term was less than seven years it was noted in this column. Each apprentice was allocated a unique serial number and this has been used as the key reference throughout the calendar.

The survival of a number of the Society's annual reports in the Wiltshire Record Office, the Wiltshire Archaeological and Natural History Society Library,[12] the Wiltshire Local Studies Library, and with the Wiltshire Society,[13] has enabled the information from the apprentice registers to be supplemented in two ways. In many of the lists of children elected for apprenticeship each year, details of the parents' residence, occupation and background are given. Additionally, each report includes a cumulative list of apprentices placed up to that year.

The annual reports listed children who had been elected for an apprenticeship. However it is clear from the apprentice registers that some of these children failed to obtain an apprenticeship. These have been calendared at the end of the main sequence, and allotted numbers **B1-62**.

The apprentice registers contain details of the amount of the premium for each apprenticeship, and the dates on which the two payments were made. The first was paid when the indenture was enacted, and the second halfway through the apprenticeship period. This has been used as a check on the apprenticeship term, which in most cases can be assumed to be seven years unless noted otherwise in the remarks column of the register. On a few occasions this latter information has been found to be in error.

ANALYSIS OF THE APPRENTICESHIP DATA

During the period 1817 to May 1923 the Society apprenticed a total of 1006 children (831 male, 175 female). A further 62 candidates failed to secure apprenticeships. Of these 1006 apprentices, some 650 were placed with masters in the Greater London area. Most of the remainder were placed with masters in Wiltshire. A few were found apprenticeships in Hampshire, Berkshire and Somerset. Two only (**447, 549**) were placed with masters outside this general Wiltshire-London axis, to masters near Manchester and in Brighton.

Almost exclusively girls were apprenticed into dressmaking, millinery, and similar trades. In Wiltshire the approved apprentice master (or mistress) was Sarah Heathcote, dressmaker and milliner, of the Parade, Trowbridge. Between 1875 and 1897 she had ten apprentices placed with her by the Society. In 1895 an Arthur Egington Heathcote was also taking girls for dress-making apprenticeships, and he may well have been a relation. By 1905 Sarah Heathcote's establishment had moved to Bridge

House in Trowbridge, and in 1907 the references are in general to Messrs Heathcote and Co., also at this address.

Similarly in Collingbourne Ducis in 1867 Henry Lay Smith (**364**) was apprenticed to James Rawlings, carpenter and machinist. In 1886 the Society placed George Charles Annetts (**617**) with H. and W. Rawlings, agricultural engineers, who were presumably the successor business to James Rawlings of 1867.

The period covered by this calendar, 1817 to 1922, embraces a time of considerable changes in the nature of society as a whole. It was an age that saw great strides in scientific developments which are in some measure reflected in the trades (and in a few cases professions) followed by the apprentices of the Wiltshire Society.

The 650 apprentices placed with London masters may be assumed to have had either one or both parents of Wiltshire birth, or that the apprentice was born in Wiltshire. In 301 cases there were clear statements that either or both the parents came from Wiltshire, and of these 49 instances gave the mother's maiden name. For example the parents of Eliza Grist (**272**) were John Grist and his wife Jane (nèe Collier), both of Dilton Marsh in Wiltshire. Similarly the parents of James Alexander Frampton (**403**) and John G. Frampton (**273**) were Edmund and Elizabeth Frampton. Their mother was Elizabeth Newham from Britford, Wiltshire.

The individual human stories which these records tell may be set against the overall pattern of Victorian internal migration from rural to urban England deducible from other sources. In 1871, for instance, according to census data,[14] 27,639 Wiltshire natives were living in London and the intra-metropolitan districts of Middlesex, Surrey, and Kent. They represented rather less than 1% of the total metropolitan population of 3.25 million, but in terms of Wiltshire's loss they were far more significant. Wiltshire in 1871 had a population of 257,177, so that for every hundred Wiltshire residents at this date another eleven Wiltshire natives were living in London. Whereas the population of England and Wales quadrupled between 1801 and 1911, Wiltshire's population during the same period increased by only 55%, and between 1841 and 1881 scarcely altered at all, despite the rapid growth of Swindon.

It has been calculated[15] that between 1861 and 1900 nearly two-thirds of Wiltshire natives in the 15-24 age bracket left the county. Most (48% of males and 59% of females) migrated internally within England and Wales, and the remainder (15% of males, 7% of females) emigrated overseas. The higher proportion of female internal migrants (many of whom must have moved to London) is reflected also in census data, which show that female Wiltshire natives in London in 1871 outnumbered males at the ratio of about 6 to 4. This imbalance was paralleled by migrants from other rural counties close to London.[16]

Statistics such as these help to place in perspective the work of the Wiltshire Society, by demonstrating the scale of migration to the capital during the later nineteenth century. Similar figures do not exist before 1851, but the problems which such migration caused, and which the Society was formed to address, clearly existed already by 1817. Indeed, it should be recalled that the nineteenth-century Wiltshire Society was the successor to an earlier Society which provided apprenticeships to the children of Wiltshiremen living in London from the later seventeenth century.

Table 1. Distribution of Apprenticeships over Trade Groups

Trade	Males	Females	Total
Clothing Manufacture, including Shoemaking	92	169	261
Building Trades	214	0	214
Engineering and Metalworking	173	0	173
Furniture Manufacture	120	1	121
Printing and Stationery	65	2	67
Watchmaking, Jewellery, and Goldworking	59	2	61
Food Trades	35	1	36
Household Goods and Services	39	0	39
Medical	6	0	6
Miscellaneous	28	0	28
Totals	831	175	1006

Table 1 analyses the distribution of apprenticeships over some arbitrary trade groupings. It is clear that the majority of girls were apprenticed to the clothing industry, of which the major employer was in dressmaking and millinery. Although boys were apprenticed into the traditional trades of shoemaking and watchmaking, these numbers were far out-weighed by those entering building and engineering trades. This latter showed a considerable up-turn towards the end of the nineteenth century, with the development of mechanised transport and manufacturing processes. The clothing trades were evenly distributed between town and county as were the building trades (see Table 2), while watchmaking, jewellery, and gold-working were almost exclusively town occupations.

Table 2. Distribution of Trade Groupings by Location (Town and County) and by Sex

Trade	Sex	County	Town	Total
Clothing Manufacture, including Shoemaking	M	39	53	92
	F	62	107	169
Building Trades	M	116	98	214
Engineering and Metalworking	M	60	113	173
Furniture Manufacture	M	41	79	120
	F	0	1	1
Printing and Stationery	M	14	51	65
	F	0	2	2
Watchmaking, Jewellery, and Goldworking	M	2	57	59
	F	0	2	2
Food Trades	M	11	24	35
	F	0	1	1
Household Goods and Services	M	12	27	39
Medical	M	0	6	6
Miscellaneous	M	5	23	28
Totals		362	642	1006

Table 3. Decennial Distribution of Apprenticeships by Sex and Location
The numbers of apprentices refer to placements in the decade preceding the year stated; the totals for 1820 and 1930 are for part decades only.

Location	Sex	1820	1830	1840	1850	1860	1870	1880	1890	1900	1910	1920	1930	Total
County	M				1		26	39	34	53	75	48	24	300
	F						1	4	10	13	30	4	0	62
Town	M	1	43	57	68	80	68	81	52	42	29	8	2	531
	F			2	8	19	16	20	22	17	8	1	0	113
Totals		1	43	59	77	99	111	144	118	125	142	61	26	1006

On an aggregate basis the ratio of boys to girls was about 5:1 both for town and county apprentices. However, as Table 3 illustrates, this varied from year to year and was probably as much influenced by numbers of applications as by any deliberate bias.

Table 4. Decennial Distribution of Annual Apprenticeship Premiums by Location and Sex *Premiums are rounded up to whole pounds; totals for decades up to 1820 and up to 1930 are for part decades only; actual expenditure before 1838 is not known.*

Location	Sex	1820	1830	1840	1850	1860	1870	1880	1890	1900	1910	1920	1930	Total
County	M				25		535	815	708	1042	1496	1023	712	6356
	F						20	85	215	260	625	75		1280
Town	M			343	1542	1625	1467	1819	1155	850	752	260	75	11888
	F				178	410	345	445	486	325	165	30		2383
Totals				343	1745	2035	2367	3164	2565	2477	3038	1388	787	21907
Cost per Apprentice		6	23	21	21	22	22	20	21	23	30			

Table 5. Relative Value of Money

	1830	1840	1850	1860	1870	1880	1890	1900	1910	1920	1930	1992
RPI	11.2	12.4	9.5	12.9	12.2	11.5	9.3	9.8	9.8	23.7	13.6	530.9
Relative value	47.2	42.7	55.9	41.2	43.6	46.1	57.2	54.5	54.5	22.4	39.0	1.0

Comparison of the annual premiums (Table 4), with the variation (approximate) of the relative value of money[17] (Table 5), shows that the Society operated in a fairly stable economic climate until the advent of the Great War. Inflation then grew rapidly with prices almost trebling by 1920, but the Society's premiums remained substantially constant numerically, and hence fell in real terms by the same ratio.

The Society reports also register a fall in the number of patrons during this period and into the 1930s.

Examination of individual apprenticeships reveals that the position becomes increasingly difficult to analyse on this gross basis. While many traditional trades took apprentices at the same premiums (numerically) as in the previous century, the newer occupations such as engineering demanded substantially higher premiums in line with the more specialised nature of the training provided and the real costs involved.

It is instructive to make comparisons between the Society and other, similar, apprenticing institutions in Wiltshire at that time. According to the Charity Commissioners' reports, in the mid-nineteenth century there were some 46 endowed charities committed to providing apprenticeships for children. Many of these dated from the late seventeenth century, and often only provided sufficient funds to apprentice one boy every two years or so. The principal Wiltshire charities which offer the closest comparison with the Wiltshire Society were the Devizes Bear Club and the Broad Town Charity.

The Devizes Bear Club dated from 1765 and continued to operate until 1877. Its history and details of its apprentices and subscribers have been described by John Hurley.[18] Apart from the fact that its sphere of interest was restricted to Devizes and the immediate environs, it also differed significantly from the Wiltshire Society in that it provided elementary education for boys from the age of eleven years to fit them for apprenticeship at the age of fourteen.

The Broad Town Charity[19] was an endowed charity established under the terms of the Dowager Duchess of Somerset's will in 1686. This charity provided apprenticeships for boys born and living in Wiltshire, and with special provisions for those from the Duchess's manors of Broad Town, Thornhill, Froxfield, Wootton Rivers and Huish. The income for the trust was derived from rents from these manors and investment of moneys left under her will.

Making exact comparisons between these three charities is limited by the available data. Hurley provides an extract from the annual accounts of the Bear Club for the year 1858, which shows the expenditure on apprenticing but not the numbers apprenticed. Similarly in that year the records of both the Broad Town Charity and the Wiltshire Society (before 1838) enable the number of boys apprenticed to be ascertained but not the cost. The average cost for the Broad Town Charity seems to have been £15 per boy (based upon those records which include the value of the premium) while that for the Wiltshire Society was £20 per child. The average payment for the Bear Club can only be estimated from a statement made in 1833 which suggests a figure of £15.

The higher average premiums paid per child by the Wiltshire Society were probably due to the higher proportion of placements in London rather than Wiltshire at that time. The premiums were substantially higher in both Wiltshire and London than those paid for parish apprentices. This undoubtedly gave the Society considerable clout in choosing masters for their apprentices, and in monitoring the progress of the apprenticeship.

EDITORIAL NOTE

The sequence of entries in this calendar follows the order in which the apprentices were indentured, and hence their appearance in the apprentice registers. The original serial number (**1-1006**) allocated to each apprentice has been retained as the key reference to the individual apprentice. The four candidates identified as exhibitioners, and the sixty-two who failed to gain apprenticeships are calendared after entry **1006**, and have been assigned entry numbers **A1-4** and **B1-62** respectively. These numbers are artificial, and do not appear in the records.

Each entry presents some or all of the following details: serial number/ entry number; apprentice name (surname, forenames); parents' forenames (and surname, if different from apprentice surname); parents' address; master's name; master's occupation; master's address; term of apprenticeship; premium; indenture date. The parents' names and address, where given, have been taken from annual reports; other details, after 1830, derive from the apprentice registers. Supplementary notes, printed in smaller type, follow many entries. These summarize all substantial additional information about the apprenticeship supplied in annual reports. All places are in Wiltshire or London unless otherwise identified.

The rules of the Society as published in the report of 1823 are transcribed as Appendix A. Appendix B is a list of governors and subscribers, 1817-1921, compiled from annual reports. It reads like a court directory of the southern counties and indicates the wide range of patronage enjoyed by the Society over a long period. Appendix C lists the presidents of the Society from 1817 to 1923.

An index (to entry numbers, except where prefixed by p. for page number) combines all personal names, place-names, and names of companies and businesses. There is a second index, of occupations.

The data have been processed using a computer data-base,[20] and a copy of the data[21] in machine-readable form will be deposited with E.S.R.C. Data Archive.

NOTES

1. Henly, H.R., 'The Wiltshire Feast' *Genealogists Magazine*, vol.24 (9), 1994, pp.393-98

2. 26 May 1817.

3. vol.87 (2), 1817, p.79.

4. May 1818

5. Bills of Mortality. The Company of Parish Clerks issued a weekly statement of the numbers of dead and the causes for the City of London and adjoining parishes, from information supplied by its members. The custom prevailed from the 16th century until 1837 when the General Register Office was established, although the Guildhall Library has some up to 1852.

6. 4th May 1820.

7. *Devizes and Wiltshire Gazette*, 18th May 1820.

8. See note 7 and Table 5.

9. WRO 1409/ box A.

10. 1912 Accounts.

11. WRO 1475/1-4

12. WA&NHS Library: bound set of reports for 1840, 1843, 1844, 1846, 1849, 1854, 1864, 1876 1877, 1885, and 1889; reports for 1823 (in WT 104), 1901 (in WT 92), 1914-15 (in WT 116), 1920 (in WT 117), 1929 (in WT 129).

13. Annual reports, held by the secretary of the Wiltshire Society, have been consulted: 1912, 1921, 1925, 1926, 1927, 1930, 1934-1952.

14. *Census of England and Wales, 1871: Population Abstracts*, vol.3, p.24; see also table in *Victoria History of Wiltshire*, vol.4, pp.339-61

15. Baines, Dudley, *Migration in a mature economy: emigration and internal migration in England and Wales, 1861-1900*, 1985, pp.230-1

16. Shannon, H.A., 'Migration and the growth of London, 1841-911/2 *Economic History Review*, vol.5, 1935, pp.79-86 (on p.84)

17. Based on data from E.H.P. Brown and S.V. Hopkins 'Seven centuries of the prices of consumables, compared with builders' wage-rates', *Economica*, vol. 23, 1956, pp. 306-10; and *Monthly Digest of Statistics*.

18. Hurley, John, *The history of the Devizes Bear Club: a social charity and school, 1756-1875*. Wiltshire Family History Society, 1995.

19. Carter, B.J., 'Apprentices of the Broad Town Charity' series of papers in *Wiltshire Family History Society Journal*, nos. 29-33.

20. Microsoft Access V2.0.

21. E.S.R.C. Data Archive, University of Essex, Wivenhoe Park. Colchester. Essex CO4 3SQ

THE APPRENTICE REGISTERS OF THE WILTSHIRE SOCIETY 1817 – 1922

CALENDAR

1 Austin, Job, son of Samuel and Sophia: to Joseph Eveleigh, organ builder, of Swan St, Minories. 12 Jan 1819

Father and mother from Wilton, where they were married April 1791.

2 Britton, Sandys, son of Thomas and Mary: to John Tipson, watch case maker, of Wells St, Stepney. 22 Jan. 1820

Father, a native of Kington, has a wife and four children to maintain, and is reduced to great poverty by failure in business.

3 Barker, Jacob, son of Catherine: to William V. Scotney, haberdasher and hosier, of Newington Causeway. 3 Feb. 1820

Mother, a native of Bulkington, was left a widow with two children, in 1814, in indigent circumstances.

4 Fulford, Thomas, son of William and Theodosia, of Denmark Court, Strand: to George Pigott, printer, of Old St. 30 Nov. 1820

Father, almost blind, from Salisbury, has a wife and six children.

5 Chamberlayne, John, son of John and Frances: to John King, printer, of Thames St. 6 Feb. 1821

Father and mother were married at Salisbury, where they both lived; had three children at the time of petitioning this society; father died before the son was apprenticed, and left his widow and family in very indigent circumstances. Free of the Stationers' Company.

6 Thorne, John, son of John and Mary, of Gould's Hill, Shadwell: to Robert Stanton, citizen and pewterer, of Blackman St, Southwark. 7 Feb. 1821

Father a native of Wanborough, and mother of Castle Eaton; kept a cheesemonger's shop in Broadway, Ludgate Hill, for 18 years, but failed. Have three children. Free of the Pewterers' Company.

7 Field, Joseph, son of William and Mary, of Marshall St: to James Bolam, carver, gilder, etc, of Lower Marsh, Lambeth. 25 Feb. 1821

Parents, from Trowbridge, have nine children; father in a bad state of health, and therefore unable to provide for his family.

8 Collar, Benjamin, son of Posthumus and Mary, of Shoe Lane: to Robert Richardson, currier, of Roll's Buildings, Fetter Lane. 14 Nov. 1821

Father a native of Bradford, with three children, is in the employ of Ive and Burbage, of Fleet St.

9 Bigwood, James, son of John and Elizabeth, of Widegate Alley, Bishopsgate: to Benjamin Dobson, organ builder, citizen and patten maker, of 22 Swan St, Minories. 3 March 1822

Father from Westbury, has a wife and four children.

10 Hillier, James, son of Thomas and Margaret, of Lion St, New Kent Rd: to Samuel Thomas Blowen, fish salesman, citizen and gun maker, of Billingsgate and Long Lane, Bermondsey. 28 March 1822

11 Gayton, Christopher, son of Charles and Catherine: to Francis Charles, engraver, of Charles St, City Rd. 4 June 1822

Father from Hilperton; nine children. Free of the Cutlers' Company.

12 Fricker, Joseph, son of John and Elizabeth, of 10 Parliament St, St George's Market, Southwark. 1 March 1823

Father, from Wingfield, is a shoemaker; five children.

13 Randall, James, son of James and Mary, of Gresse St, Rathbone Place: to John Mellor, boot and shoe maker, of Kentish Town. 26 June 1823

Both parents from Westbury. Father, a spinner but reduced to poverty, has nine children.

14 Dixon, James, son of John and Elizabeth, of Church St, Soho: to Mrs Ann Oaten (late Shave), pastry cook, of Curzon St, Mayfair. 20 June 1823

Parents from Broad Chalke. Father, a journeyman carpenter, has four children.

15 Woodman, Henry, son of James and Elizabeth, of Mitre St, Lambeth: to Frederick Morris, coach joiner and window blind maker, of King St, Holborn. 12 July 1823

Parents from Chippenham, formerly in good circumstances in that town.

16 Reynolds, Edward, son of Edward, of Great James's St, Lisson Green: to John Whitbourne, chair-maker, of Northumberland St, Marylebone. 7 Sept. 1823

Father, a currier, a native of Corsham, was in business at Bradford Has a wife and seven children, neither [*sic*] of whom is enabled at present to earn a livelihood. Parents' home also given as William's Place, Marylebone.

17 Blatch, Frederick, son of Maria: to John Souter, bricklayer, of Exeter St, Chelsea. 23 Jan. 1824

Mother, a widow, a native of Calne.

18 Cook, Charles Arthur, son of Richard Cook, of Castle St, Southwark: to William Clark, plumber and glazier, of Little Guildford St, Southwark. 2 Feb. 1824

Parents from Devizes.

19 Crine, Thomas, son of John Crine, of the New Rd: to Francis Field, hot-presser, of Addle St, Cheapside. 4 Feb. 1824

Father from Broad Chalke.

20 Fulford, Charles, son of William and Theodosia, of Denmark Court, Strand: to John Chamberlain, boot and shoe-maker, of Whitehorse Yard, Drury Lane. 24 April 1824

Son of the parents named in **4**. Father, almost blind, from Salisbury, has a wife and six children.

21 Prior, Charles, son of William and Sarah: to William Ogan, boot and shoe-maker, of Hackney, Middlesex. 30 April 1824

Parents from Trowbridge. Father, a journeyman carpenter, has twelve children.

22 Paxton, James, son of William and Frances, of Cornwell St, St George's in the East: to Robert Cumming, boot and shoe-maker, of Red Lion St, Spitalfields. 15 Nov. 1824

Mother a native of Corsham. Parents reduced to great distress by failure in business.

23 Ayers, William, son of Joseph and Mary, of Durham Place, Chelsea: to John Parton, boot and shoe-maker, of 33 Paradise Row, Chelsea. 7 Feb. 1825

Parents, from Westbury, have six children.

24 Rapson, John, son of Charles and Mary, of Poppin's Court, Fleet St: to John Rackham, coach-maker, of 14 Longacre. 29 April 1825

Parents from Salisbury. Father, a printing compositor, is afflicted with bad health, and has five children.

25 Tibbs, John, son of Diana, of Carpenter's Row, Edgeware Rd: to Thomas Hildersley, turner, of 17 Noel St, Soho. 29 April 1826

Father a native of Amesbury; mother, from Salisbury, was left a widow with four children, two of them deaf and dumb, and one blind.

26 Peirson, Joseph, son of William and Ann, of Hamilton Row, Battle Bridge: to William Hurford, tailor, of 12 Little Guildford St, Russell Square. 1 May 1826

Mother a native of Heytesbury; father a journeyman tailor. They have twelve children living.

27 Roots, James, son of John Corn Roots, of Pell Place, Wellclose Square: to James Tweed, cabinet maker, of 13 Globe Rd, Mile End Rd. 2 May 1826

Father, a journeyman tailor and a native of Salisbury, is lately left a widower with five children.

28 Newman, Henry Adams, son of Elizabeth, of 134 Bishopsgate St: to William Goodbourn, draper, of 7 Paternoster Row, Spital Fields. 7 Feb. 1827

Father, a native of Westbury, left his widow in great distress. Free of the Drapers' Company.

29 Lanham, George Staples, son of John and Ann, of 35 Bow St, Covent Garden: to George James Bennett, hairdresser, of King St, Hammersmith. 1 May 1827

Father a native of Salisbury; mother of Swallowcliffe. They have six children and are in indigent circumstances.

30 White, Thomas, son of James and Ann, of 7 Sheep Lane, Hackney: to John Thompson, painter and glazier, of Holloway. 1 May 1827

Father a native of Wilton; mother of Salisbury. They have five children.

31 Stokes, Joseph William, son of Hannah, of 10 Thomas St, Oxford St: to Edwin White, carver, of 59 Old St. 7 Feb. 1828

Mother is a widow, a native of Bradford; father, of Damerham, left her unprovided for.

32 Bryant, Robert, son of Robert, of 18 Manners' Gardens, Chelsea: to William Patrick Grey, cabinet maker, of 48 Wardour St, Soho. 7 Feb. 1828

Father is a shoemaker, a native of Bradford, and has seven children.

33 Field, John Moor, son of Mary, of Garden Row, London Rd: to Henry Jones, carver and gilder, of 9 Camomile St. 27 March 1828

Mother is a widow, father lately dead. Parents were both from Trowbridge, with nine children. Free of the Shipwrights' Company.

34 Spencer, Ambrose, son of Joseph, of 15 Great Hermitage St: to William Ogan, boot and shoe maker, of Hackney, Middlesex. 14 April 1828

Father, a painter, native of Marlborough, has lost the use of both his hands, and has a wife and five children.

35 Peirson, Henry, son of William and Ann, of Hamilton Row, Battle Bridge: to Thomas Harris, tailor, of 1 Northam's Buildings, Somer's Town. 18 April 1828

Mother a native of Heytesbury; the father a journeyman tailor. They have twelve children living.

36 Hillier, Jesse, son of Thomas and Margaret, of Lion St, New Kent Rd: to Thomas Tucker, fishmonger, of Billingsgate and Waterloo Rd. 18 April 1828

37 Whitmarsh, Charles Awdry, son of Charles, of 14 Sion Square: to Henry Hall, hairdresser, of 57 Marchmont St, Brunswick Square. 9 Feb. 1829

Father, a harness maker, is a native of Amesbury, and has four children; mother and son were born at Marlborough.

38 Peers, George, son of Thomas, of 1 Wellington St, Bethnal Green: to James Stembridge, cooper, of 28 Goswell St. 9 Feb. 1829

Father a cooper. Mother a native of Pewsey, her father having been a farmer there; she has five children.

39 Grant, Edward, son of Hanibal, of 1 Vauxhall Walk: to Doulton and Watts, potters, of Lambeth. 23 March 1829

Father a navigator. Parents are both natives of Rowde.

40 Read, William Henry, son of William, of 9 Garden Walk, Clerkenwell: to William Stocker, tailor and draper, of 66 High St, St Giles. 18 April 1829

Father a rug-maker; mother a native of Bradford, and has very bad health; they have five children.

41 Haines, Charles Seward, son of Daniel, of 120 Eastfield St, Limehouse: to William Syer, cabinet maker, of 12 South St, Finsbury Market. 18 April 1829

Father, a shoemaker, and son are both natives of Warminster. Parents have seven children and are in very reduced circumstances.

42 Clark, Thomas, son of Christiana, of 8 Seymour Row, Euston Square: to James Harmer, plasterer and modeller, of 11 Pitt St, Tottenham Court Rd. 22 July 1829

Mother a widow. Parents were both natives of Box.

43 Marchant, George Cooper, son of Robert, of 8 Popham St, Islington: to Robert Guy Swift, carver and gilder, of 40 Holywell Lane, Shoreditch. 22 July 1829

Father a list shoemaker. Parents are both natives of Bradford, and have six children.

44 Chequer, William Thomas, son of Mary, of 17 Back Church Lane, St George's in the East: to Joseph Cooke, gold beater, of 1 Palatine Place, Commercial Rd. 9 Nov. 1829

Mother a widow. Father, a native of Marlborough, was a whitesmith, and lately died in a lunatic asylum, in extreme distress.

45 Spackman, John, son of Thomas John Savage Spackman, of Great Sutton St, Clerkenwell: to John Richardson, fishmonger, of Shoe Lane and Clapham. 28 Jan. 1830

Mother a native of Aldbourne; father, a dairyman, of Marlborough. They have nine children and an orphan nephew dependent on them. Free of the Fishmongers' Company.

46 Blackford, Robert, son of Jane Blackford (now Newsham), of 10 South Wharf Rd, Paddington: to Edward Burge, boot and shoe maker, of 24 Queen St, Bryanstone Square. 12 March 1830

Mother a native of Swindon; father of Marlborough.

47   Collar, George, son of George, of 8 Adam's St, Manchester Square: to George Griffen, cabinet maker, of 9 Talbot Court, Gracechurch St. 6 July 1830

Father a native of Bradford, has seven children. Free of the Haberdashers' Company.

48   Badham, John Alexander, son of John, of 90 Cromer St: to Thomas Dean, printer, of 40 Threadneedle St. 6 July 1830

Mother, from Cholderton, has a large family, and the father afflicted with rheumatism. Free of the Stationers' Company.

49   Fleming, James: to Thomas Goulden, bricklayer and builder, of Forest Row, Dalston. 19 July 1830

Apprentice is an orphan. Father was a tradesman at Wilton, and mother lately died in distress in London.

50   Reynolds, George Hooper, son of Edward, of William's Place, Marylebone: to Richard Lewis, printer, of 50 Bunhill Row. 7 Feb. 1831

Brother of **16**. Father a native of Corsham.

51   Lane, John Leach, son of James, of 18 Peter St, Soho: to Frederick Stocken, coach maker, of 28 and 29 Little Queen St. 19 April 1831

Father, a harness maker, from Melksham; the mother from Corsham.

52   Roberts, Stephen, son of William, of Hornsey Rd: to Richard Smith, carpenter, of 11 Hull's Terrace, John St, St Luke's. 3 May 1831

Mother a native of Atworth, and has seven children. Free of the Carpenters' Company.

53   Badham, Jane Ann Penelope, daughter of John, of 90 Cromer St: to Mrs. Allsop, milliner and dressmaker, of 274 Regent St. 4 May 1831

Mother, from Cholderton, has a large family; father afflicted with rheumatism [*see* **48**].

54   Swatton, William, son of George, of Artillery Passage: to James Porter, cabinet maker, of 13 Caroline St, Camden Town. 12 July 1831

Father, a furniture broker, from All Cannings, has four children.

55 Cook, George, son of Richard, of Castle St, Southwark: to James Foan, leather pipe and bucket maker, of 23 Short St, Lambeth. 21 Nov. 1831

Brother to **18**. Parents from Devizes.

56 Kendall, Alfred, son of William, of Tothill St: to Joseph Peter Hutt, tin-plate worker, of 105 Goswell St. 6 Feb. 1832

Parents both from Melksham.

57 Pitman, John Miles, son of William Pitman, of George St, Marylebone: to George Buckthorp, gold-beater, of 5 Tabernacle Square. 7 March 1832

Father, a shoemaker, is a native of Bradford, and has five children. Free of the Goldsmiths' Company.

58 Little, Stephen, son of Joanna Little, of Clark's Buildings, St Giles: to William Warman, cooper, of Ball's Pond Rd. 16 April 1832

Mother from Wroughton, and lately left a widow with four children.

59 Hopkins, John, son of Nicholas, of James St, Kennington: to William Hooper, boot and shoe maker, of James St, Kennington. 14 Aug. 1832

Father a native of Westbury, and has nine children.

60 Goodman, James, son of Charles, of 8 Lombard St, Fleet St: to George Forse, chair and cabinet carver, of 18 Tash St, Gray's Inn Lane. 19 Nov. 1832

Father from Trowbridge.

61 White, John, son of Mary, of Macclesfield St: to Luke Broomhead, manufacturing cutler, of Union St East. 11 Dec. 1832

Mother is from All Cannings, and father was a native of Woodborough. He met with an accident which caused his death, and left his widow with seven children, six of whom are now living.

62 Lawrence, Henry Fraser, son of Thomas, of Catherine St, Vinegar Yard, City Rd: to John Draysey, copper-plate printer, of 14 Primrose St, Bishopsgate St. 4 March 1833

Father, a native of Wilton, is lame, and is otherwise afflicted. Free of the Clockmakers' Company.

63 Crine, James, son of John, of the New Rd: to Francis Field, hot presser, of Addle St. 6 March 1833

Brother of **19**. Father from Broad Chalke. Free of the Goldsmiths' Company.

64 Gillmore, Walter, son of Stephen, of Tottenham St: to John Molesworth Thomas, cabinet maker, of 2 Sussex St, London University. 19 April 1833

Father is from Marlborough, and has six children.

65 Spicer, William, son of James and Sarah, of 14 Alfred Court, Paul's Alley, Red Cross St, Cripplegate: to Samuel Allen, cabinet maker, of 5 Prince's St, Barbican. 1 May 1833

Father is from Preshute, and has a family of six children. Free of the Dyers' Company.

66 Fox, Charles Albert Benett, son of Mary Fox, of Little Union St, St George in the East: to John Allum, cork manufacturer, of Vauxhall Walk, Lambeth. 20 Aug. 1833

Father was native of Ebbesbourne, and mother of Salisbury. She is a widow, and has lost the use of her limbs; she has five children.

67 Blanchett, Edward Frederick, son of Sarah, of Furnival's Inn: to John Denham, mathematical instrument maker, of 11 Philip St, Kingsland Rd. 28 Jan. 1834

Father was born at Wootton Bassett, and died in 1827, leaving his widow with four children.

68 Purnell, Abraham, son of Joseph and Mary, of Alfred St, St Dunstan's, Stepney: to George Keyworth, cutler, of Vine St, Piccadilly. 23 April 1834

Mother is from East Knoyle, and has seven children.

69 Lowe, James, son of James and Susanna, of Fleur De Lis Court, Spitalfields: to Cornelius Lawler, stationer, of Old Broad St. 30 May 1834

Mother a native of Bradford. Free of the Farriers' Company.

70 Bond, Thomas, son of Sarah Ann, of New St, Kingsland Rd: to Benjamin Bird, cabinet maker, of New Inn Yard, Shoreditch. 17 Nov. 1834

Mother a widow; father was a native of Marlborough.

71 Todd, Joseph Jee, son of John and Arabella, of 15 Bath St, City Rd: to Charles Roope, linen draper, of Sloane St, Chelsea. 21 Nov. 1834

Mother is from Everleigh, and has six children.

72 Reynolds, John, son of Thomas and Ann, of Singleton St, City Rd: to Henry Kitchingman, fishing rod maker, of Skinner St, Bishopsgate Without. 5 Feb. 1835

Father a native of Westbury, and mother of Hindon; they have six children. Free of the Turners' Company.

73 Wyatt, Thomas, son of Thomas and Ann, of 15 Silver St, Golden Square: to John Reinerus Gortz, tailor, of 70 Quadrant, Regent St. 10 Feb. 1835

Father is from Devizes, and has five children.

74 Goodman, Charles Peter, son of Charles, of 8 Lombard St, Fleet St: to Charles Garner, cabinet maker, of 62 Coppice Row, Clerkenwell. 29 June 1835

Brother to **60**. Father is from Trowbridge.

75 Pidding, William, son of James and Catherine, of Goldsmith's Terrace, Hackney Rd: to J.C. Wooster, cabinet maker, of Ashford St, Pitfield St, Hoxton. 1 July 1835

Father is from Marlborough, and has six children.

76 Wait, George, son of Thomas and Sarah, of Little Guildford St, Russell Square: to George Young Hadley, locksmith and bell-hanger, of 3 Skinner St, Bishopsgate. 2 July 1835

Father from Broad Hinton; mother from Chilton; and the boy was born at Marlborough. Free of the Blacksmiths' Company.

77 Tanner, William: to Frederick Fisher, butcher, of Noble St, Cheapside. 7 Oct. 1835

An orphan. Father, who was born at Corsley, and mother both died in summer 1834.

78 Lane, Mary Elizabeth, daughter of Sarah, of Smart's Buildings, Holborn: to Mary Durston, milliner, of Little Queen St, Lincoln's Inn Fields. 20 Nov. 1835

Mother, a widow, is a native of Corsham. Father, from Melksham, died in 1834, leaving his widow with five children.

79 Wilkins, Charles, son of William, of Commercial Rd, Pimlico: to George Underton, brass turner, of Museum St, Bloomsbury. 24 Nov. 1835

Father, from Tisbury, has eight children.

80   Merritt, Charles, son of Jane, of 8 Cecil Court, St Martin's Lane: to George Theophilus Trickett, bookbinder, of 24 Great Smith St, Westminster. 29 June 1836

Father, who was from All Cannings, died in 1834, leaving his widow with seven children.

81   Goodfellow, James, son of William, of Spencer's Terrace, Brewer's Green, Westminster: to William Mose, shoemaker, of Seymour Place, Bryanstone Square. 7 July 1836

Father, a native of Chilmark, is a widower and has five children.

82   Sympson, Edmund, son of Ann, of Draper's Place: to Charles Allen, saddler, of 22 Little Newport St. 8 July 1836

Father, from Hindon, died in 1832, leaving his widow with six children.

83   Giles, John, son of Edmund, of Griffin St, Lambeth: to William Davis, mother of pearl turner, of 28 Fleet St. 21 July 1836

Parents both from Marlborough, where the boy also was born. Father left a widower with ten children, six of whom are living.

84   Humphries, James, son of John and Ann, of Somer's St, Back Hill: to William Slade, tailor, of Little Saffron Hill. 25 July 1836

Parents are both from Westbury, and have three children. The boy, who is a cripple, was born at Westbury.

85   Cogswell, Henry James, son of Philip James, of Queen's Head Court, Newgate St: to Frederick Summers, gold beater, of London Wall. 7 Dec. 1836

Father, native of Trowbridge, has nearly lost his sight, and has two children.

86   Davis, William, son of George, of North St, City Rd: to Joseph Trevallion, chair and couch maker, of Clifton St, Finsbury. 1 May 1837

Father, from Bradford, is a widower with four children, and is frequently unable to work, being afflicted with rheumatism.

87   Scott, John, son of John and Mary, of Drummond St, Euston Square: to George Merrifield, turner, of Great Turnstile, Holborn. 3 May 1837

Father from Melksham, mother from Lacock; they have five children. Free of the Turners' Company.

88 Gibbs, John, son of John and Ann, of 5 Foster's Buildings, Lambeth Marsh: to John Day, boot and shoe maker, of 17 Commercial Rd, Blackfriars Rd. 27 July 1837

Father from Warminster, has four children.

89 Cogswell, John, son of William and Lucy, of 20 Thomas St, Kennington Common: to John Beezley, tailor, of Yate's Court, Carey St. 19 Dec. 1837

Father, from Trowbridge, has five children.

90 Hutchins, William, son of Charles, of 16 Mead's Row, Westminster Rd: to Robert James Pearl, dyer, of 3 Queen St, Edgeware Rd, Tottenham. 7 yrs, £25. 9 Jan. 1838

Father, native of Bishop's Cannings, is a widower, and has three children. First indenture cancelled by magistrate for master's misconduct; reapprenticed to T. McGill, 2 Windmill St, Tottenham Court Rd, dyer.

91 Beckett, John William, son of John and Mary, of 37 Green St, Bethnall Green: to George Wood, musical instrument maker, of Compton St, Soho. 7 yrs, £25. 15 Feb. 1838

Father from Upton Lovell; mother from Heytesbury. They have four children.

92 White, Mark, son of Mary, of Macclesfield St: to James Jackson, watch case maker, of Galway St, St Lukes. 7 yrs, £25. 8 March 1838

Brother of **61**. Mother is from All Cannings, and father was a native of Woodborough. He met with an accident which caused his death, and left his widow with seven children.

93 Gillingham, Thomas, son of Thomas and Elizabeth, of 4 Harrison St, Gray's Inn Rd: to Thomas Fry, engineer, of 4 Poland St, Oxford St. 7 yrs, £25. 16 July 1838

Father from Tisbury; mother from Marlborough. They have five children.

94 Latter, William Thomas, son of John and Harriet, of 1 Bond St, Commercial Rd, Lambeth: to John Dore, plumber, of 17 Exeter St, Clerkenwell. 7 yrs, £25. 17 July 1838

Mother from Chippenham, and in very ill health; has had ten children, two of whom are living.

95 Snook, Robert, of West (*Bishop's*) Lavington: to Edward Masey, brass and cock founder, of 8 Back St, Horseley Down. 7 yrs, £28. 4 Feb. 1839

Applicant an orphan, who has four brothers and sisters unprovided for.

96 Vincent, William, son of Mary, of 28 Arlington St, Clerkenwell: to Benjamin Thorn, upholsterer, of 1 Bagnigne Wells Rd. 7 yrs, £25. 5 Feb. 1839

Father and mother both natives of Westbury. Mother a widow with five children. Free of the Skinners' Company.

97 Knott, Joseph, son of George and Naomi, of 12 Merlin's Place, Spa Fields: to Charles Lapthorne, cordwainer, of 33 St Helena Place, Spa Fields. 7 yrs, £23. 23 April 1839

Both parents from Devizes; mother is a cripple. Assigned to Thomas Bamfield.

98 Pearce, Richard, son of Richard and Ann, of 4 Nettleton Court, Nicholl Square: to Frederick Summers, gold beater, of Little Britain. 7 yrs, £25. 1 May 1839

Father, from Mildenhall, of advanced age and in ill health, has four other children dependent on him. Free of the Goldsmiths' Company.

99 Pritchard, John, son of Harriet, of 6 Golden Lion Court, Aldersgate St: to Albert Whitby, tailor, of Exmouth St, Clerkenwell. 7 yrs, £25. 1 July 1839

Father was from Devizes; mother is a widow in very ill health, and has five children. Reported that the lad died 23 May 1843 (mother's letter).

100 Clark, Frederick, son of Ann, of 12 Little Britain: to George Drew, turner, of Prince's St, Marylebone. 7 yrs, £25. 23 July 1839

Father was from Salisbury; mother is a widow with seven children.

101 Davis, Richard, son of Richard and Sarah, of 14 Jane St, St George's in the East: to John Chambers, gun maker, of 6 Union St, Whitechapel Rd. 7 yrs, £25. 19 Aug. 1839

Father from Bromham; mother, now a widow, from Westbury. They have four children, one a cripple.

102 Greenland, William George, son of Edward and Mary Ann, of 1 Bromley Buildings, Bread St Hill, Thames St: to Benjamin Blakesley, carpenter and trunk maker, of 17 Friday St, Cheapside. 7 yrs, £20. 1 Oct. 1839

Parents, from Westbury, have six children. Free of the Haberdashers' Company.

103   Frampton, William George, son of Elizabeth, of 63 Barbican: to William Nathaniel Somersall, silversmith, of 53 Bartholomew Close. 7 yrs, £25. 4 Dec. 1839

Mother a widow; father, who was from Salisbury, was afflicted with insanity and died in 1837, leaving a widow and five children. Free of the Vintners' Company. Assigned to Richard Hunt, of Bond St, silversmith.

104   Randall, John Charles, son of Sarah, of 8 Freeman Place, Kennington: to William Hall, barge builder, of Steward's Lane, Battersea. 7 yrs, £25. 25 July 1840

Father was from Devizes; mother, from Trowbridge, a widow with four children. Free of the Shipwrights' Company.

105   Townsend, Richard, son of Elizabeth, of 3 Fleet Lane, Farringdon St: to Joseph Pickard, turner, of 17 Broad St, Bloomsbury. 7 yrs, £25. 4 Aug. 1840

Mother, a widow from Melksham, has four children. Apprentice convicted of felony, 16 April 1844; second moiety not paid.

106   Welchman, Sarah Bennett, daughter of Isaac Thomas and Elizabeth, of Hackney Rd: to Emma Brown, milliner, of 34 Ludgate St. 7 yrs, £25. 5 Aug. 1840

Mother from Melksham; father in ill health. They have five children.

107   Humphrys, George Frederick, son of John, of 47 Great Guildford St, Blackfriars Rd: to John Brees, ironmonger, of West St, Smithfield. 7 yrs, £25. 12 Nov. 1840

Father, from Hannington, is a widower with five children. Indenture cancelled by Lord Mayor's Court (master's misconduct). Reapprenticed to Samuel Ryder, of 7 Swan St, Dover Rd, Boro'. Free of the Armourers' Company.

108   Hussey, Joseph, son of James and Elizabeth, of 11 Harlington St, Waterloo Rd: to Gerrard Willett, picture frame maker, of 10 Water St, Strand. 7 yrs, £25. 4 Jan. 1841

Father is from Trowbridge, where apprentice was born; he has brought up his four orphan brothers and sisters, besides his own family.

109   Davis, Richard, son of Mary, of 2 Cumberland St, Fulham Rd: to Horatio Ockerby, law stationer, of Chancery Lane. 7 yrs, £25. 12 Jan. 1841

Father was from Bromham; mother is a widow with seven children. Free of the Stationers' Company.

110 Bowsher, Henry, son of Henry and Mary Ann, of 9 Albany St, Camberwell: to Joshua Waggett, cordwainer, of 35 Ernest St, Regents Park. 7 yrs, £25. 18 Jan. 1841

Mother, from Sutton Veny, has seven children.

111 Griffin, Thomas, son of Robert and Sarah, of 71 London Wall: to Montague Alexander, millwright, of Marlborough. 7 yrs, £25. 4 Feb. 1841

Father from Ogbourne St Andrew; mother from Marlborough. They have four children.

112 Jones, Alfred, son of John and Mary Ann, of 39 Great Sutton St, Clerkenwell: to Charles Seales Warner, gas fitter and brassfounder, of 16 Artillery Lane, Bishopsgate. 7 yrs, £14. 8 April 1841

Father, from Wilton, has five children. Intended for a Mercer's premium but in consequence of delay was unable to obtain one, and was therefore apprenticed by the Society.

113 Purnell, Joseph, son of Joseph and Mary, of 5 White Horse Lane, Stepney: to Henry Kitchinman, turner and fishing rod maker, of 64 Skinner St, Bishopsgate Without. 7 yrs, £25. 2 June 1841

Brother of **68**. Parents, of advanced age, have several children dependent on them. Free of the Turners' Company.

114 Jeffery, Charles Wilson, son of Charles and Hannah, of Hackney: to Maria Frances Knock, bookbinder, of 8 Well St, Cripplegate. 7 yrs, £25. 7 June 1841

Father, from Wilton, has seven children dependent on him. Indenture cancelled by magistrate 10 April 1843. Reapprenticed to William Taylor, Clapham, Surrey, carpenter and builder, 30 April 1844, for remainder of original term.

115 Little, Ann Margaret, daughter of Jane, of 17 Boston St, Blandford Square: to Frances Powell, milliner, of 16 Charles St, Manchester Square. 3 yrs, £25. 13 July 1841

Father was from Rowde; mother, from Corsham, a widow with four children.

116 Tull, Hannah, daughter of Mary, of 1 Langley Place, Commercial Rd: to Charlotte Kirkby, milliner and dressmaker, of Maidenhead St, Hertford. 3 yrs, £20. 28 Sept. 1841

Mother, a widow from Fisherton Delamere, has ten children dependent on her. Assigned to Thomas Roberts, 17 Hardwick Place, Commercial Rd, draper.

117 Humphreys, Henry, son of Frances, of 13 Cross St, Islington: to James Shuffell, gold beater, of Queen's Head Lane, Islington. 7 yrs, £25. 30 Nov. 1841

Father was from Hannington; mother a widow with seven children. Assigned to William Bayley, of Goswell Rd, gold beater.

118 Jones, Robert, son of John and Mary Ann, of 39 Great Sutton St, Clerkenwell: to Joshua Henry Dorrell, tailor, of 37 Old St Rd. 7 yrs, £25. 1 Dec. 1841

Father, from Wilton, has five children. Free of the Goldsmiths' Company.

119 Haynes, Alfred William Butcher, son of Daniel and Marianne, of 4 John St, Stepney: to Henry Orme, last and jointed clog maker, of 36 Mile End Rd. 7 yrs, £25. 21 Dec. 1841

Parents, from Warminster, have four children; mother in ill health. Indenture cancelled 15 Nov 1842 as directed; £5 returned.

120 Dare, Jane, daughter of Harriet, of 1 Church Lane, Kensington: to William Rhind, milliner, of 109 Sloane St. 3 yrs, £25. 21 Dec. 1841

Parents from Swindon; father was a butcher.

121 Pepal, Mary Ann, daughter of John and Elizabeth, of 62 Park St, Lambeth: to Ann Jones, Jane Jones, and Celia Dent, milliners and dressmakers, of 9 Vere St, Oxford St. 3 yrs, £25. 22 March 1842

Mother, from Salisbury, is in very ill health. Assigned to S. Piggott, The Quadrant, Regent St, 16 Sept 1842, and reapprenticed to Mrs Allsop, Regent St.

122 Deverell, Henry, son of Charles and Elizabeth, of 10 Chapel St, Milton St, Cripplegate: to Samuel Smith Noble, carpenter, of 1 Little Moorfields. 7 yrs, £25. 21 June 1842

Parents, from Westbury, have seven children; apprentice born at Melksham. Reapprenticed to B. Blakesley, 47 Friday St, 7 Feb 1844; assigned to Paul Phillips, 17 Addle St, 15 Dec 1845. Free of the Founders' and Lorimers' Company.

123 Viner, Elizabeth, daughter of Elizabeth, of Addle Hill: to Thomas Smith, milliner and dressmaker, of St Paul's Churchyard. 4 yrs, £25. 5 July 1842

Father was from Westbury; mother a widow with six children.

124 Fricker, Frederick William, son of John and Louisa, of 25 Smith St, Somer's Town: to George New, grocer, of 1 Marlborough Rd, Brompton. 7 yrs, £25. 7 July 1842

Father from Bradford, where apprentice was born. Father has sustained an injury in his eyes. Free of the Grocers' Company.

125 Barton, William Joseph, son of William and Esther, of 14 Jubilee Place, Commercial Rd: to William Hayns, carpenter, of Grundy St, Poplar. 7 yrs, £25. 26 July 1842

Mother from Warminster; father, in very ill health, has five children.

126 Turner, Reuben, son of Stephen, of 3 Green Dragon Court, Snow Hill: to John Lewis, bookbinder, of 9 Gough Square, Fleet St. 7 yrs, £25. 5 Oct. 1842

Father, from Tisbury, has brought up a family of eleven children. Free of the Goldsmiths' Company.

127 Edwards, James Hayward, son of Samuel and Harriet, of 9 Hare Court, Aldersgate St: to Walter Morisse, silversmith and polisher, of 5 Jewin Crescent. 7 yrs, £25. 5 Oct. 1842

Father, from Trowbridge, was a sailor, and has bad eyesight. Free of the Goldsmiths' Company.

128 Hutley, Henry, son of Samuel and Sarah, of 9 New North St, Red Lion Square: to William Henry Davis, mother of pearl turner, of 3 Bentinck Place, High St, Portland Town. 7 yrs, £25. 6 Jan. 1843

Mother, a widow from Devizes, has ten children.

129 Horne, Thomas Forbes, son of Robert Forbes and Emma Horne, of 3 Woolpack Place, Homerton: to John Hull, coach maker, of Church St, Hackney. 7 yrs, £25. 19 Jan. 1843

Father, from Little Bedwyn, has six children.

130 Tidman, Josiah James, son of Ambrose and Sarah, of Old Ford, Bow: to Robert James, carpenter, joiner and packing-case maker, of 2 Brewer St, Golden Square. 7 yrs, £25. 14 Feb. 1843

Father, from Wilton, has six children and is in very ill health. On enquiry on 12 April 1852 of Mr James, he stated the apprentice left him 3 or 4 years ago. He could not say where he had gone but supposed to America with his uncle, who had broken up and gone to America.

131 Arnett, Thomas, son of Alice, of 21 George's Row, St Luke's: to William Roberts, manufacturer of window blinds and flower stands, of 21 South Row, New Rd, St Pancras. 7 yrs, £25. 13 June 1843

Mother, from South Wraxall, has three children; her eye-sight is failing.

132 Fulford, James Charles, son of James and Rachel, of 13 Broad Wall, Stamford St, Blackfriars: to Messrs Levy, Robson and Franklyn, letter press printers, of Great New St, Fetter Lane. 7 yrs, £25. 8 Aug. 1843

Outdoor apprentice. Father, from Salisbury, has seven children. [*Another report states that father from Heytesbury, mother from Hindon*]

133 Fennell, Henry, son of Paul and Mary Ann, of 35 Harlington St, Waterloo Rd: to James Moore, watermen's and lightermen's, of 16 Hatfield St, Stamford St. 7 yrs, £25. 14 Dec. 1843

Father, a widower from Bromham, is in ill health; he has six children and maintains an infirm sister. Free of the Watermen's and Lightermen's Company and of the Stationers' Company.

134 White, Charles Henry Edward, son of Martha, of 7 Regent's Place, Westminster: to George Grafton Tottem, working jeweller and silversmith, of College St, Chelsea. 7 yrs, £25. 25 Jan. 1844

Father from Castle Combe; mother, from Hilperton, is in ill health. Father went abroad 14 years ago, and has not been heard of since. Reapprenticed to George H. Allen, 13 King St, Soho, jeweller and goldsmith, 23 July 1846, Tottem having become bankrupt.

135 Newcombe, Frederick Evan: to William Lakeman, hatter, of 44 High St, Shadwell. 7 yrs, £25. 31 Jan. 1844

An orphan. Mother was from Swindon; father was a gentleman of independent property, but died in poverty, leaving three children unprovided for, one a cripple.

136 Steadman, Charles, son of Benjamin and Jane, of College House, College St, Belvidere Rd, Lambeth: to John Tapling Fisher, statuary and stone mason, of 14 King St, Whitehall. 7 yrs, £25. 9 Feb. 1844

Parents, both from Warminster, have six children.

137 Hill, Alexander, son of Jane, of 31 Pilgrim St, Walworth: to William Haughton, draper, haberdasher and laceman, of 13 Black Prince Row, Walworth. 5 yrs, £25. 25 April 1844

Mother, a widow from Codford St Peter, has five children dependent on her.

138 Rushen, William David, son of Mary Bruce, of 36 Camomile St: to John Bickley, watchmaker, of 7 Half Moon Crescent, White Conduit Fields, Islington. 7 yrs, £25. 11 May 1844

Father from Ramsbury; mother from Wiltshire, and children dependent on her.

139 Lewis, William John, son of William, of 9 Layton Grove, Southwark: to Richard Hoe, carpenter, trunk and case maker, of 44 Leadenhall St. 7 yrs, £25. 2 July 1844

Father, from Chippenham, has had much illness in his family. Free of the Joiners' Company.

140 Tiley, James, son of Joseph, of 7 William St, Clerkenwell: to Robert Hoddy, pocket-book and leather case maker, of 27 Rosamond St, Clerkenwell. 7 yrs, £25. 9 July 1844

Father from Bromham; children all dependent on the parents.

141 Chandler, Henry Joseph, son of Henry, of 17 New St, Lambeth Walk: to William Cobley, gold-beater, of 3 St John's Ct., King St, Snow Hill. 7 yrs, £25. 2 Oct. 1844

Father, from Highworth, in ill health; has a wife and six children dependent on him. Free of the Painter-Stainers' Company.

142 Hacker, Thomas, son of Thomas, late of Guildford St, Southwark: to John Pear, barber, of 32 Poultry. 7 yrs, £25. 7 Jan. 1845

Father, now deceased, was from Broad Hinton; mother, from Marlborough, has all the children dependent on her. Free of the Barber's Company. On enquiry 23 Oct 1852 at 32 Poultry of Mr Pear, he stated Hacker only remained with him about 2 or 3 years and went from him to W Nicholls, of Kennington, Surrey. Second moiety not paid.

143 Downs, Thomas, son of William, of 8 Grove, Brooksby Walk, Homerton: to George Lakeman, cabinet manufacturer, of Grove Passage, Hackney. 7 yrs, £25. 21 Jan. 1845

Mother from Salisbury; father has a complaint in the brain; all the children dependent on the parents.

144 Hancock, Thomas, son of Edward, of 3 Market St, St John St, Clerkenwell: to Henry Williams, house painter, of 12 Great Distaff Lane. 7 yrs, £25. 2 April 1845

Father, from Box, has suffered much illness in his family. Free of the Painter-Stainers' Company.

145 Howard, Samuel Lewis, son of Samuel, of 21 Kinnerton St, Knightsbridge: to Thomas Joyce, engraver, etc, of 6 Wells St, Falcon Square. 7 yrs, £25. 4 April 1845

Both parents from Bradford. Mother almost disabled by a complaint arising from over-exertion.

146 Hibberd, Benjamin Bladud, son of Thomas, of 7 Stanford Place, Kingsland Rd: to Messrs H. and M.D. Grissell, iron founders, of the Regent's Canal Iron Works. 7 yrs, £25. 8 July 1845

Applicant born at Woolley, Bradford. Parents have eight children.

147 Sympson, Alfred, son of Betsey, of 4 Queen St, Pimlico: to Rowland Riley, tailor, of 19 Basinghall St. 7 yrs, £22 5s. 18 Aug. 1845

Father from Hindon; parents have had six children. Indenture cancelled 22 July 1848 at Guildhall. Rebound 14 Feb. 1849 to Henry Jordan, 3 Upper Ebury St, Pimlico, tailor.

148 Haynes, John, son of John, of Stockwell: to Henry Thacker, cooper, of Bunhill Row. 6 yrs, £22 5s. 8 Dec. 1845

Parents from Warminster. Father servant to Mr Gay at Stockwell.

149 Newcombe, Phillipa Ellen: to Elizabeth Hunt, straw hat manufacturer, of 102 Great Russell St. 3 yrs, £12 5s. 23 Feb. 1846

Apprentice is an orphan and a cripple. Mother was from Swindon. Father was a gentleman of independent property, but died in poverty leaving three children unprovided for. Second moiety relinquished by Miss Hunt.

150 Purchase, William, son of Elizabeth, of 3 Cumberland St, Chelsea: to Charles Baker, cabinet maker and carpenter, of 10 Upper Ebury St, Pimlico. 5 yrs, £20. 18 March 1846

Mother (formerly Elizabeth Avery) from Trowbridge; father died from cholera. Indenture cancelled in 1847.

151 Fanning, Thomas Digby, son of Mary, of 4 John St, Whitechapel: to Arthur John Wadsworth, truss manufacturer, of 8 Bell Yd., Gracechurch St. 7 yrs, £20. 20 April 1846

Father, many years messenger at the Lambeth Police Court, died in 1842, leaving his family totally unprovided for. Mother from Market Lavington.

152 Applegate, Wm: to Benjamin Blakesley, carpenter, of 47 Friday St. 7 yrs, £20. 5 May 1846

Apprentice an orphan; parents from Westbury. Free of the Haberdashers' Company.

153 Shelton, Simeon, son of Morris and Rachel, of 5 Stockwell St, Old Kent Rd: to John Rogers, blacksmith and locksmith, of Canterbury Place, Old Kent Rd. 6 yrs, £20. 18 May 1846

Father from Wootton Bassett; mother (formerly Rachel Tuck) from Broad Hinton. Both in bad health, and have four children dependent on them.

154 Arnold, James Henry, son of Sarah, of 135 Kent St, Borough: to William James Ellis, engraver and copper plate printer, of 2 Great Dover St, Borough. 7 yrs, £25. 7 Sept. 1846

Mother, from Mildenhall, has four children dependent on her. Father died seven years ago. Free of the Clock-makers' Company.

155 Hurdle, Charles Frederick, son of Jeremiah, of Denton St, Somers Town: to Charles Taylor, fret cutter, of 9 Carburton St, Portland Road. 6 yrs, £20. 21 Sept. 1846

Father from Heytesbury, mother from Hindon; six children dependent on them [see **238**].

156 Barton, Elizabeth Sarah, daughter of Esther, of 2 Swatton Place, Stepney: to George Symes, milliner and dressmaker, of 5 Keys Place, Bromley, Middlesex. 3 yrs, £20. 23 Nov. 1846

Mother, from Warminster, in ill health; has three children dependent on her.

157 Pullen, William, son of James, of Charles St, Hampstead Rd: to Benjamin Blakesley, carpenter, of 47 Friday St. 7 yrs, £23. 8 Dec. 1846

Parents from Trowbridge; five children dependent on father. Free of the Haberdashers' Company.

158 Neal, Daniel Henry, son of Elizabeth, of Upper Berkeley St, Marylebone: to William Postill, working boot and shoe maker, of 4 Meards Court, Wardour St. 7 yrs, £20. 28 April 1847

Father from Warminster.

159 Sims, Daniel, son of Jane, of Highgate: to Thomas Ell, carpenter, of 9 Pierrepoint Row, High St, Islington. 6 yrs, £20. 18 May 1847

Parents from Westbury; three children dependent on mother.

160 Crook, James Stratton, son of Joseph, of 5 Great Russell St, Bermondsey: to Charles Lake, carpenter and builder, of 104 Long Lane, Bermondsey. 6½ yrs, £20. 9 June 1847

Father, from Marlborough, is in bad health.

161 Whitehead, Francis Henry, son of Thomas, of 30 Cumberland Market: to Thomas J. Morris, brazier, tin-plate worker and plumber, of 16 Shipyard, Strand. 6 yrs, £20. 28 June 1847

Father, from Wootton Bassett, has ten children. Cancelled 30 Nov. 1848.

162 Deverill, William, son of Elizabeth, of 14 Acorn St, Bishopsgate St: to William Creasey, tailor, of 21 London Wall. 6½ yrs, £20. 1 July 1847

Mother, from Westbury, has four children dependent on her. Apprentice called 20 Aug. 1850 to say he had left his master for 6 months.

163 Carter, Edwin, son of James, of 11 College St, Belvidere Rd, Lambeth: to Daniel Haynes, boot and shoemaker, of 4 John St, Whitehorse Lane, Stepney. 6 yrs, £20. 6 July 1847

Father, from Warminster, has eight children dependent on him. Indenture to Haynes cancelled. Reapprenticed 1 Aug. 1851 to J.J. Tyson, 10 New Cut, Lambeth, boot and shoe maker.

164 Hancock, Frederick, son of William, of 3 New Charles St, City Rd: to Thomas Debenham Mills, cabinet maker, of 11 Frederick Place, Goswell Rd. 6 yrs, £20. 29 Dec. 1847

Father, from Marlborough, has been bankrupt in trade. Indenture cancelled 12 Feb. 1849 at Clerkenwell.

165 Randall, Samuel George, son of William, of Queen's Head Court, Gray's Inn Lane: to John Easterling, gas fitter and brass manufacturer, of 10 Exeter St, Strand. 6 yrs, £20. 11 Jan. 1848

Father, from Trowbridge, has had great losses in trade. Reapprenticed 5 Dec. 1849 to Thomas Dawson jun, carriage lamp manufacturer, of 28 Great St Andrew St, Seven Dials.

166 White, Henry William, son of Henry, of Carlton Cottages, Spa Rd, Bermondsey: to Thomas Joyce, wood engraver and printer's type cutter, of 6 Wells St, Falcon Square. 6 yrs, £20. 18 Jan. 1848

Father, from Warminster, has been much out of employ, and is in ill health.

167 Haines, Henry Samuel, son of Henry, of St Leonard St, Pimlico: to Samuel Newman, carpenter and builder, of 5 Leonard St, Pimlico. 5½ yrs, £20. 28 March 1848

Father, from Warminster, has three children, and a very afflicted wife.

168 Mines, Philip, son of Peter, of Halstead St, Brixton: to Robert Lockhart Wilson, carpenter and joiner, of 11 Loughboro Place, Brixton. 6 yrs, £20. 8 May 1848

Father, from Warminster, has three children, and wife in infirm health.

169 Coleman, John Joseph, son of John, of Great Russell St, Bermondsey: to Joseph Broome, carpenter and blind maker, of 10 Parsonage Row, High St, Newington Butts. 6½ yrs, £20. 6 July 1848

Mother from Wylye, Wilts; four children dependent on father. Reapprenticed 7 Feb. 1851 to Charles Lake, builder and carpenter, of 104 Long Lane, Bermondsey.

170 Tice, Henry John, son of Samuel, of Arlington St, Sadler's Wells: to Alfred Wilson, clock case maker, of 17 Percival St, Goswell Rd. 7 yrs, £20. 10 July 1848

Parents from Wilton; father has worked for 25 years past for Mr Moore, Clerkenwell.

171 Townsend, Herbert Luke, son of Samuel, of Marchmont St: to John Giles, mother of pearl turner and worker, of 7 Baron St, Pentonville. 7 yrs, £20. 20 July 1848

Father, from Westbury, a surgeon, has had great losses.

172 Hammon, Joseph Francis, son of Nairn Henrietta, of York Terrace, Chelsea: to Mary Ann Cutter, pastry cook and confectioner, of 214 Strand. 6 yrs, £20. 25 July 1848

Mother a widow, daughter of Rev M. Norris, formerly of Hindon, in greatly reduced circumstances, with six children dependent on her. Indenture cancelled at Bow Street Police Court 18 July 1849.

173 Broad, Alfred, son of Mary, of Rodney St, Pentonville: to William Henry Johnston, copper plate engraver and printer, of 1 Chester Place, Waterloo Rd. 6 yrs, £20. 14 Dec. 1848

Parents from Cricklade. Reassigned 24 Sept. 1850 to Osborn Crawford, Red Lion St, copper plate engraver.

174 Arnold, George Merritt, son of Sarah, of 135 Kent St, Southwark: to Thomas John Smith, pocket-book maker and pen stationer, of 83 Queen St, and 14 Pancras Lane, Cheapside. 7 yrs, £20. 18 Dec. 1848

Mother, a widow, from Mildenhall, keeps a small shop; had a son apprenticed by the Society in 1846 [*see* **154**]. Free of the Girdlers' Company.

175 Alley, Samuel James, son of Ann, of Wellington St, Blackfriars Rd: to Edward Hawkins, hat manufacturer, of 1 Church St, Blackfriars Rd. 6 yrs, £20. 23 Dec. 1848

Mother, a widow from Trowbridge, has six children dependent on her, and receives no assistance from the parish.

176 Taylor, Richard Stephen, son of John, of Norwood: to George Staples, carpenter, of 1 Park Rd, Lower Norwood, Surrey. 6 yrs, £20. 23 June 1849

Father is a police constable; mother from Durrington.

177 Foreman, Richard, son of George, of Barnet: to Thomas A'Court, coach builder, of Barnet. 6 yrs, £20. 21 July 1849

Father, from Warminster, has seven children dependent on him. Mother of the apprentice called on 31 May 1858 and stated that her son and his master separated, the latter having become insolvent. Second moiety of indenture not paid.

178 Young, Francis S., son of Fanny, of 25 Gloster Terrace, Vauxhall Bridge: to George Bridges, carpenter, of 24 Newcastle St, Strand. 5½ yrs, £20. 8 Dec. 1849

Father was from Devizes; mother, a widow, has four children dependent on her.

179 Palmer, William J., son of Samuel, of 19 Crescent St, Euston Square: to John Newman, cabinet maker and tambour frame maker, of 4, Cross St, Golden Square. 5½ yrs, £20. 12 Dec. 1849

Parents from Wilton. Father, a journeyman tailor, has a wife and six children dependent on him. John Newman went insane in 1851 and was sent to an asylum in Colney Hatch. Apprentice reassigned 3 Aug. 1852 to E. William Fielder, 9 Little Marlbro' St, turner.

180 Harris, Charles, son of William, of 37 Upper Marsh, Lambeth: to John Stevens, engraver and printer, of 42 Gibson St, Waterloo Rd. 6 yrs, £20. 24 Dec. 1849

Mother from Malmesbury. Parents, in bad health, have eight children.

181 Shipman, George, son of Jane, of 22 Marshall St, London Rd: to William Henry Palmer, gold-beater, of 16 Spencer St, Goswell Rd. 7 yrs, £20. 2 Jan. 1850

Parents from Potterne. Mother, a widow, is married again, and keeps a shop; has six children dependent on her. Free of the Goldsmiths' Company.

182 Arnett, Henry, son of Thomas, of 37 Baltic St, St Luke's: to John Jacobs, furrier, of 11 East St, Hoxton. 5½ yrs, £20. 11 Jan. 1850

Parents both dead. Mother from South Wraxall. Apprentice was educated at Langbourne Ward School.

183 Howard, Henry George, son of Samuel, of Kinnerton St, Knightsbridge: to Elias Octavius Symons, builder, of 3 Exeter St, Sloane Street. 7¾ yrs, £20. 11 Jan. 1850

Parents from Bradford. Father works as a carpenter, and has eight children dependent on him.

184 Phillips, John, son of Charles, of 8 Mortimer Market: to Paul Phillips, carpenter, of 17 Addle St Aldermanbury. 7 yrs, £20. 7 Feb. 1850

Father, from Devizes, out of employment, has six children. Free of the Founders' Company.

185 West, Catherine, daughter of John, of Brunswick Rd, Camberwell: to John Nicholson, milliners and dressmaker, of 1 Grove Place, Camberwell. 3 yrs, £20. 23 April 1850

Parents, from Corsham, have ten children.

186 Milverton, John, son of John, of 19 Upper James St, Camden Town: to Benjamin J.M. Greenhill, scale maker and weighing machine manufacturer, of 221 Hoxton Old Town. 6 yrs, £20. 2 May 1850

Mother from Axford; father is clerk to a barrister, and has eight children. Apprentice was drowned in 1851.

187 Lewis, James, son of James and Anne, of Sun Court, Moorgate St: to John Lewis, bookbinder, of 9 Gough Square, Fleet St, 7 yrs, £20. 3 July 1850

Father, from Chippenham, is a labourer, and has three children. Free of the Goldsmiths' Company. See also **241**.

188 Haines, James, son of James, of Belgrave House, Wandsworth Rd: to James Knapp Dare, carpenter, of Stockwell Green. 7 yrs, £20. 9 July 1850

Father, from Warminster, is a gentleman's servant, and has two children.

189 Duran, James, son of Anne, of Hereford Place, Kennington: to Henry Fairbank, engineer and machinist, of 121 Old St, St Lukes. 6 yrs, £25. 11 Nov. 1850

Mother, a widow from Trowbridge, has four children.

190 Atkinson, Edwin Pierson, son of W.H., of 32 Winchester St, Pentonville: to William Andrew Johnson, manufacturing goldsmith and jeweller, of 10 Wellington St, Goswell Rd. 7 yrs, £20. 21 Dec. 1850

Mother from Heytesbury; six children in the family.

191 Cock, George Augustus, son of W.H., of Shepperton Cottages, Islington: to George Wells, builder, of Surrey House, Coleman St, Camberwell. 6 yrs, £20. 21 Jan. 1851

Mother, from Stratton St Margaret, has three children. Master also of Peckham Grove, Camberwell.

192 Pitt, Jane Matilda: to William Axford, milliner and dressmaker, of 4 Maddox St. 3 yrs, £25. 29 Jan. 1851

Father from Westport St Mary.

193 Sympson, Luke, son of Betsy, of 13 Queen St, Pimlico: to Richard Stevens, ivory turner, of 30 Hungerford Market. 6 yrs, £20. 8 Feb. 1851

Father was from Hindon, an appraiser; six children in family. Noted that on enquiry matters between master and apprentice were going smoothly.

194 Ricketts, Joseph, son of H. of Park St, Kennington Cross: to Jesse Davis, carpenter and joiner, of Mill Lane, Brixton Hill. 5 yrs, £20. 13 Feb. 1851

Father, from Holt, has seven children.

195 Griffin, James John, son of Jesse, of 15 Cambridge Rd, Mile End: to James Pells, horse-hair manufacturer, of 10 Matilda St, Old Bethnal Green Rd. 5 yrs, £20. 8 May 1851

Father, from Avebury, had two children.

196 Rogers, Naish Richmond, son of Samuel, of 5 Finsbury Square: to Robert Neate, butcher and slaughterer, of 21 Hungerford Market. 5½ yrs, £20. 2 June 1851

Father, from Cherhill, is a cabinet-maker. On enquiry 22 Jan. 1857 found that apprentice had long since left his master.

197 Reynolds, Charles, son of Henry and Ann, of Union Place, City Rd: to John Capes, artist brush manufacturer, of 6 Canonbury Terrace, Islington. 6 yrs, £20. 11 Sept. 1851

Parents from Westbury; the candidate, aged 14 yrs in May 1850, was also born in Westbury. Father is a bright-smith; mother (formerly Ann Naish) and most of the children dependent on the father. Six children in family.

198 Sheppard, William, son of James and Sarah, of 26 Little Trinity Lane, Thames St: to James Caesar, lighterman, of 6 Queenhithe. 7 yrs, £20. 11 Sept. 1851

Mother (formerly Sarah Hussey), from North Bradley, died of cholera in Sept. 1849. Father, from Trowbridge, by trade a butcher but out of employ, has six of the children dependent on him. Candidate aged 14 yrs in June 1850. Seven children in family. Free of the Watermans' Company. Caesar died, and clerk of company made transfer to John Hasler, at Mr Crawshay, Paul's Wharf.

199 Alley, Eliza Ellen, daughter of James and Ann: to Eliza Boot, dress and mantle maker, of 10 Wellington St, Blackfriars Rd. 2 yrs, £20. 14 Nov. 1851

Aged 14 yrs in Oct. 1850. Mother, a widow from Trowbridge (formerly Ann Eyres); father, a labourer, died ten years ago. One of the sons apprenticed by the Society in 1848 [see **175**]; the rest of the children dependent on the mother, who receives no assistance from the parish. Six children in family.

200 Howell, John, son of John and Hannah, of 3 Vincent Place, Westminster: to George Jennings, plumber, of 29 Great Charlotte St, Blackfriars Rd, 6 yrs, £20. 15 Nov. 1851

Aged 14 yrs in Jan. 1851. Five children in family. Father, from Chilmark, is a stone-mason, but much out of work and unable to provide for his family, only one of whom earns anything. The mother much afflicted with asthma and often confined to the house.

201 White, George, son of James and Hannah, of 53 Godfrey St, Chelsea: to Richard Bourchier, tea dealer and grocer, of 10 Gloster Place, Kings Rd, Chelsea. 6 yrs, £20. 26 Nov. 1851

Aged 14 yrs in March 1852. Mother (formerly Hannah Knapp) from Bradford; father is a baker. Ten children in family, nine wholly dependent on parents for support.

202 Hammon, Albert Benjamin, son of Joseph and Nairn Henrietta, of 6 York Terrace, Chelsea: to William Robertson, wholesale confectioner, of 38 Queen's Rd West, Chelsea. 5½ yrs, £20. 6 Dec. 1851

Father died in 1847; mother (formerly N.H. Norris, daughter of Rev M. Norris, formerly incumbent of Hindon) is in greatly reduced circumstances. Five of her children are dependent on her for support, the other was apprenticed by the Society in 1848 [*see* **172**].

203 Arnold, Richard, son of Richard and Sarah, of 135 Kent St, Borough: to William Warr Paull, carpenter, builder and undertaker, of 106 Great Dover Rd. 7 yrs, £20. 15 Jan. 1852

Aged 14 yrs in Sept. 1851. Mother (formerly Sarah Shipman), from Mildenhall, left a widow 12 yrs ago. She keeps a small shop in the Borough. Four children in family; the two eldest boys have been apprenticed by the Society [*see* **154, 174**]. All the children were left dependent on mother.

204 Weightman, John, son of William and Eliza, of 6 Butler St, Spitalfields: to William King, carpenter and builder, of 8 Upper Chapman St, St George in the East. 5 yrs 4 months, £20. 9 March 1852

Aged 14 yrs in July 1850. Three children in family. Mother (formerly Eliza Elliott) from Bradford; father is a journeyman carpenter, who has had eight children, but three only are living. He is without means to apprentice his son.

205 Bath, Edward, son of Thomas and Esther, of 53 Augustus St, Regent's Park: to Benjamin Blakesley, carpenter and packing case maker, of 17 Old Change. 7 yrs, £20. 1 June 1852

Aged 14 yrs in Sept. 1851. Four children in family. Father, who was born at Box, and served his time to Mr Thomas Shell of that place, is unable to depend on his trade in the winter months; mother, who is ailing, was formerly Esther Tyler of Atworth. Free of the Haberdashers' Company.

206 Hall, Jehu, son of John, of 6 East St, Walworth Gardens: to Thomas West, carpenter and builder, of Albert Cottage, Albert St, Penton Place, Walworth. 7 yrs, £20. 5 July 1852

Parents, from Westbury, have three children supported by the mother, who is a charwoman.

207 Coleman, Henry James, son of John and Harriett, of 8 Amelia St, Old Kent Rd: to Thomas Cox, builder, of 1 Brunswick Rd, Camberwell. 4 yrs, £10. 3 Aug. 1852

Aged 14 yrs in Aug. 1851. Three children in family. Mother (formerly Harriett Read) from Wylye; father is a labouring man and unable to do constant work, from being afflicted with rheumatic gout. Children dependent on parents, who have not the means of apprenticing them. Transferred 18 March 1856 to William Walkins, 17 James St, Commercial Rd, Peckham, bricklayer.

208 Wigmore, Charles, son of William and Hannah, of 11 Robert St, Lower Marsh, Lambeth: to John Winn, gas fitter, of 25 Charlotte Place, Blackfriars Rd. 6 yrs, £25. 2 Aug. 1852

Aged 14 yrs in April 1851. Five children in family. Mother (formerly Hannah Little), from Seend, is in declining health; father, from East Knoyle, a journeyman carpenter, has had 12 children. Only five are living, three of whom dependent on father, who is afflicted with lameness. Apprentice called on 13 Aug. 1858 to say he was working with Winn for 28s. a week.

209 Chandler, Thomas William, son of Henry, of 16 New St, Lambeth Walk: to Messrs Nash and Miller, barge builders, of Upper Fore St, Lambeth. 7 yrs, £20. 29 Nov. 1852

Father, from Highworth, is a journeyman baker and has five children.

210 Colcroft, Thomas Richard, son of Thomas and Eliza, of Metropolitan Buildings, Old Pancras Rd: to John L. Pain, carpenter, of Old Pancras Rd. 7 yrs, £20. 30 Dec. 1852

Father is an attendant at the British Museum; mother, formerly Eliza Bray from Marlborough, has seven children [see **235**]. Pain became bankrupt in Nov. 1854, and apprentice transferred to John Scott, of 27 Chepstow Villas, West, carpenter and joiner.

211 Haynes, George William: to Zechariah Artis, zinc, tin and iron plate manufacturer, of 269 High St, Poplar. 7 yrs, £20. 9 March 1853

Apprentice is an orphan. Father, from Warminster, left three children orphans, another of whom, Henry Samuel, was apprenticed by the Society in 1848 [see **167**].

212 Pitt, Charles, son of William, of 3 Archer St, Bond St, South Lambeth: to Daniel Wayman, smith and farrier, of 19 Vauxhall Terrace, Vauxhall Walk. 5½ yrs, £20. 5 May 1853

Father in the employ of the South Western Railway. Apprentice born at Marlborough. Parents have eight children, of whom one is in the General Post Office and three at service. Transferred 13 Dec. 1855 to David Cadwell, Golden Cross Yard, Kennington, blacksmith and farrier.

213 Sillitoe, George, son of Robert and Mary, of 3 Hare Court, Aldersgate St: to Charles Helme, carver and gilder (indoor), of 49 Aldersgate St: 7 yrs, £20. 13 May 1853

Mother, formerly Mary Lewis, from Chippenham; father is a journeyman packing-case maker. Parents have six children. Candidate has been at school.

214 Haynes, Edgar Albert, son of Edgar and Emma Sophia: to Richard Mullins, optical instrument maker, of 39 Green St, Bethnal Green. 7 yrs, £20. 5 Aug. 1853

Apprentice is an orphan. Mother from Warminster; father, a journeyman carpenter often out of employ, died leaving four children of whom the apprentice was the eldest [*see* **233**]. Transferred to Samuel Angus, Upper North St, Poplar, stone-mason.

215 Brunker, William, son of John, of 10 Studd St, Islington: to George Barclay, compositor, of 28 Castle St, Leicester Sq. 7 yrs, £20. 14 Feb. 1853

Parents, from Westbury, have three children; father is a stamper in the Post Office.

216 White, Mark, son of George and Elizabeth, of 31 Banner St, St Luke's: to Robert Cockburn, packing case maker, of 16 Bull and Mouth St. 7 yrs, £20. 4 Oct. 1853

Father, from Bromham, in the employ of Whitbread the Brewer for 30 yrs; mother, formerly Elizabeth Swatton, from All Cannings. They have five children living, out of nine. Free of the Joiners' Company.

217 Batt, Caroline Dinah, daughter of Dinah, of 29 Carnaby St, Golden Sq: to Sophia Salmon, milliner and dressmaker, of 3 Argyle St, Regent St. 2 yrs, £25. 12 Dec. 1853

Mother, formerly Dinah Waldron, from Chiseldon, was left a widow with six children, two of whom are unprovided for. She keeps a small china shop.

218 Sheppard, Emily, daughter of James: to John Whatley, waistcoat maker, of 48 Bridge St, Southwark. 3 yrs, £20. 14 Dec. 1853

Father, from Trowbridge, is a journeyman butcher; mother died in 1849, leaving seven children. Second moiety not paid, as the apprentice died.

219 Fowles, Frederick J., son of Charles, of 41 St Mary at Hill: to John William Grove, printer, of 22 Harp Lane, Tower St. 7 yrs, £20. 9 March 1854

Father, wine cellarman at London Docks, is from Salisbury, and resided for some years at West Harnham as licensed victualler, but was unfortunate. Has five children. Free of the Fishmongers' Company.

220 Bruckin, Thomas Henry, son of Thomas, of 5 Maidenhead Court, Cannon St: to James Parsons, mathematical instrument engraver, of 11 Upper Stamford St, Blackfriars. 7 yrs, £20. 2 March 1854

Mother (formerly Caroline Hayns) from Warminster; six children in family. Free of the Grocers' Company.

221 Lee, William: to William Goodwin, bookbinder, of 7 Ireland Yard, Doctors Commons. 5½ yrs, £20. 30 May 1854

222 Durnford, Daniel George, son of Daniel, of 104 Lillington St, Vauxhall Bridge Road: to William Spottiswoode, the Queen's printer, of Lew St Square. 7 yrs, £20. 13 June 1854

Father, journeyman tin-plate worker, from Devizes; three children in family. Free of the Stationers' Company.

223 Mayhew, Henry Albert, son of Henry and Martha, of 28 Shaftesbury Place, Aldersgate St: to Henry Debaufer, gasfitter etc, of 10 and 11 Creed Lane. 7 yrs, £25. 13 July 1854

Father a journeyman tailor; mother, formerly Martha Bryant from Marlborough. Five children in family, of whom two are provided for. Free of the Lorimers' Company.

224 Blanchard, James, son of Joseph, of 47 Brook St, Lambeth: to John Trigg, chronometer and watch jeweller, of 10 President St East, St Lukes. 7 yrs, £20. 24 July 1854

Father a journeyman carpenter from Trowbridge; eight children in family. Transferred 17 July 1855 to Edmund Farmer, 40 King's Square, St Luke's, watch jeweller.

225 Colcroft, Frances M., son of Thomas and Eliza: to George Cowle, milliner and dressmaker, of 14 Waterloo Place. 3 yrs, £25. 17 Aug. 1854

Mother from Marlborough [*see* **235**].

226 Butler, George Augustus: to Charles Plaskett, watch and clock maker, of 31 Raven St, Whitechapel Rd. 7 yrs, £25. 22 Aug. 1854

Parents from Aldbourne. Master wrote 21 March 1859 that his apprentice had absconded.

227 Gathen, Sarah: to Frederick Richards, dressmaker and milliner, of Church Place, Hackney. 3 yrs, £20. 28 Nov. 1854

Mother from Salisbury.

228 Mustoe, Job William, son of William and Mary Ann, of 2 Bowling Square, Lower Whitecross St: to Richard Hoe, carpenter, of 44 Leadenhall St. 7 yrs, £20. 5 Sept. 1854

Father a carpenter; mother (Mary Ann Hayward), from Bradford, has nine children, two in situations as errand boys, the rest dependent on the parents. Free of the Joiners' Company.

229 Figgins, Vincent, son of Hannah, of 6 Teale St, Hackney Rd: to Thomas Joyce, wood engraver, of 6 Wells St, Cripplegate. 7 yrs, £20. 5 Dec. 1854

Mother a widow; father was from Devizes. Six children in family; one daughter is married, two others are in service, and the others assist their mother as a washerwoman.

230 Fulford, Henry, son of James, of 60 Holland St, Blackfriars Rd: to Thomas C. Johns, printer, of Wine Office Court, Fleet St. 7 yrs, £20. 5 Dec. 1854

Father, a journeyman printer from Salisbury, has five young children. An elder son, James Charles, was apprenticed by the Society in 1843 to Messrs Levy, Robson and Franklin [*see* **132**], and is now a working journeyman. Free of the Stationers' Company.

231 Young, John, son of John, of 1 Oak Terrace, Lower Norwood: to Mrs Amy Grist, flour and tea dealer, of Westow St, Upper Norwood. 7 yrs, £20. 23 Jan. 1855

Father, a city missionary from Warminster, has five children. Reapprenticed to F. Ledger, 3 Catherine St, compositor.

232 Carter, Albert Fachney, son of Sophia, of 18 Caroline Place, Bayswater: to William Appleton, tinman, locksmith, bell-hanger and gas-fitter, of 68 Drury Lane. 6 yrs, £20. 26 March 1855

Widowed mother a laundress; father was from Cricklade. Seven children in family.

233 Haynes, Edwin Charles, son of Edgar and Emma Sophia: to Robert Williams, plumber, painter etc, of 44 High St, Poplar. 6½ yrs, £20. 26 July 1855

Candidate, aged 14 yrs in Dec. 1854, is an orphan. Mother (Emma Sophia Hayns), from Warminster, died six years ago, leaving four children; father died in 1853. An aunt has taken charge of the candidate, but has no means to apprentice him. A brother, Edgar Albert, was apprenticed by the Society in Aug. 1853 [*see* **214**].

234 Pullen, Frank, son of James and Martha, of 17 Sherborne St, Blandford Square: to Frederick James, trunk and portmanteau maker, of 226 Oxford St. 7 yrs, £20. 6 Sept. 1855

Father left his family in 1851 for America, and has not since been heard of. Mother (Martha Avens), from Trowbridge, is dependent on her three daughters, who go out to needlework. A son, William, was apprenticed in 1846 [*see* **157**], and in Dec. 1854 reported himself as doing piece-work for Mr Jones in London Wall. Transferred 14 June 1859 to Henry Pound, 64 Leadenhall St, trunk and portmanteau maker.

235 Colcroft, Jane Tower, daughter of Thomas and Eliza: to George Cowle, milliner, of 4 Waterloo Place. 3 yrs, £25. 7 Nov. 1855

Aged 14 yrs in Oct. 1855. Seven children in family. Father, late attendant at British Museum, is dead; mother (formerly Eliza Bray) from Marlborough. Thomas Richard Colcroft and Frances Mary Colcroft, two of the children, were apprenticed by the Society in 1852 and 1854 respetively [see **210, 225**].

236 Seager, Frederick, son of Thomas and Christiana, of 35 Brook St, Holborn: to William Heath, brass finisher and gas-fitter, of 25 Poppins Court, Fleet St. 7 yrs, £20. 21 Nov. 1855

Father is and has been for the last 16 years a letter carrier in the London District Post Office. Four of the children and his wife, who is in very delicate health, dependent on him. Mother (Christiana or Keziah Hall), born at Melksham, and daughter of Thomas Hall of Westbury. Parents have resided for 26 years in London, and have 7 children, of whom the apprentice is the second.

237 Kilminster, Albert Richard, son of James and Ann, of 7 New Montague St, Spitalfields: to Henry Bishop, cabinet and general carver, of 47 Baldwin St, City Rd. 6 yrs, £20. 21 Nov. 1855

Age 14 yrs in Feb. 1855. Four children in family. Father, from Calne, is a journeyman tailor, which is a precarious employment regulated by the seasons. He has a failing eyesight, and no other source of income wherewith to support his wife and children, who are dependent on him. Mother (Ann Davis) from Derry Hill.

238 Hurdle, James Alexander, son of Jeremiah and Maria, of 4, Eve Terrace, Old St Pancras Rd: to Samuel Young, coach builder, of Trematon Mews, Albion St, Caledonian Rd, King's Cross. 6¼ yrs, £20. 5 Dec. 1855

Aged 14 yrs in March 1855. Father, a working carpenter from Heytesbury, has a large family, part of whom are still dependent upon him. He has long been suffering from palsy, and is incapable of work. Mother (Maria Hall) is from Hindon. Another son, Charles Frederick, was apprenticed by the Society in Sept. 1846 [see **155**].

239 Tucker, Mary: to Samuel Moore, dressmaker, of 6 University St. 3 yrs, £20. 12 Dec. 1855

Indenture to Moore cancelled; reapprenticed 8 Sept. 1856 to B. Austin, 2 Stafford St, Lew? Rd, milliner and dress maker.

240 Stagg, Joseph, son of George and Mary, of 8 St James's Terrace, Blue Anchor Rd, Bermondsey: to Messrs Bevington and Morris, curriers etc, of Rouel Tannery, Blue Anchor Road. 7 yrs, £20. 15 Dec. 1855

Aged 14 yrs Oct. 1855. Five children in family. Parents from Marlborough. Mother, formerly Mary Hillier, is dead; father a worker in the tan-yard of Messrs Bevington and Morris, who give him a good character. He has to support his children, of whom the candidate is eldest born.

241 Lewis, Alfred, son of James and Ann, of 4 Blue Hart Court, Moorgate St: to William Lock, bookbinder, of 117 Borough Rd, Southwark. 7 yrs, £20. 30 April 1856

Aged 14 years Jan. 1856. Father, from Chippenham, is a casual labourer and much out of employ; his wife has delicate health, and much fine needle-work has impaired her sight. James Lewis, another son, was apprenticed by the Society in 1850 to J. Lewis, Gough Square, book-binder [*see* **187**], and the father is anxious for his brother to reap similar benefits. Transferred 12 Oct. 1860 to Robert Spencer jun, Bridgewater Gardens, Barbican, bookbinder.

242 Reynolds, Alfred, son of Henry and Ann, of 20 Buttesland St, Hoxton: to Charles Botten jun, brassfounder, of Crawford Passage, Clerkenwell. 5¾ yrs, £20. 3 May 1856

Parents from Westbury. Father is a common engineer; four of the children and his wife are nearly dependent on him. Mother formerly Ann Naish. Master became bankrupt in 1860. Transferred 5 Dec 1860 to R.L. Howard, 85 Upper Whitechapel St, engineer.

243 Hancock, Henry James, son of Edward, of 3 Market St, Clerkenwell: to E.H. and W. French, watch chain makers, of 31 Spencer St, Clerkenwell. 6 yrs 8 months, £20. 20 May 1856

Father a journeyman mason from Box.

244 Dawson, Joseph William, son of Joseph and Caroline, of New St, Brompton: to Thomas Spratley, saddler and harness maker, of 2 Wandsworth Rd. 7 yrs, £20. 12 June 1856

Parents keep a coffee house in New St, Brompton, which enables them to maintain their children but not to apprentice them. Candidate conducted himself well at the National School, and received awards for good conduct. Mother, formerly Caroline Beauchamp, from West Dean. Spratley called 17 Feb. 1859 and said apprentice had run away. He called again 26 April and said that apprentice had never returned and he did not know where he was.

245 Mundy, Henry, son of James, of 5 Potter's Cottages, Archbishop's Rd, Brixton Hill: to Edward Leigh, carpenter etc, of New Park Rd, Brixton Hill. 5¾ yrs, £20. 15 July 1856

Father a carpenter; apprentice was born at Marlborough.

246 Harvell, William Henry, son of Thomas and Mary Jane: to George Samuel Yearly, grocer and cheesemonger, of 11 Green St, Bethnal Green. 7 yrs, £20. 15 July 1856

Aged 14 yrs in July 1855. Four children in family. Father is a mechanic of limited means, and has to bring up and educate his four sons by his own labour; mother, Mary Jane Haines, from Warminster. Candidate has for the last five years been at a free school at Bow. Indenture cancelled at Worship St, 18 Aug. 1858, and apprentice sent to prison for one month for stealing from his master.

247 Stagg, Mary C.: to Teresa Maria Moody, dressmaker, of St James's Place West, Winchester. 3 yrs, £20. 4 Aug. 1856

248 Johnson, Henry, son of James and Honour, of 24 Branch Place, Hoxton New Town: to Messrs Henry and Martin Delagarde Grissel, vicemen and turners, of Regent's Canal Iron Works. 6 yrs, £25. 1 Sept. 1856

Aged 14 yrs in June 1855. Five children in family. Mother was formerly Honour Fryer from Steeple Ashton. Father, also from Wiltshire, has a large family to support on small means, five of whom are quite incapable of work. He states that his son, the candidate, possesses moral and religious principles beyond his years.

249 Haines, Thomas, son of Charles and Betsy: to John Tyler, lighterman, of Waterman's Arms, Milwall. 7 yrs, £20. 13 Nov 1856

Aged 14 yrs in May 1854. Seven children in family. Father, deceased, from Warminster, was a journeyman carpenter; apprentice is the eldest child. Free of the Waterman's Company.

250 Roadway, Mary Ann: to Sophia Salmon, milliner, dressmaker and mantle maker, of 3 Argylle St. 2 yrs, £25. 20 Nov. 1856

251 Hussey, Ann Elizabeth, daughter of Isaiah and Susannah, of 151 St John's St, Clerkenwell: to Messrs Moran and Quin, jewellers and miniature case liners, of 65a Poland St. 5 yrs, £25. 16 Dec. 1856

Aged 14 yrs in Feb. 1856. Father, from Trowbridge, died in 1845, aged 26. Mother was left with two children totally unprovided for; one child has died and she has with difficulty supported herself and the candidate by needlework.

252 Shipway, Jane: to Maria Richards, dressmaker, of 26 Great Ormond St. 2 yrs, £20. 13 July 1857

253 Lamport, Charles William, son of Amelia Lovell, of 3 Hertford St, Haggerston: to Robert Grimes, tailor, of 108 Vauxhall Walk. 6½ yrs, £20. 13 July 1857

Aged 14 yrs in Dec. 1856. Two children in family. Father died before the birth of the candidate. Mother, formerly Amelia Barnes from St Edmund's, Salisbury, had two children by her first husband, Charles Lamport, and married again. Her present husband is a weaver.

254 Innes, Robinson, son of James, of 3 Stamford Place, Hatfield St, Blackfriars Rd: to Henry Ingle, smith and engineer, of 102 and 12 Shoe Lane. 6 yrs, £20. 15 July 1857

Mother formerly Harriet Sutton from Devizes.

255 Fairclough, Matthew P., son of Ann, of 15 Hampden St, Harrow Rd: to James Meadow, carpenter and cabinet maker, of 11 Alexander St, Westbourne Park Rd. 5¾ yrs, £20. 21 July 1857

Mother a widow, formerly Ann Withers from Mildenhall.

256 New, Thomas J., son of Thomas, of 8 Upper Victoria Rd, Holloway: to William Hussey, lever escapement maker, of 30 Sudeley St, City Rd. 5 yrs, £20. 23 Sept. 1857

Father from Westbury.

257 Payne, Walter, son of Philip, of 84 Southwark Bridge Rd: to William Payne, hairdresser, of 1 Warwick Lane. 6½ yrs, £20. 13 Oct. 1857

Father from Trowbridge.

258 Guy, Samuel C., son of Samuel, of 8 North Bruton Mews: to George South, shoeing smith, of 40 New Bond St. 5¾ yrs, £20. 20 Oct. 1857

Father from Chippenham.

259 Dawson, Thomas George, son of Joseph, of 7 New St, Brompton: to George Foxley, carpenter, glazier and painter, of 31 King St, Regent St. 6 yrs, £20. 11 Feb. 1858

Brother to **244.**

260 Edmonds, Thomas, son of Abraham, of 4 Yeoman's Row, Brompton: to G. Foxley, plumber etc, of 31 King St, Regent St. 6 yrs, £20. 11 Feb. 1858

Father from Calne. Mr Foxley said 11 Aug. 1861 the apprentice had left him and enlisted.

261 Bull, James, son of Mary Mayell, of 10 Claremont Cottages, Peel St, Kensington: to Thomas Smith, coachbuilder and wheelwright, of Great Ilford. 5¼ yrs, £20. 17 Feb. 1858

Son by first husband; mother formerly Mary Webb of Broughton Gifford.

262 White, Henry St Thomas, son of Isaac, of 10 City Rd: to James Henry Rowley, architect, of 17 St Helen's Place. 4 yrs, £25. 2 July 1858

Parents from Corsham; mother formerly Cecilia Osborne.

263 Bull, Jacob, son of Mary Mayell, of 10 Claremont Cottages, Peel St, Kensington: to George Foreman, wheelwright, of 28 Gray St, Webber St, Blackfriars. 6½ yrs, £25. 31 July 1858

Son by first husband; mother formerly Mary Webb from Broughton Gifford, The master, George Foreman, left his business and could not be found. Supposed he went abroad taking his part of the indenture with him. Boy reapprenticed 12 Jan. 1860 to Stephen Balls, 28 Hornton St, Kensington, wheelwright. £5 added to the premium.

264 Hibburd, Ann, daughter of Ann, of Battersea Rise: to Charles John Greenwood, dress and mantle maker, of 175 Manor St, Clapham. 2 yrs, £20. 31 July 1858

Mother a widow, formerly Ann Goatley from Marlborough.

265 Hopkins, Thomas, son of Elizabeth, of 21 Little Guildford St, Russell Sq.: to William Guy, builder, carpenter etc, of 25 Brunswick St, Blackfriars Rd. 6¼ yrs, £20. 24 Sept. 1858

Mother a widow; father was from Corsley. Reapprenticed 7 Jan. 1862 to Geo Pigott Moore, carpenter and builder, of 9 Sutherland Place, Bayswater.

266 Fletcher, Charles, son of Sarah, of 2 Trinity Buildings, Great Tower St: to Frederick Henry Sutton, wholesale stationers etc, of 34 Crutched Friars. 7 yrs, £20. 28 Oct. 1858

Mother a widow; father was from Wilton. Free of the Ironmongers' Company.

267 Edwards, Martha, daughter of Samuel, of Royal Hospital, Greenwich: to Benoni Austin, milliner etc, of 2 Stafford St, Marylebone Rd. 3 yrs, £20. 27 Nov. 1858

Father from Trowbridge.

268 Johnson, Edward, son of James, of 24 Branch Place, Hoxton: to James Appleton, engineer lathe and tool maker, of 100 Old St, St Luke's. 6 yrs, £25. 18 Dec. 1858

Father an engineer from Trowbridge. Reapprenticed 27 Sept. 1859 to H. Fairbank, engineer, 69 Old St. E. Johnson called 17 May 1862 to say magistrates had cancelled his indenture.

269 Weston, William, son of John, of 4 Windsor Court, Monkwell St, Cripplegate: to William Hussey, lever escapement maker, of 30 Sudeley St, Islington. 5¾ yrs, £20. 31 Jan. 1859

Father a turncock from Bromham. Reapprenticed 29 July 1861 to H. Palmer, of 2 High St, Peckham, lever escapement maker.

270   Blundy, Charles William, son of George, of 22 Prince St, Riley's Park, Bermondsey: to Henry Putley, cooper, of 40 St Mary at Hill. 7 yrs, £20. 7 Dec. 1858

Father a carpenter from Devizes. Free of the Coopers' Company.

271   Butcher, Henry J., son of William and Ann, of 1 Pye's Cottages, Rouse's Gardens, King's Rd, Chelsea: to Charles Oak Savage, goldbeater, of 112 Gt Titchfield St, Oxford St. 7 yrs, £20. 28 March 1859

Father a labourer; mother formerly Ann Willis from North Bradley. Parents paid £5 in addition to the £20 premium. Master reported 13 April 1861 apprentice had absconded.

272   Grist, Eliza, daughter of John and Jane, of 55 Brandon St, Walworth: to Emily Evans, milliner and dressmaker, of 150 Dover Rd. 3 yrs, £20. 24 June 1859

Parents from Dilton Marsh. Father a labourer; mother formerly Jane Collier.

273   Frampton, John G., son of Edmund and Eliza, of 43 Hereford St, Lisson Grove: to William Death, gilder etc, of 30 Praed St. 6 yrs, £20. 14 July 1859

Father a railway labourer; mother formerly Eliza Newham from Britford.

274   Hayns, Henry Eliel, son of Jemima, of 47 St Ann's Rd, Bow Common: to Joseph D'Aguila Samuda, joiner etc, of Poplar. 6 yrs, £20. 9 Aug. 1859

Mother a widow, formerly J. Eacott from Warminster.

275   Lovell, Mary, daughter of Henry, of 2 Hertford St, Haggerston: to George Trought, waistcoat maker and tailor, of 4 Cotton Row, Marlborough Rd, Dalston. 5 yrs, £20. 30 Aug. 1859

Father from Salisbury.

276   Buckpitt, Mary, daughter of Elizabeth, of 46 Henry St, Woolwich: to Mary Ann Whormby, dressmaker, of 16 Ogilby St, Woolwich. 3 yrs, £20. 18 Oct. 1859

Mother a widow; apprentice was born at Bratton.

277   Burt, William George, son of Ann Lavinia, of 57 Charlotte St, Fitzroy Square: to Samuel B. Webber, manufacturing jeweller, of 30 Poland St, Oxford St. 6 yrs, £20. 4 Nov. 1859

Mother, a widow, is a milliner, formerly A.L. Dyer from Trowbridge.

278 Whitworth, Thomas, son of Thomas and Elizabeth: to Thomas Docking, cooper, of 10 Montague Villas, West Green Rd, Tottenham, and at Whitbread's Brewery. 7 yrs, £25. 7 Nov. 1859

Father a servant to Messrs Whitbread, brewers; mother formerly Elizabeth Briant from Hilperton.

279 Shipway, Fanny, daughter of Joseph, of 9 York Terrace, Vine St, Lambeth: to Maria Richards, dressmaker, of 8 King St, Holborn. 2 yrs, £20. 19 Nov. 1859

Father a bricklayer from Overton; sister to **252.**

280 Higgins, Thomas, son of Stephen, of 168 Grange Rd, Bermondsey: to Samuel Morris, currier etc, of Rowel Tannery, Blue Anchor Rd, Bermondsey. 7 yrs, £20. 16 July 1860

Father a carman from Chippenham.

281 Freeman, John Jacob, son of Aaron, of 12 Cowper St, Finsbury: to Jesse Chessum, carpenter and builder, of 89 Leonard St, Finsbury. 6½ yrs, £20. 23 July 1860

Father a paper enameller from Liddington.

282 Drake, Samuel, son of Elizabeth, of 31 Georgiana St, Camden Town: to Alexander Paton, manufacturing goldsmith and jeweller, of 9 Upper Charles St, Northampton Square. 6 yrs 4 months, £20. 27 Oct. 1860

Mother a widow; father was from Rowde.

283 Sillitoe, Charles, son of Robert, of 11 Nettleton Court, Nicholl Square, Aldersgate St: to Frederick Summers, gold-beater, of 19 Little Britain. 7 yrs, £20. 7 Nov. 1860

Father a journeyman packing-case maker; mother formerly Mary Lewis from Chippenham. Brother to **213**. Free of the Goldsmiths' Company. Apprentice died 26 March 1864, per Mrs Sillitoe.

284 Coulson, William Philip, son of William and Charlotte, of 44 Acton St, Gray's Inn Rd: to Thomas Titmus, boot and shoe maker, of 16 Upper Bingfield St, Caledonian Rd. 6¾ yrs, £20. 22 Nov. 1860

Father a tailor; mother formerly Charlotte Pearson from Heytesbury.

285   Smith, John Silver, son of Sarah, of Wilton: to John Miles, carpenter and wheelwright, of Collingbourne Ducis. 7 yrs, £20. 5 Feb. 1861

Mother, a widow, formerly Sarah Palmer from Collingbourne. County apprentice.

286   Mundy, George, son of James and Mary, of 3 Alma Place, Brixton Hill: to James Maxwell, plumber etc, of 9 Loughborough Place, North Brixton. 5½ yrs, £20. 7 March 1861

Mother formerly Mary Brown from Marlborough; father from Cheverell.

287   Cole, Emily Rebecca: to Charles Wayne, milliner, of 332 Oxford St. 2 yrs, £20. 16 March 1861

Mother formerly Frances Dyer from Trowbridge.

288   Dawson, Susanna Eaton, daughter of Caroline: to Marianne Coles, milliner, of 4 Brompton Place. 2 yrs, £20. 27 March 1861

Mother formerly Caroline Beauchamp from West Dean. Transferred 28 Oct. 1862 to H.J. Jones, of 17 South Audley St, dressmaker.

289   Alexander, Arthur, son of George, of 75 Lant St, Borough: to John Acton White, waterman etc, of 28 East Lane, Bermondsey. 7 yrs, £20. 9 April 1861

Father a coffee-shop keeper from Pewsey. Free of the Watermen's Company.

290   Mildenhall, George, son of Frederick, of Collingbourne Kingston: to Henry Ponting, builder and carpenter, of Collingbourne Ducis. 7 yrs, £20. 10 May 1861

Father is a carpenter. County apprentice.

291   Roberts, Joshua, son of Maria Burchell, of 93 Webber Row, Blackfriars Rd: to Josiah Spargo, coppersmith and brazier, of 96 Great Suffolk St, Borough. 6 yrs, £20. 7 June 1861

Apprentice attained the age of 21 in Feb. 1867. Mother formerly Maria Gold from Great Bedwyn. Transferred to H. Maples, of 8 Cross St, Clapham, brazier and coppersmith.

292   Amor, Una Maria, daughter of Hannah, of 54 Stratton Ground, Westminster: to Edward B. Taylor, military embroiderer, of 35 Gerrard St, Soho. 4 yrs, £25. 15 July 1861

Mother formerly Hannah Card from Salisbury.

293 Saunders, Edward William, son of John E., of 2 William St, Bethnal Green: to Henry Hill, lock manufacturer, of 14 Union Place, Stepney Green. 6 yrs, £20. 26 July 1861

Father a dock labourer from Cricklade.

294 Dodds, Horace, son of James and Matilda, of 2 Glaucus St, Bromley, Middlesex: to William Oakley, iron-founder, of High St, Bromley, Middlesex. 6 yrs, £20. 31 July 1861

Father a colour-maker; mother formerly Matilda Hayns from Warminster.

295 Blandford, John Edward, son of Edward, of 13 Heath St, Commercial Rd East: to Henry Clifford, whitesmith etc, of 4 Bloomsbury Terrace, Commercial Rd East. 5¾ yrs, £20. 19 Oct. 1861

Father a shoemaker from Warminster.

296 Watts, William Burrow, son of George, of 61 Roupell St, Lambeth: to Finlay Thompson, millwright engineer, of 12 Queen St, New Cut, Lambeth. 6 yrs, £25. 1 Nov. 1861

Father a labourer; apprentice born in Salisbury.

297 Haynes, Thomas Henry, son of Thomas and Catherine, of Alvington, Devon: to Michael Cunningham, oil and colour man, of 11 Commercial Place, Kentish Town. 7 yrs, £20. 16 Dec. 1861

Father a gentleman's servant; mother formerly Catherine Newman Hancock from Corsham.

298 Wilkins, Henry Charles, son of Charles, of 2 Ranelagh Cottages, Commercial Rd, Pimlico: to Nathaniel Wood Lavers, glazier and painted glass manufacturer, of Endell St, Bloomsbury. 6½ yrs, £20. 24 March 1862

Father from Tisbury.

299 Prince, Charles Tidd, son of Emily, of 4 Carter St, Poplar: to John Stewart, iron-founder, of Russell St, Blackwall. 6½ yrs, £20. 27 March 1862

Mother, a widow, formerly Emily Tabor from Warminster.

300 Hayns, George, son of Jemima, of 52 St Ann's Rd, Bow Common: to Thomas Blundell, coppersmith, of 7 Conant Place, West India Dock Rd. 5½ yrs, £20. 11 April 1869

Mother, formerly Jemima Eacott, a widow from Warminster.

301 Freeman, James Mitchell, son of Aaron, of 56 Buttesland St, East Rd, Hoxton: to Benjamin N. Blakesley, packing case maker, of Old Change. 6½ yrs, £23 15s. 1 April 1862

Father from Liddington. Free of the Haberdashers' Company.

302 Eatwell, John, son of John, of 14 Great Barlow St, High St, Marylebone: to Joshua Sanders, tailor, of 16 Gt Quebec St, Marylebone Rd. 7 yrs, £20. 30 May 1862

Father from Broad Hinton.

303 Francis, Arthur Huntley, son of Rebekah, of Warminster: to J.M. and W. Martin, printers, of Warminster. 6 yrs, £20. 24 June 1862

Mother is the widow of the master of the Warminster National School. County apprentice.

304 Orchard, Henry, son of John, of Warminster: to William and Thomas Webb, cabinet makers, of Warminster. 6 yrs, £20. 2 June 1862

Father is a tailor. County apprentice.

305 Gillingham, Henry Charles, son of Henry and Dorcas, of 34 Hampden St, Harrow Rd: to John Thomas, plumber, painter and gas-fitter, of 16 Albert Terrace, Portchester Square. 7 yrs, £20. 1 July 1862

Mother formerly Dorcas Grace from Salisbury; father is a railway labourer.

306 Kiddle, Jane, daughter of James, of 1 St John's Place, Spa Rd, Bermondsey: to George Dyke, milliner and dressmaker, of Yeovil, Somerset. 4 yrs, £20. 30 July 1862

Parents from Urchfont (*Erchfont*).

307 Lewis, Alfred James, son of William, of 3 Peter St, Southwark Bridge Rd: to James Howell, accounts book manufacturer, of 3 West St, Smithfield. 6½ yrs, £20. 15 Sept. 1862

Father a carpenter from Chippenham. Apprentice is a brother to W.J.Lewis [*see* **139**]. Transferred 24 Aug. 1864 to William Richardson, vellum binding and account book manufacturer. Reapprenticed, 17 March 1866 to W. Franklin, 18 New Park Rd, Southwark, coppersmith, for 3 yrs.

308 Hopkins, Harriett Sarah, daughter of Elizabeth, of 21 Little Guildford St, Russell Square: to Anne Roberts, dressmaker, of 40 Leighton Grove, Gloster Place, Kentish Town. 3 yrs, £20. 13 Oct. 1862

Mother is a widow; father was from Corsley. Apprentice is a sister to T. Hopkins **(265)**.

309 Cumner, Ebenezer Alfred, son of Mary Ann, of 9 Aland Rd, Kentish Town: to Thomas Lycett, chronometer finisher, of 66 St Paul St, New North Rd. 5½ yrs, £25. 22 Nov. 1862

Mother is a widow; father was from Milton Lilbourne.

310 Eatwell, Robert Josiah, son of Robert, of 20 Murray St, Camden Square: to Henry John Garnett, gas fitter and brass finisher, of 6 Westbourne Grove. 6¾ yrs, £25. 14 Feb. 1863

Father is a brick-layer from Broad Hinton. Transferred 22 Aug. 1864 to Henry Hawes, 6 Warden Rd, Kentish New Town, smith and bell-hanger.

311 Bruckin, James Arthur, son of Thomas and Caroline, of 5 John St, Blackfriars Rd: to Louis Martin, lamp manufacturer, of 6 Tenison St, York Rd, Lambeth. 6¾ yrs, £20. 2 March 1863

Mother formerly Caroline Haynes from Warminster. Apprentice is brother to Thomas Henry Bruckin **(220)**.

312 Mills, Arthur, son of Henry, of Bramshaw, Wilts: to Francis Try Henbest, builder and wheelwright, of Fordingbridge, Hants. 5 yrs, £25. 6 Jan. 1863

County apprentice.

313 Watts, George, son of George, of 61 Roupell St, Lambeth: to John Dorrell, boot and shoe maker, of 33 Waverley Rd, Harrow Rd. 6 yrs, £20. 1 April 1863

Father is a labourer. Apprentice was born at Salisbury, and is brother to **296**. Father called 5 Oct. 1864 to say his son the apprentice had died.

314 Goodfellow, Henry William, son of Ann, of Fovant: to William Burrough, shoemaker, of Fovant. 6 yrs, £20. 15 June 1863

County apprentice.

315 Coombs, John William: to John Pitt, carpenter and wheelwright, of Pitton, near Salisbury. 6¾ yrs, £20. 3 June 1863

316   Saunders, John Joseph: to Jabez Dent, chair maker, of 6 Wolverly St, Bethnal Green Rd. 6 yrs, £20. 1 July 1863

317   Munday, Julia Ann: to John Foster Reed, milliner and dressmaker, of 22 The Pavement, Clapham Common. 2 yrs, £20. 9 July 1863

318   Daniell, John: to John Barnden, carpenter and joiner, of Warminster. 5¾ yrs, £20. 6 July 1863

319   Carpenter, Mark: to John Abbott, carpenter, of Keyford, near Frome, Somerset. 5½ yrs, £20. 27 July 1863

Apprentice died 1 July 1865.

320   Prince, Emily: to Eliz. A. Brenchley, dressmaker, of 48 Bromley St, Commercial Rd East. 3 yrs, £20. 3 Nov. 1863

321   Elliot, Alfred John: to Edwin Ballen, plumber, of 2a Chichester Place, Harrow Rd. 5½ yrs, £20. 26 March 1864

322   Hider, William: to K.G. Woodham (for Price's Patent Candle Co. Ltd.), coppersmith, of Battersea. 5¾ yrs, £20. 18 April 1864

323   Eatwell, Robert: to George Pulman, compositor and printer, of 24 Thayor St, Manchester Sq. 5¾ yrs, £20. 19 April 1864

324   Scammell, Samuel, of Donhead St Mary: to Robert Ball, coachmaker, of Shaftesbury, Dorset. 6 yrs, £25. 24 May 1864

325   Wright, Kate: to William Smith, draper and milliner, of 6 New Bridge St, Vauxhall. 3 yrs, £20. 14 June 1864

Parents from Salisbury.

326   Young, William Henry: to George H. Dowling, carpenter, builder and joiner, of Surbiton Rd. 7 yrs, £25. 6 July 1864

Father from Warminster.

327   Whitworth, Robert, son of Elizabeth: to J.T. Farnham, engineer and machinist, of 26 Union St, Kingsland Rd. 6 yrs, £25. 11 July 1864

Mother, formerly Elizabeth Bryant, from Hilperton.

328 Young, Albert William: to John Allen, smith and engineer, of 17, Little Trinity Lane. 6½ yrs, £20. 1 Aug. 1864

Father from Fisherton Anger. Reapprenticed 1 July 1868 to William Chambers, of 17 Little Trinity Lane, smith.

329 Mersh, Francis, son of Mary A. Mersh: to Frances Jane Summers, widow, goldbeater, of 19 Little Britain. 6½ yrs, £25. 1 Aug. 1864

Mother, formerly Mary A. Fricker, from Corton. Mrs Mersh called 12 March 1866 to say that the apprentice had run away and gone into the Navy.

330 Hussey, James John: to John Compton Merryweather, pattern maker, of 63 Longacre and York St, Lambeth. 6 yrs, £25. 18 Aug. 1864

Father is from Trowbridge.

331 Barnes, Thomas John, son of Mary Barnes: to Robert Barlow, carpenter and builder, of 5 High St, Kingsland. 6 yrs, £20. 17 Oct. 1864

Mother, formerly Mary Lawrence, from Ramsbury.

332 Amor, Alice M.: to Hannah Mcdonald, widow, needlewoman, of Coburg House, 9 Manor St, Chelsea. 4 yrs, £20. 23 Jan. 1865

333 Marks, Gilbert: to Macdonald Neal, compositor, of 61 St John's Square, Clerkenwell. 7 yrs, £25. 12 May 1865

334 Gough, Henry: to John Bracher, joiner, of Fonthill, Tisbury. 6 yrs, £20. 27 June 1865

335 Wild, George Robert: to Thomas Baker, blacksmith, of Compton Iron Foundry, Newbury, Berks. 6½ yrs, £25. 29 June 1865

336 Turner, James: to Martin Meaden, coachbuilder, of Warminster. 7 yrs, £25. 22 July 1865

337 Biggs, Alfred: to Charles Brieant, carpenter and wheelwright, of Pitton, near Salisbury. 7 yrs, £25. 26 July 1865

338 Truckle, Albert: to J.H. Holley, of 3 Slaidburn St, King's Rd, Chelsea. 6½ yrs, £20. 21 Sept. 1865

339 Harding, Annie J., to Anne Roberts, of 40 Leighton Grove, Kentish Town, dress and mantle maker. 2 yrs, £20. 1 Nov. 1865

340 Gregory, Frederick George: to Messrs Charles and Robert Warner, engineers, of 8 Crescent, Cripplegate. 6 yrs, £20. 7 Oct. 1865

341 Kiddle, James: to Thomas Bevington Sparrow, engineer, of Bermondsey. 5¾ yrs, £20. 13 Nov. 1865

342 Adams, James, of Highworth: to Rev Edward Rowden, vicar of Highworth. 5 yrs, £25. 16 Feb. 1866

Apprenticed at Highworth as pupil teacher in National School, 5 years from 1 June 1865. Also named as masters are Edgar Hanbury, of Eastrop Grange, Highworth; and George Baker, churchwarden, of Highworth.

343 Heale, Lavinia M.: to Mary Richards, dressmaker, of 33 South Audley St. 2 yrs, £25. 20 April 1866

344 Hider, Walter James: to Frederick Robinson, foundry engineer and pattern maker, of Battersea. 6 yrs, £20. 14 May 1866

345 Young, James: to Edward Edwards, plumber, of Warminster. 6¾ yrs, £20. 5 June 1866

346 Wright, Louisa: to Caroline Austen, dressmaker, of 4 Belgrave Place, Wandsworth Rd. 2 yrs, £25. 3 July 1866

347 Batchelor, William Henry, son of Henry, of Warminster: to Edward Watts, rope, twine and sack manufacturer, of Seloin St, Warminster. 5¾ yrs, £20. 3 July 1866

Brother to **434**.

348 Barnes, Edward: to John Pogson, brass finisher and gas fitter, of 6 Jubilee St, Mile End. 6½ yrs, £25. 9 July 1866

Pogson died March 1868; Reapprenticed 17 June 1868 to W.G. Wade of 2 Grange St, Hoxton, gas-fitter etc.

349 Gaisford, William Jabez: to James Benjamin Manning, engineer, of Burdett St, Limehouse. 5 yrs, £25. 16 July 1866

350 Alexander, Elizabeth: to Mrs Chandler, milliner and dressmaker, of 173 Great Dover St. 3 yrs, £20. 27 July 1866

351 Amor, Eustace J.: to William Keith, carpenter, of 18 Montpelier St, Brompton. 5¾ yrs, £20. 13 Aug. 1866

352 Speck, Henry: to Joseph Armstrong, manager of G.W.R. Works, blacksmith, of New Swindon. 7 yrs, £20. 1 Aug. 1866

353 Sillitoe, William: to Thomas Illman, packing case maker, of Noble St, Little Britain. 7 yrs, £20. 14 Sept. 1866

Free of the Joiners' Company.

354 Mott, William Thomas: to John Grimes, pewterer and B. fitter [*?brass fitter*], of 33 Whitechapel Rd. 5¾ yrs, £25. 17 Oct. 1866

Cancelled; reapprenticed from 17 Aug. 1868 to F. Skinner, of 56 Jubilee St.

355 Smith, Isaac: to Abraham Blick, carpenter and joiner, of 1 Albert Terrace, Church Row, Acton. 6 yrs, £25. 18 Oct. 1866

356 Smith, Edwin: to Charles Hinton, tailor, of Codford St Peter. 7 yrs, £20. 13 Nov. 1866

357 Cowderoy, John: to Pickard and Stoneman, cabinet makers, of 10 Spencer St, New Inn Yard, Shoreditch. 6¼ yrs, £25. 18 Dec. 1866

Master called 29 Nov. 1869 to say apprentice had run away.

358 Maxfield, William: to William Scammell, carpenter, of Warminster. 6¾ yrs, £20. 1 April 1867

359 Marks, Adela: to M. Snead and E. Lomer, dressmaker, of 6 Grey Terrace, Great Dover Rd. 4 yrs, £25. 15 May 1867

360 Pepperell, Harry: to Frederick Richard Fisher, carpenter, of Salisbury. 6 yrs 4 months, £20. 9 May 1867

361 Breewood, Albert: to Henry Nixon, plumber, of 28 Clapham Rd. 6½ yrs, £20. 1 Aug. 1867

362 Toop, Albert: to William Woodhams, grocer, of Croydon. 5 yrs, £20. 18 Sept. 1867

363 Freeman, Stephen Isaac: to James Harvey, packing case maker, of 11 Fore St. 7 yrs, £23. 6 Aug. 1867

Free of the Barbers' Company.

364 Smith, Henry Lay, son of Alfred, of Collingbourne Ducis: to James Rawlings, carpenter and machinist, of Collingbourne Ducis. 6½ yrs, £20. 1 Oct. 1867

Father a journeyman carpenter. Reapprenticed 23 Oct. 1873 to William Carter, of East Stratton, Hants, tea dealer, for 2 years and 181 days.

365   Pitney, Henry: to Thomas Thompson, plumber, of Castle Combe, near Grittleton. 7 yrs, £20. 17 Oct. 1867

366 Davis, Robert: to Jos. Barter, carpenter, of Sutton Veny. 5¾ yrs, £20. 19 Oct. 1867

367 Bailey, Frank, son of Jacob and Amelia, of 3 Edward St, Greenwich: to James Marshall, joiner etc, of 8 Orchard Place, Trafalgar Rd, East Greenwich. 7 yrs, £25. 18 Dec. 1867

Father is a letter-carrier. Parents are from Trowbridge, mother formerly Amelia Paradice. Apprentice is brother to **423-4**.

368 Churchill, James: to Carson and Toone, iron-founders, of Warminster. 7 yrs, £20. 29 June 1867

369 Dancy, John: to K.G. Woodham (Price's Patent Candle Co. Ltd.), carpenter, of Belmont, Battersea. 6½ yrs, £20. 3 Jan. 1868

370 Gregory, William Alexander: to William Gibbs, glass embosser etc, of 114 Old St, St Lukes. 6 yrs, £20. 18 Feb. 1868

371 Prince, William: to James Sheffield, carpenter and joiner, of 109 Chrisp St, Poplar. 6½ yrs, £20. 20 Feb. 1868

Transferred 6 June 1871 to William Parsons of 1 Parsfield Terrace, Dewsbury Rd, Poplar.

372 Lammas, William Thomas: to Armstrong and Downton, brass finisher etc, of 2 West India Dock Rd. 6 yrs, £20. 11 June 1868

373 Newnham, Alfred John: to James Ruddock, mason and carver, of 5 West St, Commercial Rd, Pimlico. 6 yrs 4 months, £20. 26 June 1868

374 Harding, Mary M.: to Anne Roberts, braiding and juvenile dressmaker, of 16 Gaisford St, Kentish Town Rd. 2 yrs, £20. 1 July 1868

375 Atkins, Sarah J.: to Elizabeth Davis, dressmaker, of St Thomas Square, Salisbury. 3 yrs, £20. 9 July 1868

Reapprenticed 15 Feb. 1869 to Mrs Sparsholt, milliner, of Winchester, Hants, for two years.

376 Brown, Joseph: to George Chivers, carpenter, of Calne. 7 yrs, £20. 23 July 1868

377 Spackman, John Jewell: to John Thomas Trumble, lighterman, of Waterman's Hall, 18 St Mary at Hill. 7 yrs, £20. 11 Aug. 1868

Free of the Watermen's Company.

378 Hussey, Frederick: to William Whieldon, engineer's pattern maker, of 190 Westminster Bridge Rd. 6 yrs, £25. 20 Aug. 1868

379 Griffin, Robert: to William Whieldon, engineer's pattern maker, of 190 Westminster Bridge Rd. 6½ yrs, £25. 31 Aug. 1868

380 Lidbury, Frederick: to Edward Hales, painter and house decorator, of Warminster. 7 yrs, £20. 13 Oct. 1868

381 Saunders, Henry: to Joseph Dent, cabinet manufacturer, of 30 Caurobert St, Bethnal Green Rd. 6 yrs, £20. 23 Dec. 1868

382 Ball, Harry: to Benjamin Parsons, carpenter and builder, of Warminster. 7 yrs, £20. 24 Dec. 1868

383 Lewington, John T.: to George Hunt, farrier, of 2 Church St, Blackfriars Rd. 5 yrs, £20. 13 April 1869

Father from Great Bedwyn. Apprentice brother to **452**.

384 Ford, Robert Thomas: to John Sedgfield, grocer, of Devizes. 4 yrs, £25. 12 April 1869

385 Francis, Frederick: to Samuel Fatt, saddler etc, of Warminster. 7 yrs, £20. 22 June 1869

386 Hawkins, George Cook: to Benjamin Treeton, of 30 Colchester St, Leman St, Whitechapel. 5 yrs, £20. 20 July 1869

Reapprenticed 15 April 1872 to Musto and Co., engineers, of Mile End New Town.

387 Freeman, Caleb Samuel, son of Esther, of 1 Charles Place, Hoxton: to Thomas Birch Mackey, bookbinder, of 5 Baches Row, City Rd. 7 yrs, £20. 27 Aug. 1869

Mother a widow; father was from Liddington. Apprentice is a brother to apprentices **281, 301** and **363**.

388 Cooper, John Knott: to William John Pearman, cabinet maker, of Devizes. 7 yrs, £20. 17 May 1869

389 Pearson, Alice E.: to H. Chester, milliner and dressmaker, of 5 Holders Terrace, Grosvenor Gardens. 3 yrs, £25. 23 Oct. 1869

Transferred to E. Stansell of 85, Oxford St.

390 Newman, Henry William, son of William George, of 26 Mount Gardens, Westminster Bridge Rd: to Richard Waygood, engineer, of Falmouth Rd, Great Dover St. 7 yrs, £25. 25 Oct. 1869

Father is an engineer from Devizes. Certificates returned 4 March 1872 to William George Newman, 5 Thornton St, South St, Walworth.

391 Hutchins, John William, son of John and Emma Elizabeth, of 34 Pell St, Cable St: to John James Toomey, packer, of 31 Bush Lane, Cannon St. 7 yrs, £20. 5 Jan. 1870

Father is a carpenter from Trowbridge. Free of the Clothworkers' Company [*see also* **431** *and* **508**].

392 Morey, Thomas, son of Sarah Ann, of 7 Smith St, Kennington Park: to William James Maxwell, plumber etc, of Elder House, Brixton Rd. 6½ yrs, £20. 1 March 1870

Mother formerly S.A.Belcher of Limpley Stoke. Certificates returned 4 March 1878 to Mrs Sarah A. Morey.

393 Cole, Thomas R.: to William Allen, pawn-broker, of 2 Prince Patrick Place, Millwall. 4 yrs, £20. 11 March 1870

Apprentice had been 3 yrs with Mr Allen.

394 Haskell, Henry J.: to D.S. Jenkins, ship owner, of 30 Lime St, EC. 4 yrs, £25. 1 April 1870

395 Townsend, Edward: to John Crispin, schoolmaster, of Warminster. 5 yrs, £20. 3 May 1870

396 Elkins, William, son of Stephen, of Chalford, Westbury: to Isaac Pearce Watts, saddler etc, of Westbury. 7 yrs, £20. 4 May 1870

Father is a labourer. Assigned 8 Dec. 1873 to Francis John Watts, son of I.P.Watts, and carrying on the same business at the same place. All certificates returned 4 March 1878 to father, Stephen Elkins of Chalford, Westbury.

397 Mott, Adelaide Jane: to Mrs Wood, dressmaker, of 624 Mile End Rd. 2 yrs, £20. 20 May 1870

398 Spackman, Mary Ann: to Mrs W. Smith, waistcoat maker, of 2a Pleasant Row, Stepney Green. 2 yrs, £20. 26 May 1870

399 Holbrook, Samuel: to Elias Boulger, tailor of Dorset House, Dorset St, Fleet St, and at 1 Mitre Court. 5¼ yrs, £20. 2 June 1870

Indenture cancelled by magistrate. Reapprenticed, 11 Nov. 1873, to Alfred John Miller, of 9 Union Square, Borough, tailor.

400 Kerley, John, son of James, of Warminster: to Messrs Carson and Toone, iron-founders, of Warminster. 6 yrs, £20. 8 June 1870

County apprentice. Certificates returned 4 March 1878 to James Kerley, c/o H.P. Jones Esq, Portway House, Warminster.

401 Toop, Ralph: to Amos Spark, plumber, of High St, Forest Hill. 5 yrs, £20. 14 July 1870

402 Mason, Thomas, son of Mary Ann, of 19a Henry St, Hampstead Rd: to Hippolyte Saleur, buhl and marquetry manufacturer and cabinet maker, of 52 Bolsolver St. 7 yrs, £25. 13 June 1870

Mother is a widow; father was from Great Bedwyn.

403 Frampton, James Alexander, son of Edmund and Elizabeth, of 6 Earl St, Edgeware Rd: to John Henry Spencer, plumber etc, of 23 John St N., Marylebone Rd. 6 yrs, £20. 12 Aug. 1870

Father is a railway porter; mother formerly Elizabeth Newham from Britford. Apprentice brother to **273**.

404 Mulcock, John Thomas, son of Sarah, of Rowde: to William Webb, carpenter, of Bromham. 6¾ yrs, £20. 18 Aug. 1870

Mother formerly Sarah Deverall. County apprentice.

405 Pitt, Harry George, son of Emma, of 36 Linton St, New North Rd: to Benjamin Griffiths, manufacturing jeweller, of 6 Ashby St, Clerkenwell. 6 yrs 4 months, £25. 13 Oct. 1870

Mother a widow; parents from Marlborough.

406 Cumner, Emily: to Thomas Wells Pembrey, draper and milliner, of Bampton, Oxon. 3 yrs, £25. 18 July 1870

407 Barnes, Joseph, son of Richard and Mary, of 9 The Grove, Homerton: to V. Cutmore, grainer, of 1 Burdett Cottages, Bow. 6 yrs 4 months, £20. 25 Nov. 1870

Father is a wine porter; mother, formerly Mary Lawrence, from Ramsbury. Apprentice brother to **331** and **348**. V. Cutmore died; no will or admon. Apprentice reapprenticed 24 March 1873 to Joseph Martin, 204 Jubilee Rd, Mile End, grainer.

408 Coulson, Cornelius, son of William, of 44 Acton St, Grays Inn Rd: to J.F. Cartwright, cabinet case-maker, of 35 Aylesbury St, Clerkenwell. 6 yrs, £20. 17 Dec. 1870

Mother, formerly C. Peirson, from Heytesbury. Apprentice is brother to **284**.

409 Miell, William Henry: to John Cumner, linen draper, of 27 Borough High St. 3 yrs, £25. 2 Jan. 1871

410 Hall, Nelson, son of Caroline, of Warminster: to William and Thomas Webb, cabinet makers etc, of Warminster 7 yrs, £20. 8 Feb. 1871

Mother is a widow. County apprentice.

411 Woodley, John: to John George Pope, carpenter of Marlborough. 5¼ yrs, £25. 28 March 1871

412 Kyte, Sydney Thomas, son of Sarah Jane, of Salisbury: to William Herbert Ady, carpenter etc, of St Anns St, Salisbury. 6¼ yrs, £20. 10 May 1871

Mother is a widow. County apprentice.

413 Lovelock, Sarah Ann: to John Draper, book-sewer, of 5 Little Tower St. 3 yrs, £20. 18 May 1871

414 Alexander, Sarah Ann: to Mrs Chandler, milliner and dressmaker, of 45 Great Dover St. 3 yrs, £20. 15 June 1871

415 Aland, Ebenezer, son of Thomas, of 26 Loman St, Gravel Lane, Southwark: to Henry Aland, engineer, of 18 Richard St, Ronpelle St, Lambeth. 7 yrs, £20. 17 June 1871

Father is a labourer from Bradford.

416 Mayhew, Alexander, son of Eliza, of 4 Gresse St, Tottenham Court Rd: to William H.J. Hodge, printer, of Black Horse Yard, Rathbone Place. 6 yrs, £20. 27 June 1871

Mother a widow, formerly Eliza Peirson from Heytesbury. Reassigned 12 April 1874 to Richard Hackett, the successor to W.H.J. Hodge.

417 Smith, Albert, son of Isaac, of 2 Elisha Terrace, Avenue, Acton: to John Robert Moon, confectioner etc, of the Broadway, Ealing. 6 yrs, £25. 4 July 1871

Father a pensioner from Knook. Apprentice is a brother to **355**.

418 Stow, John, son of Robert, of Salisbury: to Charles Harding, saddler etc, of Silver St, Salisbury. 6¼ yrs, £20. 1 July 1871

Father is a working saddler. County apprentice.

419 Bowman, Elizabeth Anne: to Elizabeth Webb, milliner etc, of 7 Lower East Hayes, Bath, Somerset. 3 yrs, £25. 1 July 1871

420 King, Joseph, son of Mary Ann, of 42 York Rd, Lambeth: to Charles William Henry Wyman, letter press printer etc, of 75 Great Queen St, WC. 7 yrs, £25. 1 July 1871

Mother is a widow; father was from Tisbury.

421 Orchard, Frederick, son of Albert, of Warminster: to Benjamin Parsons, carpenter etc, of Warminster. 6½ yrs, £20. 12 July 1871

Father is a tailor. County apprentice.

422 Pitt, William Hilson, son of William John, of 1a Devonshire Place, Upper Kennington Lane: to John William Fowler, working jeweller, of 2 Kennington Park Rd. 6 yrs, £25. 4 Sept. 1871

Father is a warehouseman from Marlborough.

423 Bailey, George, son of Jacob and Amelia, of 3 Edward St, Greenwich: to William Bromley, ironmonger, of 23 Nelson St, Greenwich. 5 yrs, £25. 11 Dec. 1871

Parents are from Trowbridge. Father is a letter-carrier; mother formerly Amelia Paradice. Apprentice brother to **367**.

424 Bailey, Harry, son of Jacob and Amelia, of 3 Edward St, Greenwich: to William Dummer, dyer and cleaner, of 2 Deptford Bridge. 5 yrs, £25. 11 Dec. 1871

Parents are from Trowbridge. Father is a letter-carrier; mother formerly Amelia Paradice. Apprentice brother to **367** and **423**.

425 Daniell, John, son of Elizabeth, of 24 Alfred St, Paddington: to John Perry Pecover, gas-fitter etc, of 17 Jonson Pl, Harrow Rd. 6 yrs, £25. 25 Jan. 1872

Mother, a widow, formerly Elizabeth Greenhill from North Bradley. Apprenticeship dissolved 11 March 1878; certificate returned to mother, Elizabeth Daniels, of 32 Kennett Row, St Peter's Pk, Harrow.

426 James, Samuel George, son of Samuel, of 6 Lynton St, Blue Anchor Rd, Bermondsey: to Daniel A. Messent, lithographer and copper-plate printer, of 8 Newgate St. 6 yrs 4 months, £20. 10 June 1872

Father from Bradford.

427 Alder, Frank George, son of Mary A., of Trowbridge: to William Smith, carpenter, of Church St, Trowbridge. 6 yrs, £20. 20 June 1872

Mother is a widow. County apprentice.

428 Lane, William G.: to M.G. Horder, grocer, of 115 Castle St, Salisbury. 3 yrs, £20. 20 June 1872

429 West, Virginia G.: to Catherine West, dressmaker, of 14 Adea Grove, N. Green Lane. 3 yrs, £25. 26 July 1872

430 Higgins, Henry E., son of Stephen, of 2 Bellevue Place, Blue Anchor Rd, Bermondsey: to William Glover, fitter and turner, of St James Rd, Old Kent Rd. 6¼ yrs, £20. 20 Aug. 1872

Father from Chippenham. Apprentice is a brother to **280**.

431 Hutchins, William Christopher, son of John and Emma Elizabeth, of 34 Pell St, St George's in the East: to A. Ohlson, coppersmith etc, of 85 New Rd, Whitechapel. 6½ yrs, £20. 21 Aug. 1872

Father, a carpenter from Trowbridge, is in delicate health, and his earnings are precarious. Apprentice is a brother to **391** and **508**.

432 Ovens, Thomas, son of James, of 55 Roscoe St, Canning Town: to Richard Foale, builder, of 3 Alexander Terrace, Barking Rd. 6 yrs, £20. 21 Aug. 1872

Parents from Devizes.

433 Curtis, Edwin J., son of Frank, of Warminster: to John Smith, grocer, of Warminster. 5 yrs, £20. 11 Aug. 1872

County apprentice.

434 Batchelor, George C., son of Henry, of Warminster: to B.W. Coates, bookbinder, of Warminster. 7 yrs, £25. 12 Aug. 1872

Brother to **347**. County apprentice.

435 Great, Joseph, son of John, of 1 Tuffnell's Place, Astey's Row, Essex Rd: to J.W. Mugliston, gold-chain maker, of 2 Tuffnel's Place, Islington. 6 yrs, £25. 29 Aug. 1872

Father from 'Charlcot' [*Chalcot in Westbury or Charlcote in Bremhill?*]. Second moiety not paid, 7 Nov. 1876, on account of boy absconding to sea.

436 Smith, Alice: to E.F. Witts, dressmaker, of 15 Lancaster Lane. 2 yrs, £20. 4 Nov. 1872

437 Brazier, John, son of James, of Woodford: to H.J. Jarvis, blacksmith, of Woodford. 5¼ yrs, £25. 21 Dec. 1872

County apprentice.

438 Smith, Agnes: to George Davies, milliner, of 229 Oxford St. 2 yrs, £25. 27 Feb. 1873

439 Frampton, Elizabeth M.C.: to Mrs E. Wright, dressmaker, of 18 Craven Rd, Westbourne Terrace. 2 yrs, £20. 24 March 1873

440 Nash, Thomas, son of Mary, of Chiseldon: to George Wiltshire, mason etc, of Bath Rd, Swindon. 7 yrs, £20. 5 April 1873

Mother is a widow. County apprentice.

441 Hider, Robert T., son of William, of 32 Benfield St, Battersea: to Edmund Alfred Pontifex, armourer and brazier, of Shoe Lane, EC. 7 yrs, £20. 24 April 1873

Mother from Potterne. Free of the Armourers' Company.

442 Whatley, John, son of Henry, of 6 Trafalgar Grove, East Greenwich: to Josiah Murrin, carpenter and joiner, of 16 Royal Hill, Greenwich. 6 yrs, £20. 28 July 1873

Father is from Wilton.

443 Smith, John, son of Elijah, of 1 Victoria Place, Tyer St, Vauxhall: to George Box, ironmonger etc, of Broad St, Lambeth. 6 yrs, £20. 22 Aug. 1873

Father from Marlborough.

444 Crisp, Thomas James, son of Walter, of 23 Mansfield St, Kingsland Rd: to Thomas Heath, beer-engine maker, of 33 Rahere St, Goswell Rd. 6 yrs 4 months, £25. 20 Sept. 1873

Father from Bradford-on-Avon.

445 Adams, Thomas, son of Mary, of Highworth: to John Gobey, grocer, of Castle St, Cirencester, Glos. 5 yrs, £20. 27 Oct. 1873

Mother is a widow. County apprentice.

446 Pitt, Robert James, son of William John, of 1a Devonshire Place, Upper Kennington Lane: to John William Fowler, working jeweller, of 2 Kennington Park Rd. 6 yrs, £25. 7 Nov. 1873

Father from Marlborough.

447 Styles, Henry, son of Susannah, of 16 Boyson Rd, Camberwell: to Edward Taylor, roll turner, of 25 Wellington St, Bradford Rd, S. Bradford near Manchester. 7 yrs, £25. 11 Nov. 1873

Mother, a widow, is from Trowbridge.

448 Hussey, William, son of Joseph, of 7 Hatfield Crescent, Clapham Junction: to William Whieldon, engineer's pattern maker, of Westminster Bridge Rd. 6½ yrs, £25. 15 Nov. 1873

Brother to **330** and **378**. Business dissolved Aug. 1877; apprentice disappeared in 1877.

449 Bennett, Frederick James, son of William, of 15 Culford Rd, Islington: to Henry John Drayton, writer, grainer etc, of 20 Clarence St, Islington. 5 yrs, £20. 16 Jan. 1874

Father from Trowbridge.

450 Annetts, Henry, son of George, of Collingbourne Kingston: to James Rawlings, machinery carpenter, of Collingbourne Ducis. 7 yrs, £20. 3 Feb. 1874

County apprentice.

451 Hill, John, son of William, of Malmesbury: to John Wadley Witton, grocer, of Malmesbury. 5 yrs, £20. 3 March 1874

Apprenticeship dissolved by mutual consent 9 March 1878; certificate returned.

452 Lewington, Sam, son of John, of 15 Water St, Blackfriars: to Edmund Symmons, bookbinder, of 23 Bouverie St, Fleet St. 5 yrs, £20. 5 March 1874

Father from Great Bedwyn. Apprentice brother to **383**.

453 Hall, John, son of Bertha, of 1 Havelock Terrace, Peckham: to Messrs Weygood and Co., engineers, of Falmouth Rd, Gt Dover St, Borough. 6½ yrs, £20 10s. 26 April 1874

Mother, a widow, from Dilton Marsh.

454 Lammas, Henry George, son of George Henry, of 5 Mary Place, East Ferry Rd, Poplar, Middlesex: to James Downton, brass finisher, of 2 West India Dock Rd, Limehouse. 6 yrs, £25. 6 May 1874

Mother is from Warminster.

455 Davis, William, son of William, of 1 Lower Uxbridge St, Notting Hill, Middlesex: to George Silman, coach builder, of 187 Fulham Rd. 7 yrs, £25. 6 May 1874

Father is from Preshute.

456 Ford, George John, son of Hannah, of the Cottage Hospital, Church St, Trowbridge: to Lois Case, drapers, of Trowbridge. 5 yrs, £20. 4 June 1874

County apprentice.

457 King, Thomas William, son of Henry, of 7 White Hart Passage, Liquorpond St, Grays Inn Rd: to Jesse Young, carpenter, of Clerkenwell Close. 5½ yrs, £20. 4 June 1874

Father from Alton [*Barnes*].

458 Bailey, Ellen, daughter of William, of 76 Rodney Rd, Walworth. SE.: to Fanny Smith, dressmaker, of 58 Union Rd, Borough. 2 yrs, £20. 15 July 1874

Father is from Dilton Marsh.

459 Cook, Frederick William, son of Charles, of Chute: to James Baiden, shoemaker, of Upton near Hungerford, Berks. 5 yrs, £25. 15 July 1874

Father is a labourer. County apprentice.

460 Price, Thomas, son of John, of Westbury: to George Grant, tailor, of Westbury. 5 yrs, £20. 15 Aug. 1874

County apprentice.

461 Young, Henry George, son of Sarah, of Warminster: to Webb and Son, upholsterers, of Warminster. 7 yrs, £20. 5 Nov. 1874

County apprentice.

462 Tanswell, Walter James, son of James Rogers Tanswell, of Sambourne, Warminster: to William Scammell, carpenter and builder, of Warminster. 7 yrs, £20. 11 Nov 1874

County apprentice. Transferred 17 June 1876 to Joseph Gaisford, of Warminster, carpenter and builder.

463 Carr, Ann, daughter of Sarah, of Upton Scudamore: to Elizabeth Butcher, dressmaker, of Brook St, New Town, Warminster. 7 yrs, £25. 18 Jan. 1875

Mother is a widow. County apprentice. Apprenticeship dissolved by mutual consent in 1878.

464 Aland, Manoah, son of Thomas, of 26 Loman St, Gravel Lane, Southwark: to George Askie, pattern and model maker, of 42 Westminster Bridge Rd, Westminster. 6 yrs 4 months, £25. 24 March 1875

Father from Bradford.

465 Field, Mary Ann Maria, daughter of William Henry Gray Field, of 2 Bennett's Buildings, White Hart St, Kennington Cross: to George Robert Bone, milliner, of 138a High St, Borough. 2 yrs, £20. 15 April 1875

Mother from Wilton.

466 Stokes, Mary Ann, daughter of Mary Ann, of Trowbridge: to Sarah Heathcote, dressmaker, of Trowbridge. 3 yrs, £20. 11 May 1875

Mother a widow. County apprentice.

467 Newman, Owen, son of James D., of 22a Fair St, St John's, Southwark: to Messrs Cassel, Petter and Galpin, printers, of Belle Sauvage Yard, Ludgate Hill. 7 yrs, £20. 20 May 1875

Father from Salisbury. Newman absconded Jan. 1879, and has gone to sea.

468 Poole, John, son of W.H., of 8 Blue Anchor Lane, Bermondsey: to James Seaton, smith, of 199 Long Lane, Bermondsey. 7 yrs, £25. 25 Jun 1875

Father is a clerk; mother from Wroughton.

469 Hart, Charles James, son of Louisa, of 9 Brighton St, Argyle Square, Kings Cross: to Frederick J. Brazier, plumber, of Seven Sisters Rd, Holloway. 6¼ yrs, £20. 21 Aug 1875

Mother a widow from Marlborough.

470 Mott, Elizabeth Catherine, daughter of Jane, of 32 Antill Rd, Bow: to George Francis Pitts, milliner, of 379 Mile End Rd, Bow. 2 yrs, £25. 25 Aug. 1875

Mother is a widow from Chute. The apprentice has been for several months in Mr Pitts' employ.

471 Trollope, Henry Charles, son of Charles, of Warminster: to James Wise, coach builder, of Warminster. 6 yrs, £20. 28 Aug 1875

Father is a journeyman butcher. County apprentice.

472 Saunders, William, son of John E., of 8 Prospect Place, Stepney Green: to Frederick Daniel Mathew, brushmaker, of 106 Upper Thames St. 7 yrs, £20. 8 Sept. 1875

Father is a labourer, from Cricklade. Apprentice is a brother to **293**, **316**, and **381**. Apprenticeship dissolved 8 March 1879 by mutual consent; apprentice tried in a second place but failed to keep it.

473 Hall, John Augustus, son of William, of Corsham: to James Boscombe, bootmaker, of Corsham. 5 yrs, £15. 16 Sept. 1875

Father is a labourer. Not sufficiently strong to do outdoor work. County apprentice.

474 Rickets, John Charles, son of John, of 10 College Avenue, Hackney: to E.A. Pontifex, brazier, of Shoe Lane. 7 yrs, £20. 30 Sep 1875

Father is a clerk from Ramsbury. Free of the Armourers' Company.

475 Sainsbury, James Charles, son of James C., of Westbury Leigh: to Thomas Cox, grocer, of Walcot St, Bath, Somerset. 6 yrs, £25. 4 Oct. 1875

Father is a yeoman. Apprentice unfit for outdoor employ. County apprentice.

476 Webb, Isaac Paul, son of Catherine N., of 12 George St, Gypsy Hill, Norwood: to W. Whieldon, engineer, of 190 Westminster Bridge Rd, Westminster. 6 yrs, £25. 20 Dec. 1875

Parents from Melksham, mother a widow. Transferred 10 March 1879 to Symonds and Co., 107 Southwark Bridge Rd.

477 Crisp, Ann Elizabeth, daughter of Walter, of 23 Mansfield St, Kingsland Rd: to William Phillips, milliner, of 90 High St, Kingsland. 2 yrs, £20. 19 Feb. 1876

Sister to **444**. Father from Bradford-on-Avon.

478 Farrell, James (Walter) Lovett, son of Patrick, of London: to Thomas Swayne, carpenter and joiner, of Chippenham. 5 yrs, £20. 19 March 1876

Father a journeyman bookseller. County apprentice. [*Apprentice's name is given as Walter L. Lovett in Annual report*]

479 Smith, Allan, son of Hannah, of Ashen Rd, Shepherds Bush: to Charles K.K. Bishop, organ builder, of 250 Marylebone Rd. 7 yrs, £25. 5 May 1876

Mother a widow from Winterbourne Stoke. Transferred 15 Nov. 1881 to E.H. Suggate, the successor of C.K.K. Bishop, to complete apprenticeship.

480 Griffen, Henry, son of George, of Steeple Ashton: to John Miles, shoemaker, of Steeple Ashton. 5 yrs, £20. 1 July 1876

Father is a labourer. Apprentice not fit for outdoor work. County apprentice.

481 Trueman, Thomas, son of Charles and Sarah, of Collingbourne Ducis: to Walter Cottle, shoemaker, of Collingbourne Ducis. 5 yrs, £25. 12 July 1876

Father is a labourer, wages 11s. per week. He has eight children, four of whom are dependent upon him. Candidate is a cripple and has been so for some years. There has been considerable delay in this case owing to the failing health of the late Rector of Collingbourne Ducis. County apprentice.

482 Elliot, Ada Elizabeth, daughter of George: to Charles Henry Seddon, milliner, of 11 Osnaburgh St, Regent St. 2 yrs, £25. 18 July 1876

Father is a carpenter from Bradford-on-Avon. Reapprenticed 10 Dec. 1877 to William Bull, of 14 Edward St, Hampstead Rd.

483 White, George, son of Joseph and Clara, of Longbridge Deverill: to Martin Brothers, printer and book-binder, of Warminster. 7 yrs, £20. 25 July 1876

Father an agricultural labourer; has a wife and three children dependent upon him. Apprentice is unfit for outdoor work. County apprentice.

484 Reynolds, Alfred, son of Alfred and Alice: to Henry Bacon, upholsterer, of Worship St, Finsbury. 6½ yrs, £25. 18 Aug. 1876

Father from Westbury, and was apprenticed by the Society in 1856 (**242**). Wages 36s. a week, and has a wife and five children dependent on him.

485 Gaisford, Jane Flower, daughter of Thomas and Sarah Jane: to Valentine Vyse, milliner, of 20 Ludgate Hill, EC. 2 yrs, £25. 4 Nov. 1876

Town apprentice. Father, from Bulkington, near Devizes, is a widower and a brother of **359**. Has four children dependent on him, of whom the second is the candidate.

486 Adlam, Walter Joseph, son of Joseph and Louisa: to Walter Dickes, chromo-lithographer, of Faringdon Rd, EC. 6 yrs, £20. 8 Nov. 1876

Father, a journeyman boot and shoe maker, has worked for one firm for the last ten years. Has six children dependent upon him. Mother (formerly Louisa Dunning) from Westbury. Town apprentice.

487 Dafter, William George, son of William and Eliza: to Thomas James Harper, upholsterer, of 11 Charles Square, Hoxton. 6 yrs, £25. 25 Jan. 1877

Father from Cricklade; mother (formerly Eliza Reynolds) from Westbury. Father a jobbing gardener, wages 14s. per week. Has two children, one of whom is partially and the other (the candidate) entirely dependent on him.

488 Baker, Walter Henry, son of George and Emma: to Messrs. Henderson and McNeil, brass finishers, of 193 Blackfriars Road. 5 yrs 4 months, £20. 29 Jan. 1877

Parents from Westbury. Father has been a milk-carrier for fourteen years in London; wages 22s. a week. Four children dependent on him, including the candidate. There have been eleven children of whom seven only are surviving.

489 Moore, James, son of James and Susannah: to Messrs. Henderson and McNeil, brass finisher, of 193 Blackfriars Rd. 6 yrs, £20. 29 Jan. 1877

Father, from Warminster, is a warehouse porter, wages 28s. a week. Has a wife and four children dependent upon him.

490 Shepherd, Charles Swithin, son of Charles and Ellen Jane: to Frederick Dray, saddler, of Heathfield, Sussex. 5 yrs, £25. 3 March 1877

Mother formerly Ellen White, from Devizes. Father is dead and the mother has since failed in business.

491 Daniells, Arthur, son of John and Eliza, of Upton Scudamore: to Messrs William Carpenter and James Penny, printers, of Frome, Somerset. 6 yrs, £20. 6 Mar 1877

The father was formerly an agricultural labourer, but is now disabled by ulceration of the leg and general ill-health. His means are 3s. 6d. per week from a club, and 4s and a loaf from the parish. He has seven children, five of whom (including the candidate) are dependent upon him. County apprentice.

492 Ricketts, Charles George Scaping, son of George and Sarah: to John Almond, carpenter and joiner, of 126 Jamaica Rd, Bermondsey. 5 yrs, £20. 16 April 1877

Father, from Chippenham, is a carpenter in humble circumstances, with one child dependent on him.

493 Crisp, George Samuel, son of Walter and Ann: to William Thomas Fisher, carpenter and joiner, of 21 Goodman's Yard, Minories. 6 yrs, £25. 16 April 1877

Brother of apprentice **477**. Father, from Bradford, is a journeyman butcher, and has four children dependent on him.

494 Baker, Frederick Robert, son of George and Emma: to William Salter, shop-fitter and carpenter, of Webber St, Blackfriars Rd. 7 yrs, £20. 18 April 1877

Brother of apprentice **488**. Parents from Westbury. Father has been a milk-carrier for fourteen years in London; wages 22s. a week. Four children are dependent on him including the candidate. There have been eleven children, of whom seven only are surviving.

495 Vince, Sarah Lois, daughter of Eli and Mary, of Trowbridge: to Emma Jane Smith, dressmaker, of Trowbridge. 3 yrs, £20. 23 May 1877

Mother formerly Mary Alesbury of Trowbridge. Father, also of Trowbridge, has been a cripple for nineteen years. He has five children, two of whom are dependent upon him. County apprentice.

496 Feltham, James, son of Charles and Selina, of Hilperton: to Isaac Hiscock, carpenter and wheelwright, of Hilperton, Trowbridge. 4 yrs, £20. 31 May 1877

Father, a journeyman baker, has seven children, five of whom (including the candidate) are dependent upon him. No application before, through ignorance of the existence of the Society. County apprentice.

497 Hibberd, Frederick Arthur Albert, son of John and Louisa, of Burcombe: to Lewis Thomas Fulker, coach builder, of Salisbury. 7 yrs, £25. 5 July 1877

The candidate is an orphan, both parents – his father, a labourer, and his mother (formerly Elderton) – being dead. The father was a publican, and died in 1870 leaving five children almost entirely unprovided for. The mother died in 1867, and the means of the family are nearly exhausted. County apprentice.

498 Adlam, John, son of John and Mary Ann, of Stratford-sub-Castle, Salisbury: to Lewis Thomas Fulker, coach builder, of Salisbury. 6 yrs, £25. 5 July 1877

The father is dead; the mother, formerly Mary Ann Goddard, has four children, two of whom (including the candidate) are dependent upon her. County apprentice.

499 Hughes, Henry, son of George and Sarah, of Steeple Ashton: to Thomas Miles, shoemaker, of Steeple Ashton. 5 yrs, £20. 24 June 1877

Father formerly of Bromham; mother, formerly Sarah Kemp, of Steeple Ashton. The father is a common day-labourer, and has eight children dependent upon him, including the candidate, who is crippled in the legs, and though fit for a trade, is not able to work as an agricultural labourer. County apprentice.

500 Smith, Arthur, son of Jeremiah and Sarah Ann, of Swindon: to George Wiltshire, carpenter and joiner, of Swindon. 4½ yrs, £20. 7 Sept. 1877

Father is an ironmonger's porter. He has five children, the youngest of whom is the candidate. The mother has been for several years an invalid. County apprentice.

501 Tasker, Thomas, son of William and Bethia: to Samuel Dennis, carpenter and house decorator, of 18 Paul St, Finsbury. 6 yrs, £20. 29 Oct. 1877

Father from Stanton; mother from Chitterne. Father, a day-labourer at 24s. a week, has two children dependent upon him. Reapprenticed 13 July 1879 to Samuel Row of 8 Beech St, Barbican, builder.

502 Hinton, Arthur, son of Arthur and Betty: to George Dear, woolsorter, of Codford. 6 yrs, £20. 12 Nov. 1877

Mother is a widow from Upton Lovell, left with eight children, two of whom are still dependent upon her.

503 Thorp, George Dann, son of George and Mary: to Frederick Sexton, cabinet maker, of 149 Southwark Bridge Rd, SE. 6 yrs, £25. 29 Nov. 1877

Mother is a widow, formerly Mary Dann of Marlborough. Three of the children are entirely dependent on her. She gets her living as a house-keeper.

504 Bennett, Thomas William, son of Charles and Sarah: to Isaac Seagrave, zinc worker, of 72 Praed St, Paddington. 6 yrs, £25. 13 Dec. 1877

Mother formerly Sarah Culley of Marlborough. Father is a cabman earning about 20s. a week.

505 Neat, Maria, daughter of Moses and Maria Emma: to John William Cole, dressmaker, of 1 Eltham Rd, Lee, SE. 2 yrs, £25. 20 Dec. 1877

Father, a journeyman whitesmith from Westbury, has two children dependent upon his earnings.

506 Dimes, Albert, son of James and Ellen: to James William Taylor, chair and sofa frame maker, of 49 Castle St East, Oxford St. 6 yrs, £20. 16 Jan. 1878

Mother formerly Ellen Pine from St Edmund, Salisbury. Father was a gold-chaser earning 30s. a week. He is now afflicted with fits and his wages very uncertain and much reduced.

507 Dowse, Albert Edward, son of Henry and Mary Ann: to Charles Binion Cooper, whitesmith, of 65 Theobald's Rd, Bloomsbury. 5¾ yrs, £25. 15 March 1878

Mother formerly Mary Ann Culley from Marlborough. Father is a carman, earning £1 a week. The candidate is partially, and another child entirely, dependent upon his earnings. Articles assigned 22 March 1881 to G.B. Coomes and Sons, of 121 Drury Lane, general iron workers.

508 Hutchins, Robert Frederick, son of John and Emma Elizabeth, of 34 Pell St, St George's in the East: to George Taylor, carpenter and joiner, of 8 Wormwood St, EC. 5 yrs, £20. 15 March 1878

Father, formerly of Trowbridge, is in delicate health, and his earnings precarious. Candidate is a brother to **391** and **431**.

509 Thomas, William Davis, son of James George and Sarah: to John Newton and Edmund Triggs, carpenters and joiners, of The Chace, Clapham. 5½ yrs, £25. 16 May 1878

Mother (formerly Davis) from Bedwyn St, St Edmund's, Salisbury. Father, a carriage fitter, wages 28s. a week, has two children dependent upon him. *(1880 Annual report:* Candidate elected to Town Exhibition. Born 14 Dec. 1862, he was educated at Clapham Parochial School and passed sixth standard in arithmetic, June 1875. He was apprenticed in May 1878 and has been working satisfactorily. The wages of the parents average 30s. a week.*)*

510   Beaven, Samuel: to James Beavan, tin-plate worker and gas-fitter, of Market Place, Trowbridge. 6 yrs, £20. 20 June 1878

511   Down, Thomas, son of Mary Ann Howard: to Latimer Clark, Muirhead and Co., telegraph instrument makers, of 29, Regency St, Westminster. 6 yrs, £30. 23 July 1878

Candidate is an inmate of Royal Victoria Patriotic School, Wandsworth. His father is dead. Mother, formerly Down, was Mary Ann Moore from Mere. She was left with four children, and has since had two more by her present husband, who is a private in the Coldstream Guards; two children are dependent on them.

512   Tanswell, William Thomas: to Sylvanus Luke, plumber, painter and glazier, of Warminster. 5 yrs, £20. 2 July 1878

County apprentice. Brother to **462**.

513   Reid, Eliza Sarah: to Sarah Ann Simpkins, dressmaker, of Sydney House, Stamford Hill. 2 yrs, £25. 8 July 1878

514   Hutchins, James: to Thomas Beazley, stonemason and builder, of Wood St, Calne. 6 yrs, £25. 31 Aug. 1878

County apprentice.

515   Poole, Arthur: to Charles Henry Kent, carpenter and builder, of 8 Paulin St, Bermondsey. 6 yrs, £30. 15 Nov. 1878

Brother to **468**; mother from Wroughton.

516   Sheppard, Lewis: to John Gane Andrews, carpenter, of Trowbridge. 6 yrs, £20. 18 Nov. 1878

County apprentice. £5 worth of tools to be given.

517   Dymock, John Abraham Joseph: to Frederick Albert Pemberton, carpenter and joiner, of 56 Horseferry Rd, Westminster. 5 yrs, £30. 7 Dec. 1878

Mother from Ogbourne St Andrew. Master died; reapprenticed 12 Jan. 1882 to John Giles, of Derby Terrace, Birkbeck St, Tottenham Ct Rd.

518   Beasant, Henry John Martin: to Edward Power, architect and surveyor, of 63 Queen Victoria St, EC. 5 yrs, £20. 7 Dec. 1878

Mother from Salisbury.

519 Hosey, Henry, son of Thomas and Louisa: to Captain J.S. Crane, of the ship *Mabel Young* of London. 1 yr, £12. 23 Dec. 1878

The mother is dead. The father, formerly of Bradford-on-Avon, worked there seven years for Messrs Edmonds and Co.; afterwards in London for 28 years for Mr Sparrow, cloth-worker, White Hart St, Minories, till he was incapacitated by paralysis. He and his son are now supported by friends. Articled on board the ship under the supervision of her owners, Millick Martin and Co., 10 George Yard, Lombard St, EC, 9 to 13 months.

520 James, Thomas Moses: to Captain J.S. Crane, of ship *Mabel Young*. 1 yr, £12. 23 Dec. 1878

Articled on board the ship under the supervision of her owners, Millick Martin and Co., 10 George Yard, Lombard St, EC, 9 to 13 months.

521 Hall, Harriett: to George F. Head, milliner, of Argyle House, Rye Lane, Peckham. 2 yrs, £20. 11 March 1879

Mother from Dilton Marsh, Westbury; sister to **453**.

522 Neat, George Thomas: to William Tytherleigh, whitesmith and general ironmonger, of 121, Clapham Park Rd. 6 yrs, £30. 18 March 1879

Indoor apprentice; left his master.

523 Barber, William: to Edwin Giles, carpenter and builder, of Ewias Harold, near Hereford, Herefordshire. 6 yrs, £30. 24 April 1879

County apprentice.

524 Eatwell, Albert William: to Henry Randall, wood turner, of 328 Euston Rd, NW. 6 yrs, £25. 8 June 1879

525 Newnham, Edwin: to Watkin Brown, engraver, of 23 Brewer St, Golden Square. 6 yrs, £25. 8 July 1879

526 Hannam, William: to Henry Musselwhite, saddler and harness maker, of Devizes. 6 yrs, £20. 10 July 1879

County apprentice.

527 Newman, Stephen William: to James Philips, engineer, of 5 and 6 Salisbury St, Jamaica Rd, Bermondsey. 7 yrs, £20. 30 July 1879

528 Scutt, William: to John Wheeler, saddler, of Basingstoke, Hants. 5 yrs, £25. 31 July 1879

County apprentice.

529 Gale, Frederick: to Frederick Telling, harness maker, of Calne. 6 yrs, £20. 14 Aug. 1879

County apprentice.

530 Adlam, Mary Jane: to Mary Salmon, dressmaker, of 97 New Bond St. 3 yrs, £20. 27 Oct. 1879

531 Schneider, Henry James: to Charles Frederick Miatt, engraver, of Percival St, Clerkenwell. 7 yrs, £25. 7 Nov. 1879

532 Looker, Ada Louisa: to Amelia Painter, dressmaker, of Swindon. 2 yrs, £20. 12 Nov. 1879

County apprentice.

533 Pullen, Edward James: to William Henry Mason, watchmaker, of 2 Portland Place, Clifton, Bristol. 6 yrs, £20. 12 Nov. 1879

County apprentice.

534 James, Walter: to James Turner, upholsterer and cabinet maker, of Warminster. 7 yrs, £25. 13 Dec. 1879

County apprentice.

535 Fruen, Isaac Richard: to Sutherland Robertson, cabinet maker, of 185 Kennington Lane, Lambeth. 6 yrs, £25. 6 June 1880

536 Rutty, William George: to William Webb, cabinet maker, of Warminster. 7 yrs, £25. 6 March 1880

County apprentice.

537   Smith, Frederick Tom: to Alexander Martin, zinc worker, of 71 Powis St, Woolwich. 5 yrs, £20. 5 March 1880

538   Brain, William Philip: to George John Farrington, printer, of Bradford-on-Avon. 4 yrs, £20. 5 April 1880

County apprentice.

539   Newman, Mary Ann: to Mary Ann Swift, milliner and dressmaker, of Westbury. 2 yrs, £20. 26 April 1880

County apprentice.

540   Burgess, Florence Ellen: to Thomas Livings, dressmaker, of Bradford-on-Avon. 2 yrs, £20. 26 April 1880

County apprentice.

541   Chapman, William Samuel: to Messrs F. and V. Head, tailors, of Marlborough. 6 yrs, £20. 17 April 1880

County apprentice.

542   Thomas, Charles Brown: to Charles Samuel Bensted, dentist, of 6 Metropolitan Buildings, Broad St, EC. 4 yrs, £25. 21 May 1880

543   Bodman, Eliza Ann: to Gilbert Edward Hunt, tailor, of Trowbridge. 4 yrs, £25. 24 May 1880

County apprentice.

544   King, William: to William Hockey, saddler, of Overton near Marlborough. 5 yrs, £25. 25 May 1880

County apprentice. Master drowned 23 Oct. 1881; lad reapprenticed to William Pratt.

545   Sheppard, Nelson: to William Smith, carpenter, of Trowbridge. 6 yrs, £20. 26 July 1880

County apprentice.

546 Poulter, Alfred Thomas: to Richard James Heard, cabinet maker, of 19 Hamilton Rd, Grove Rd, Victoria Park. 7 yrs, £25. 10 July 1880

Master absconded. Magistrate would not cancel indenture because Heard had not been served with a summons. Every effort was being made to serve him. Second moiety paid 10 March 1881 to Messrs Killick and Co. The Society sent Poulter to sea in one of Killick's ships.

547 Selman, William Henry: to Henry Neal Earl, carpenter, of 55 Ledbury Rd, Bayswater. 5 yrs, £20. 10 July 1880

The master absconded; reapprenticed 5 March 1883 to John Brooks, of Cheldon Rd, Fulham.

548 Cole, Joseph James: to George Baker, tin and iron plate worker, of 47 Featherstone St, City Rd. 6 yrs, £10. 9 Aug. 1880

549 Wheeler, Eliza Annie: to Bessie Caroline Terry, dressmaker, of 12 Temple St, Brighton, Sussex. 2 yrs, £20. 6 Sept. 1880

550 Adams, William Augustus: to John Dalby Hobson, carpenter and builder, of Gladstone Terrace, York Rd, S. Lambeth. 6 yrs, £20. 25 Nov. 1880

551 Buckland, Bertie Edward: to William Mansfield White, chaser and embosser, of 7 Upper St Martin's Lane. 7 yrs, £30. 21 Feb 1881

552 Moore, James Willis: to Charles Welch, plumber etc, of High Rd, Tottenham. 6 yrs, £20. 21 Mar 1881

553 Pearce, William, son of John and Jane, of Marlborough: to John Dobson, tailor, of Marlborough. 7 yrs, £20. 30 May 1881

County apprentice. Mother, who is a widow, earns her livelihood by working as a charwoman, but does not earn more than 12s. a week. Candidate is entirely, and her other three children partly, dependent on mother.

554 Weller, William Edward, son of William and Louisa: to George Sydney Waterlow, stationer, of Finsbury Stationery Works. 7 yrs, £10. 14 June 1881

Mother, formerly Margaret Pearce, was born at Imber. Candidate is the eldest of three delicate children. Father is a journeyman bricklayer, deaf and not in good health.

555   Bush, George, son of William and Elizabeth Jane: to William Webb, cabinet maker, of Warminster. 7 yrs, £20. 9 July 1881

Both parents were born at Warminster. There is no provision for the children beyond the weekly wages of the father, who works sometimes in a malt-house and sometimes as a mason's labourer, at weekly wages averaging 14s.

556   Oatley, Samuel John: to Robert William Trowbridge, lighterman, of 10 Lea Marsh Place, Orchard St, Blackwell Green. 6 yrs, £20. 18 July 1881

557   Quelch, Thomas Francis, son of William and Ellen: to Walter Edward Newman, hairdresser, of Egham, Surrey. 4 yrs, £20. 15 Sept. 1881

The mother, formerly Ellen Roff, was born at Marlborough. She is a widow, with three children wholly dependent on her, of which the candidate is the eldest. Indentures assigned to G.H.Barrow, of 7 Queen St, Wolverhampton, hairdresser.

558   Down, Arthur, son of Thomas and Mary Ann: to James Pullen Seagrave, zinc worker, of 10 and 46 Rochester Row, Westminster. 6 yrs, £25. 5 Sept. 1881

Father and mother both born at Mere. Father, a private in the Coldstream Guards, died in 1868, and the mother has since married again. There are six children. Candidate is brother to apprentice **511**.

559   Burgess, Gertrude Fanny, daughter of Henry George and Eleanor Jane Burgess: to Thomas Livings, milliner and draper, of Bradford-on-Avon. 2 yrs, £20. 5 Sept. 1881

The mother was born in Bradford-on-Avon, and is now a widow, with four children entirely dependent on her earnings, which amount to 10s. a week.

560   Kimber, Robert Edward, son of Robert and Maria: to R.N. and R.H. Hoskins, carpenters and builders, of Hungerford, Berks. 7 yrs, £20. 12 Sept. 1881

Father was born at Ramsbury; the mother at Christian Malford. The father is dead, and her two children are entirely dependent on the widow.

561   Whatley, Mary Ann, daughter of Henry and Mary: to Sarah Jane Mcilroy, dressmaker and mantlemaker, of 9 Warwick St, Deptford. 3 yrs, £20. 22 Oct. 1881

Mother, formerly Mary Hopkins, was born at Market Lavington, and the father at Wilton. They have three children entirely dependent upon them; wages when in work 24s. a week.

562   Hart, Frederick Thomas, son of William and Louisa: to Frederick James Brazier, plumber etc, of 50 Seven Sisters Rd, Holloway. 7 yrs, £25. 2 Dec. 1881

Mother, formerly Louisa Culley, was born at Marlborough. The candidate is now a newspaper boy in the employ of Messrs. Smith. He wishes to be apprenticed to a plumber. Father is 64 years of age.

563   Baker, William Arthur, son of George and Emma: to W.H. Allen and Co., engineers, of York St, Lambeth. 5 yrs, £25. 9 Dec. 1881

Father, George Baker, was born at Westbury. He is 57 years of age, and is employed at Messrs Peek and Freane, biscuit makers, at 18s. a week. Seven children.

564   Norris, Caroline Ann, daughter of Martha: to Mary Bartholomew, dressmaker, of 2 Churchley Villas, Upper Sydenham. 2 yrs, £20. 20 Jan. 1882

The mother, formerly Martha Grist, was born at Dilton Marsh, near Westbury. The father is at present in receipt of 25s. a week, but is not in good health.

565   Watts, George William, son of William Burrough and Janet Frances Watts: to Thomas Sheppard, gas-fitter and plumber, of 24 Bucklersby, EC. 6 yrs, £25. 28 June 1882

Father was born at Salisbury, and was apprenticed by this Society to a millwright. He is earning 30s. a week, but is not strong, and has all his seven children dependent upon him.

566   Smith, Sarah Ellen: to John Hall, milliner, of 41 Wilton Rd, Belgravia. 2 yrs, £25. 1 July 1882

Father, born at Calne, is a wheelwright employed by Mr Taylor at the Pimlico repository. He has seven children dependent upon him.

567   Naish, Celia Caroline, daughter of John Isaac and Jane Naish, of Bradford-on-Avon: to Mary Ann Livings, milliner and dressmaker, of Bradford-on-Avon. 2 yrs, £20. 10 July 1882

Mother is a widow. Her two children are entirely dependent on her, and her means are very small.

568   Lamborn, Charles Albert, son of William and Sarah, of Devizes: to Charles Romain, cabinet maker, of Market Place, Devizes. 5 yrs, £20. 11 July 1882

Father is a journeyman cabinet-maker. He has suffered a good deal from bad health, and for some time was a patient in Savernake Cottage Hospital. He suffers still from a bad leg, which interferes considerably with his trade.

569 Wise, Martha Jane Henrietta, daughter of William and Martha: to Messrs Derry and Toms, drapers and milliners, of 107 Kensington High St. 2 yrs, £20. 14 July 1882

Mother is a widow, a native of Ramsbury. Father was born at Little Bedwyn, and died in 1877, leaving his widow entirely dependent on her own exertions to support her five children. She gets her living by going out cooking. She wishes to apprentice her daughter to a dressmaker.

570 Gregory, Ernest Ambrose, son of Thomas Stephens and Mary Jane Gregory, of West Tytherton: to Francis Burnett, miller, of Calstone Mill, Calne. 2 yrs, £25. 28 July 1882

Father lives at West Tytherton, and has six children entirely dependent on him. His means amount to £50 per annum.

571 Bailey, Thomas Henry, son of John and Elizabeth: to J. Batson and Sons, fancy cabinet manufacturers, of 42 Brewer St, Golden Square. 6 yrs, £25. 8 Nov. 1882

Mother is a native of Chippenham. Her first husband, who was a native of Devizes, died in 1869, leaving the family of four children quite unprovided for. The mother married a journeyman shoemaker in 1871 with two children. His wages do not exceed £1 per week.

572 Oatley, Arthur Frederick, son of Samuel and Caroline: to Henry Smith, foreman lighterman, of 10 Glenhurst Rd, Brentford, Essex. 5 yrs, £20. 29 Nov. 1882

Father, born at Melksham, is suffering from chronic rheumatism, and can do no work. Six of his children are living at home. One of his sons has been apprenticed by the Society [see **556**]. The mother is not at all strong.

573 Dredge, Frederick, son of Thomas and Sarah, of Brixton Deverill: to Carson and Toone, iron-workers, of Warminster. 3 yrs, £20. 22 Dec. 1882

Father's wages as a farm labourer are 8s. a week, and three children are dependent on him. Father is 52 years of age, and partially crippled.

574 Coombs, Francis John: to Thomas Shepherd, builder, of 1 Fox Lane, Dalston. 5 yrs, £25. 1 March 1883

575 Humphries, George Herbert, son of James and Mary Felicia, of Codford St Mary: to Maurice Draper, harness and saddle-maker, of West Lavington. 5 yrs, £25. 30 April 1883

Father's earnings are 14s. a week. Candidate is the eldest of six children, who are all, with the exception of the candidate, entirely dependent on the father.

576 Rawlings, James: to Samuel Hobbs, blacksmith, of Trowbridge. 6 yrs, £20. 2 June 1883

577 Reynolds, Ada Mary: to Henry Vale, cigar manufacturer, of 2 Victoria Park Square. 6 yrs, £10. 12 July 1883

578 Wareham, Bertha: to Martha Maton, dressmaker, of Salisbury. 3 yrs, £30. 14 July 1883

579 Green, Albert Edward: to Charles Stent, mechanical dentist, of 5 Coventry St. 5 yrs, £25. 4 Aug. 1883

Indentures assigned 15 Dec. 1885 to Mrs Stent on the death of her husband.

580 Chapman, David: to John Knight, plumber etc, of 62 Marsham St, Westminster. 4 yrs, £25. 18 Aug. 1883

581 Bowman, William Henry: to G. and E. Hays, coach-builders, of Malmesbury. 5 yrs, £25. 1 Oct. 1883

582 Coller, Elizabeth: to Sarah Ann Simpkins, dressmaker, of Sidney House, Hampstead Hill. 1 yr, £25. 11 Oct. 1883

583 Bray, James: to Messrs Ford and Tait, letter-press and machine printers, of 52 Longacre. 7 yrs, £25. 12 Oct. 1883

584 Rawlins, Isaac: to William Thomas Webb, cabinet maker, of 49 Blue Boar Row, Salisbury. 6 yrs, £28. 30 Oct. 1883

585 Smith, Elizabeth: to Georgina Elmer, dressmaker, of 16 Lombard St, Pimlico. 2 yrs, £25. 4 Feb. 1884

586 Jones, Florence Annie: to James Mayston, draper, of Bradford-on-Avon. 2 yrs, £20. 5 Feb. 1884

587 Crisp, Daniel James: to Robert Dunn, printer, of 155 Kingsland Rd. 5 yrs, £20. 29 April 1884

Reassigned 26 June 1886 to John Pope Field, 155 Kingsland Rd, Pimlico, printer.

588 Butler, Charles James: to Henry Ansell, tailor, of Calne. 3 yrs, £20. May 1884

589 Maidment, Harry George John: to James Perkins, mason, of Withycombe, Somerset. 4 yrs, £25. 18 June 1884

590 Compton, William: to Robert Henry Targett, lithographer and general printer, of Playhouse Yard, Whitecross St, Middlesex. 5½ yrs, £25. 8 July 1884

591 Young, Walter Charles: to Edward Maundrell, iron-founder and engineer, of Calne. 6 yrs, £20. 6 June 1884

592 Read, Annie Lily: to James Maystor, draper, of Denmark House, Bradford-on-Avon. 2 yrs, £20. 7 June 1884

593 Watts, Robert Stevenson: to Eli S. Ferrer, sanitary engineer, of 24 Elbrook Rd, St Peter's Park. 5½ yrs, £25. 2 Aug. 1884

594 Mead, Agnes Helena: to Mary Ann Wordsworth, dressmaker, of 25 Wigmore St. 2 yrs, £25. 2 Aug. 1884

595 Bell, Mary A.J.: to Mary Ann and Jane Cox, dressmaker, of 133 Great Dover St, Borough. 2 yrs, £25. 2 Aug. 1884

596 Butcher, James Gilbert: to Charles East, tailor, of 95 Clifton St, Finsbury. 5 yrs, £25. 21 Aug. 1884

597 May, Frederick McTier: to William John Pierman, upholsterers, of 24 Maryport St, Devizes. 5 yrs, £20. 22 Aug. 1884

598 Wise, Frederick James: to Clark and Copping, saddlers, of 22 Gloucester Rd, South Kensington. 6½ yrs, £25. 13 Nov. 1884

599 Dancy, Oscar: to Charles Cash, at Messrs Butler and Hutchinson, jewellers, of 6 and 8 Charterhouse St. 6 yrs, £20. 2 March 1885

600 Chapman, Charles Frank, son of Charles and Ann, of Marlborough: to Henry James Deacon, carpenter and wheelwright, of Russell Square, High St, Marlborough. 6 yrs, £20. 9 May 1885

Father is a journeyman dyer earning £1 a week. His eldest son was apprenticed by this Society four and a half years ago [see **541**]. Indenture transferred 6 April 1889 to John Davis, of Avebury, carpenter and wheelwright.

601 Tucker, Frederick James, son of James and Mary Ann, of Warminster: to John Wallis Titt, engine maker of Warminster. 5¼ yrs, £20. June 1885

Father is a shoe-maker. His weekly earnings do not average more than 14s. Five of the children are more or less dependent upon him for support.

602 Rudman, William Frederick, son of William and Elizabeth: to Jacob Bonn, telegraph instrument maker, of 12 George St, Euston Rd. 4 yrs, £25. 27 June 1885

Father was born at Bradford-on-Avon. He is employed at the Royal Arsenal, Woolwich as a hammerman, wages 23s. 6d. per week. His three children are wholly dependent upon him.

603 Newman, Samuel Bradley, son of John and Sarah Jane: to Frederick Shaw, printer, of Dock Head, Bermondsey. 6 yrs, £25. 23 July 1885

Both parents were born in Salisbury. Father is a lamp-lighter earning 20s. a week. Mother has been a cripple for over seventeen years, and the three children are entirely dependent on the father.

604 Smith, George William, son of George and Benjamina: to Messrs Hadgrove and Ponder, upholsterers, of 3 Short St, Tabernacle Square, EC. 5 yrs, £25. 30 July 1885

Father was born at Calne. For the last eighteen years he has been employed at Taylor's Repository, Pimlico. Two of his children have been apprenticed by the Society. The other six are dependent on their parents. Visitor reported 21 March 1889 that boy had left and joined militia.

605 Newman, Louisa, daughter of James Davies and Jane Newman: to Charles Harrison Venning, general draper, of 330 Caledonian Rd, Islington. 3 yrs, £20. 10 July 1885

Father was born at Salisbury. He was an ex-police constable in receipt of a pension, and died in 1878, leaving his four children totally unprovided for.

606 Chapman, Juanita Mary Isabel, daughter of John and Mary Ann, of Old Swindon: to John Walton, draper, milliner and costumier, of Hull, Yorks. 3 yrs, £20. 31 July 1885

Mother is a widow. Father, who was a mechanical engineer, died in 1883 of consumption, leaving five daughters wholly unprovided for, the eldest being only thirteen years of age.

607 Burgess, Maud Mary, daughter of Henry George and Eleanor Jane, of Bradford-on-Avon: to Mary Ann Livings, milliner, of Bradford-on-Avon. 2 yrs, £20. 6 July 1885

Mother is a widow. Her husband, who was a solicitor's clerk, died suddenly in 1878, leaving his wife and children totally unprovided for. Mother has now four children dependent upon her for support, one of whom has very weak eyesight. Mother's earnings amount to about 8s. a week.

608 Whatley, Henry Joseph, son of John and Isabella Sarah: to Robert Woodger Bowers, printer, of 89 Blackfriars Rd, SE. 5 yrs, £20. 26 Sept. 1885

Father was born at Dilton Marsh, Westbury. He is an engineer earning 24s. a week. The applicant was five years ago run over by a tram-car, and in consequence of injury to his leg it had to be amputated. All the children are dependent on the father.

609 Giddings, Arthur John, son of Richard and Priscilla, of Bradford-on-Avon: to Enoch Wootten, grocer, of 17 Silver St, Trowbridge. 3 yrs, £20. 1 Sept. 1885

Mother is a widow. Her means are very small being only the interest on £400. She has nine children all unprovided for, with the exception of the eldest daughter, who is in a situation. Father, who died in 1880, was a farmer, and the £400 was all that remained after settlement of his affairs.

610 Chapman, Christopher Charles, son of Samuel and Clara Bannister Chapman, of Trowbridge: to John G. Andrews, carpenter, builder and general undertaker, of Trowbridge. 5 yrs, £20. Sept. 1885

Mother, a widow, resides at Trowbridge. Father died in 1883 leaving his widow with six children under the age of twelve, all dependent on the mother's earnings.

611 Blowey, Miriam Amor, daughter of William and Fanny Sophia: to Martin Evans Blackaller, general and fancy draper, of Buckingham Palace Rd. 2 yrs, £21. 19 Oct. 1885

Mother was born at Whiteparish, and has been living in London twenty-five years. She was left a widow nine years ago, quite destitute, but has maintained herself and children by teaching and needlework during that time. She is now prevented from working through failing health and feeble sight.

612 Bailey, Frederick Horace, son of George and Mary Ann: to William Elselow, carpenter and joiner, of Abberville, Cavendish Rd, Clapham Park. Surrey. 6 yrs, £25. 30 Oct. 1885

Father was a boot-maker and died in 1875. Mother was born in the parish of Southwick. For some time she supported herself and family by a mangle and received from the parish 3s. 6d. a week. She is now crippled with rheumatism and unable to work. The eldest girl is in service, the second boy aged eighteen is an imbecile and an invalid, and the third, a boy of sixteen, is earning 8s. a week.

613 Crisp, Florence Martha, daughter of Walter and Ann: to Mary Catherine Sturge, upholsterers, of 22 Curtain Rd, Shoreditch. Middlesex. 2 yrs, £20. 15 Dec. 1885

Father was born at Bradford-on-Avon, and died last year, leaving his wife and children totally unprovided for, one of whom, apprenticed by the Society, has since died. Mother has no means of support, except a small allowance from the earnings of the eldest children.

614 Griffin, Alfred George: to Henry George Winslow, baker and grocer, of High St, Steeple Ashton. 5 yrs, £20. 2 June 1886

615 King, Kate Louisa: to Mesdames Thorpe and Alford, dressmakers, of 52 Hereford Rd, Westbourne Grove. W. 2 yrs, £25. 19 June 1886

616 Wakeley, Alfred Herbert: to Charles David Bull, draper, of Trowbridge. 3 yrs, £20. 5 Aug. 1886

617 Annetts, George Charles: to Messrs H. and W. Rawlings, agricultural engineer, of Collingbourne Ducis. 4 yrs, £20. 18 Aug. 1886

618 Simmonds, Charles Lovell: to Messrs W.T. Wright and T. Davies, manufacturing gold and silver smiths, of 145 Oxford St W. 6 yrs, £25. 8 Sept. 1886

619 Smith, George: to Charles Richard Burns, general draper, of Lavington House, White St, Market Lavington. 5 yrs, £20. July 1886

Indenture transferred 18 June 1887 to Messrs W. and S. Sloper, of Devizes and Marlborough, outfitters. Master reported 25 April 1889 that boy had been convicted of embezzlement.

620 Butcher, Henry: to Matthias Pearce, baker, of 2 Church Rd, Leyton, Essex. 5 yrs, £20. 26 Oct. 1886

Reapprenticed: see **634**.

621 Ball, Edwin: to Gilderoy Wilson Scott, basket manufacturer, of 45 Old Compton St, Soho Sq. 5 yrs, £20. 8 Dec. 1886

622 House, Henry Francis: to Benjamin Parsons, carpenter, of Warminster. 6 yrs, £20. 16 Dec. 1886

623 Adlam, Sarah Ann: to William Johnston, book-binder, of 38 St Andrew's Hill, London. 2 yrs, £20. 19 Jan. 1887

624 Smith, Clara: to Sarah Heathcote, milliner, of the Parade, Trowbridge. 2 yrs, £20. 7 Feb. 1887

625 Gilbert, Mary Ann Golding: to Madam Anna Pottier, dressmaker, of 142 New Bond St, W. 2 yrs, £20. 8 May 1887

Visitor reported 15 March 1889 that the girl had never been with her mistress.

626 White, William Harry: to William Brooks, cabinet maker, of 49 St Mark's Rd, Notting Hill. 4 yrs, £20. 7 May 1887

627 Young, Joseph William: to Mr George Chivers, carpenter and builder, of Anchor, Calne. 6 yrs, £20. 4 June 1887

628 Rudman, John George: to Messrs James and Thomas Beaven, leather manufacturers, of Holt, Bradford. 5 yrs, £20. 9 June 1887

629 Couzens, Ada Ellen: to Thomas Tuckes, milliner, of 133 Upper St, Islington. 2 yrs, £25. 11 June 1887

630 Wise, Alfred Abraham: to Philip Howard, harness maker, of 56 Pembroke Rd, Kensington N. 5 yrs, £25. 15 July 1887

631 Ovens, David: to Edward Lester, carpenter and blind maker, of 242 Barking Rd, Canning Town. 6 yrs, £20. 19 July 1887

632 Webb, James Lewis: to Samuel Holding, tailor, of 71 London St, Greenwich. 6 yrs, £25. 16 Sept. 1887

633 Moore, William Frederick: to William Jackson Gaskill, printer, of 17 Paternoster Square, London EC. 7 yrs, £20. 20 Oct. 1887

634 Butcher, Henry: to William Reading, cooper, of 106 Broadway, Plaistow, Essex. 5 yrs, £10. 5 Nov. 1887

See **620**. Apprentice's first master, Mr Pearce, having failed, he was apprenticed with the second moiety. Visitor reported April 1889 that the boy had only stayed with his master a short time. Second moiety not paid.

635 Keates, George Argus: to William Samuel Stuckey, grocer, of 36 Fore St, Trowbridge. 3 yrs, £20. 8 Dec. 1887

636 Rogers, Reginald Charles: to William Smith, builder, of Eldon Works, Harleyford Rd, Surrey. 3 yrs, £20. 14 Dec. 1887

637 Fisher, James Dacey: to Richard Thorn, builder, of Broad Green, Croydon, Surrey. 4 yrs, £25. 26 April 1888

638 Moore, Walter Frank: to Frank Curtis, carpenter and joiner, of 11 Portway, Warminster. 5 yrs, £25. 14 May 1888

639 Crook, Albert Edward: to Benjamin Hillier, builder, of High St, Marlborough. 7 yrs, £20. 4 July 1888

640 Oatley, Joseph Daniel: to Joseph Duebuck, lithographic transfer writer etc, of 74 Little Britain, EC. 7 yrs, £20. 17 July 1888

641 Howard, Emma: to Martha Earl, dressmaker, of 43 Alderney St, Warwick Sq. 2 yrs, £25. 12 Oct. 1888

642 Phelps, Jacob James: to John Surty, tailor, of 32 Fore St, Trowbridge. 5 yrs, £20. 29 Sept. 1888

643 Poole, Rosanna Sophia: to Olivia Murray, shirt-maker, of 747 Old Kent Rd. 4 yrs, £20. 20 Nov. 1888

644 Newman, John Henry Richard: to Henry Strudwick, dressing bag manufacturer, of 2 Long Lane, Smithfield, EC. 5¾ yrs, £25. 6 Dec. 1888

645 Smith, Albert Edward: to John Arundel Leakey, pianoforte maker, of 10 Balmoral Grove, Caledonian Rd N. 5 yrs, £20. 22 Jan. 1889

646 Taylor, George Henry, son of Samuel and Sarah Ann, of Calne: to John Gale, tailor, of High St, Calne. 5 yrs, £20. 9 May 1889

Father is a grocer's porter, in receipt of 15s. a week. They have six children, the two eldest earn respectively 2s. and 1s. a week; the others are entirely dependent upon their parents.

647 Curtis, Frederick William, son of Thomas and Elizabeth, of Warminster: to John Henry Neat, painter, plumber, glazier and paper-hanger, of 1 George St, Warminster. 4 yrs, £15. 10 May 1889

Father is a journeyman painter by trade. He has four children living, entirely dependent upon him. His earnings do not average more than £1 a week in the summer, and much less in the winter. He is very anxious to apprentice his son to a useful trade, but is unable to do so from want of means. County apprentice.

648 Lucas, Walter Edward, son of James and Sarah, of Trowbridge: to William Collins, letter press printer, of Fore St, Trowbridge. 7 yrs, £20. 13 May 1889

Father died in July 1884 leaving his wife and four children unprovided for. The eldest child is sixteen and the youngest four years. Mother is in delicate health, and the only means of support are the earnings of the two elder children.

649 Hindon, Rosanna, daughter of James and Mary Jane, of Steeple Ashton: to Sarah Heathcote, dressmaker, of the Parade, Trowbridge. 2 yrs, £20. 25 May 1889

Father's earnings, as an agricultural labourer, amount to 12s. a week, with a cottage. They have seven children living. The candidate is a cripple. She has been educated in a public elementary school, and her parents are anxious to apprentice her to a dressmaker, in order that she may earn her own livelihood. County apprentice.

650 King, Louise Martha, daughter of Charles and Martha: to Mesdames Thorpe and Aldford, dressmakers, of 117 Westbourne Grove, N. 2 yrs, £25. 16 July 1889

Mother was born at Ramsbury. Father is a signalman on the Great Western Railway, and has five children, three of whom are dependent on the joint earnings of the parents, which amount to 29s. a week. Mother and children are in delicate health, one of the latter being an imbecile. One of the children has been already apprenticed by the Society.

651 Smith, Florence Helen, daughter of George and Mary, of Christchurch, Bradford-on-Avon: to Sarah Maud Byfield, milliner, of 5 Old Bond St, Bath, Somerset. 2 yrs, £20. July 1889

Father died in 1883 leaving his wife and seven children. Mother now supports herself and the three children now dependent upon her by charring.

652 Ball, George, son of John and Sarah Jane: to Messrs G.W. Scott and Son, basket manufacturers, of Old Compton St, Soho Square. 5 yrs, £20. 25 Nov. 1889

Father was born at Warminster, and is a basket-maker by trade. He has six children, four of whom are entirely dependent upon him. The wages now paid in the trade, he states, are not so good as formerly, and the work is not so certain. The candidate has an elder brother apprenticed by the Society.

653 Gerrish, Stenson Herbert, son of Job and Martha, of North Bradley: to Samuel Beaven, tailor, of 34 St Georges Terrace, Trowbridge. 5 yrs, £20. 13 Jan. 1890

Father died nine years ago leaving five children. Mother is in receipt of £16 a year as postmistress, out of which she has to pay £4 10s. for rent. She also occasionally earns a little by needlework. Her only means of maintaining herself and the three children now at home are her earnings, and the wages of one of the children, which amount to 6s. a week. County apprentice.

654 Smith, Benjaminea, daughter of George and Benjaminea: to James Turnbull Spence, silk mercer, of St Paul's Churchyard. 2 yrs, £20. 28 Feb. 1890

Father was born at Calne, and is now employed at Taylor's Depository, Pimlico, where he has been for the last 22 years. The present candidate is the fourth child, three having already been apprenticed by the Society.

655 Winter, Thomas George Henry, son of Thomas and Mary: to Benjamin Startup, plumber, of 50 Carter Lane, EC. 5 yrs, £20. 11 March 1890

Mother was born at Bratton, Westbury. Father of the candidate is dead, and the mother has married again. Her present husband, who was manager of a public house, is now out of employment, and has two children of his own to provide for besides the candidate.

656 Pollard, Henry Alfred, son of Frederick Henry and Margaret Eleanor: to John Fleming, plumber, of Sedley Place, Oxford St, W. 5 yrs, £20. 15 April 1890

Father was born at Chippenham, and is a labourer employed by the Great Western Railway Company. All his seven children are dependent upon him for their support.

657 Sheppard, Eustace Augustus: to John Feltham, tinman and gas-fitter, of 36, Round Stone St, Trowbridge. 2 yrs, £12. 21 May 1890

658 Hunt, Frederick: to James Allcock, gold and silver engraver, of 20a, Aldermanbury, EC. 5 yrs, £20. 1 June 1890

659 Jennings, Florence Louisa, daughter of John and Ann, of Bradford-on-Avon: to James and Edwin Gardner, drapers and milliners, of 13, 14, and 15 Stall St, Bath, Somerset. 2½ yrs, £20. 12 Aug. 1890

Mother, a widow, has twelve children, five of whom are dependent upon her. Father died in 1884, leaving his wife and children unprovided for, their only means of support now being a very small outfitter's business. The elder children are not in a position to assist their mother and the rest of the family.

660 Bush, Herbert Henry: to Frank Curtis, carpenter, of Warminster. 7 yrs, £20. 6 Sept. 1890

661 Cowdry, Ella Medora Eliza: to Helen Caroline and Richard Alfred Moody, dress and mantle makers, of 20 Queen's Rd, Battersea, SW. £20. 9 Sept. 1890

662 Hancock, Mary Louisa: to Olive Kerr, milliner and dressmaker, of 38 Duke St, Grosvenor Square. 1 yr, £10. 3 June 1890

663 Fisher, Harry Edwin: to James Woodcock, tailor, of 68 Derby Rd, Croydon, Surrey. 5 yrs, £20. 22 Oct. 1890

664 Hindry, George Edward, son of Henry Thomas and Mary: to Electrical Engineering Corporation Ltd, engineer, of Yiewsley, Middlesex. 5½ yrs, £20. Nov. 1890

Mother was born at Longbridge Deverill. Father, a coachman in service, died in 1876, leaving his wife and two children without any means of support. Mother then went into service, and has since maintained herself and family. The candidate, who has just left the Orphan Working School, Haverstock Hill, is desirous of being apprenticed to an engineer.

665 Biggs, Frank, son of John and Sarah, of 19 Orpingley Rd, Holloway, London N: to William Howie, plumber etc, of 15 Garlick Hill, Cannon St, EC. 7 yrs, £20. 12 Nov. 1890

Mother (formerly Sarah Holder) of Lacock, born 1851; father, a painter's labourer, earns 24s. per week. The parents were married on 14 June 1874 and have six children, namely Frank aged 13, Frederick 11, Ellen 9, Alice 7, William 5, and Edith 1½ yrs or thereabouts, all of whom are dependent upon the father. Frank Biggs was born on 3 May 1875 at Bath. Petition prepared by Edward R. Henly, solicitor of Calne, in 1888.

666 Bray, George Henry Alexander: to Walter Hazell, of Hazell, Watson Viney Ltd., printers, of 52, Long Acre, WC. 7 yrs, £20. 12 Feb. 1891

667 Young, Ernest Octavius: to Edward Ward Maundrell, turner and fitter, of the Foundry, Calne. 6 yrs, £20. 22 May 1891

668 Waters, Herbert: to Joseph Gaisford, carpenter and joiner, of 39 George St, Warminster. 7 yrs, £20. 23 May 1891

County apprentice.

669 Harraway, Walter Lewis: to Harvey James Chambers, saddler, harness and collar maker, of High St, Marlborough. 7 yrs, £20. 26 Nov. 1891

670 Skillen, Edward Henry: to Messrs Baker and Lucas, upholsterers, of 6 London Mews, London St, Middlesex. 5 yrs, £20. 5 June 1891

671 Pike, Joseph: to Messrs Henry Howell and Co., cane and stick manufacturers, of 180 Old St, EC. 6 yrs, £20. 28 June 1891

672 Wise, Edward Charles: to George Turkington, boot and shoe maker, of 35 Abingdon St, Kensington. 5 yrs, £20. 24 July 1891

673 Butcher, Ann: to Emily Lucy Holloway, dressmaker, of 17 Redcliffe Rd, South Kensington. 2 yrs, £20. 25 July 1891

674 Carter, Robert Henry: to Messrs B. Parsons and Son, carpenters and joiners, of Warminster. 6 yrs, £20. 23 July 1891

675 Hopkins, Richard Henry: to John Davis, carpenter and wheelwright, of Marlborough. 6 yrs, £20. 27 July 1891

Reassigned 27 Oct. 1891 to George Bevis of Russell Square, Marlborough, farrier, carpenter, and wheelwright.

676 Gooding, Eleanor Mabel: to Egbert William Killick, draper and silk mercer, of High St, Hungerford, Berks. 2 yrs, £20. 29 July 1891

677 Avon, Richard Marshal: to William Albert Wyatt, painter and house decorator, of Market Place, Westbury. 4 yrs, £20. 31 July 1891

678 Hancock, Frederick William: to John Knight, plumber, of 62 Marsham St, Westminster. 5 yrs, £20. 3 Sept. 1891

679 Moors, William: to Messrs Wenham and Sons, engineers, of 66 Wigmore St, W. 4 yrs, £20. 25 Jan. 1892

680 Mullings, Harry: to The Pulsometer Engineering Company Ltd, of Nine Elms Iron Works, Nine Elms, Middlesex. £20. 10 March 1892

681 Hunter, Samuel Henry: to Frederick John Thick, plumber and gas-fitter, of 73 Torbay Rd, Willesden Lane. 5 yrs, £20. 14 March 1892

682 Redman, Charles John: to John D. Feltham, tinman, gasfitter etc, of Roundstone St, Trowbridge. 4 yrs, £20. 13 April 1892

683 Biggs, Frederick John: to Edward Alfred Beer, sanitary plumber and hot-water engineer, of 24 Liverpool Rd, N. 5 yrs, £20. 13 April 1892

684 Cox, Walter: to Charles Perkins, newspaper proprietor and printer, of High St, Marlborough. 6 yrs 4 months, £20. 23 May 1892

County apprentice.

685 Bodman, William Edward: to Edward Orchard, carpenter and builder, of the Rose and Crown, Keevil, Trowbridge. 5 yrs, £20. 22 July 1892

686 Carter, William Henry: to Ponton John Ponton, builder, of Warminster. 5 yrs, £20. 22 July 1892

687 Cox, William Henry: to William Rawlings, agricultural engineer, of the Bourne Iron Works, Collingbourne Ducis. 7 yrs, £20. 21 July 1892

Apprentice dead, Oct. 1895.

688 Wheeler, Tom Edwards: to Harry Butler, tailor, of the Square, Calne. 4 yrs, £20. 13 Aug. 1892

689 Walkerdine, George: to George William Newbery, account book ruler etc, of Angel Court, Barbican. 7 yrs, £20. 12 Aug 1892

690 Pearce, Louis Giles: to Alfred John Pope, engineer, brass and iron founder, of Boreham Rd Foundry, Warminster. 6 yrs, £20. 29 Aug. 1892

County apprentice.

691 White, Mary: to Madame Elise and Co. Ltd., court dressmakers, etc, of 170, Regent St. 3 yrs, £20. 28 July 1892

692   Barnett, Lillian Maud: to Sarah Heathcote, dressmaker, of the Parade, Trowbridge. 2 yrs, £20. 26 Sept. 1892

693 West, Maud Emily: to Matthew Henry Rackstraw, general draper, of Upper St, Islington. 2 yrs, £20. 14 Oct. 1892

694   Stevens, Sidney Thomas: to John and Frank Gayton, house decorators, of Trowbridge. 3 yrs, £20. 11 Jan. 1893

695 Hunt, Philip: to John William Lowrie, cabinet maker, of 81/2 Morris Rd, Crisp St, Bromley, Kent. 5 yrs, £20. 29 April 1893

Mr Lowrie having retired, he refunded the £10, 3 Jan. 1896, and indentures were cancelled.

696 Davidge, William Maurice: to William Hansford, carpenter and joiner, of Ansty, near Salisbury. 5 yrs, £20. 1 May 1893

697 Taylor, Florence Isabel: to Sarah Heathcote, dressmaker and milliner, of the Parade, Trowbridge. 2 yrs, £20. 29 June 1893

698 Tucker, Ernest: to Thomas Arney, tailor, of Bank St, Melksham. 4 yrs, £20. 3 July 1893

699 Bryant, Frederick Charles: to George Portch, tailor, of 4 Trowbridge Rd, Bradford-on-Avon. 4 yrs, £20. 25 July 1893

700 Dear, Charles Thomas: to Messrs W. Glover and W.H. Hobson, mechanical engineers, of Albert Iron Works, St James Road, Old Kent Rd. 6 yrs, £20. 21 Jul 1893

701 Packer, Sidney James: to William Henry Hunt, printer and stationer, of 92 High St, Poole, Dorset. 3 yrs, £25. 24 July 1893

702 Bayley, Ellen Amelia: to Emily Lucy Holloway, dressmaker, of 17 Bedford Gardens, Kensington. 2 yrs, £20. 28 Sept. 1893

These indentures have been cancelled [*after Sept. 1894*] owing to the girl's eyesight being bad.

703   Cowdry, Fanny Elizabeth: to Caroline Lane, dressmaker, of 13 Clyeton St, Wandsworth Rd. 3 yrs, £20. 28 Sept. 1893

704   Scott, Robert: to Samuel Baverstock, tailor, of 44 Vicarage St, Warminster. 6 yrs, £20. 1 Jan. 1894

County apprentice.

705   Walters, Albert: to William Baker Stevens, coach builder, of Castle Carriage Works, Trowbridge. 7 yrs, £20. 24 Feb. 1894

County apprentice.

706   Henstridge, Charles Henry: to Henry Hare, wheelwright and carpenter, of West St, Wilton. 5 yrs, £20. 28 Feb. 1894

County apprentice.

707   Burfitt, Alice Mabel: to Ellen Mary Howson, court dressmaker, of 86 Gloucester Rd. 2 yrs, £20. 31 March 1894

708   Ranger, Francis Carl Edward: to Andrew Smith, pianoforte manufacturer, of 36 North Rd, Cattle Market. 7 yrs, £20. 25 July 1894

709   Head, John Ernest Sydney: to Henry Joseph Bailey, carpenter and joiner, of Burbage. 6½ yrs, £20. 28 July 1894

County apprentice.

710   Haywood, David Edmund: to Messrs Benham and Sons, Ltd, engineers, of 66 Wigmore St, W. 5 yrs, £20. July 1894

711   King, Mabel Julia: to Sarah Heathcote, dressmaker, of the Parade, Trowbridge. 2 yrs, £20. 4 Sept. 1894

712   Rogers, Archibald John Seager: to Messrs Tilk and Smith, engineers etc, of High St Iron Works, Melksham. 5 yrs, £20. 8 Sept. 1894

County apprentice.

713 Dew, Harry Froome: to John Ham, builder, plumber etc, of 71 Denmark Hill, SE. 5 yrs, £20. 16 Oct. 1894

[*after April 1897*] This indenture cancelled before a magistrate at Lambeth County Court.

714 Simmons, Lewis Stanley: to Walter Raymond, silversmith, of 179 Wardour St, Oxford St W. 5 yrs, £25. 1 Nov 1894

715 Hunt, Philip: to Messrs R.L. Guy and Co., fancy and general cabinet makers, of 56, City Rd, EC. 5 yrs, £20. 22 Nov 1894

716 Presley, Herbert: to Uriah White jun, shoeing and jobbing smith, of 3 North St, Warminster. 7 yrs, £20. 1 May 1894

County apprentice.

717 Harvey, William John: to Benjamin Davey, coach builder and wheelwright, of 6 High St, Lewisham, SE. 6 yrs, £20. 19 Feb 1895

718 Mullings, George Wentworth: to Pulsometer Engineering Co. Ltd, engineers, of Nine Elms Works, Nine Elms, SW. 6 yrs, £20. 31 Mar 1895

719 Ball, Sarah Jane: to Ellen Elizabeth Stokes, dressmaker, of 102 St Mary's Rd, Peckham, SE. 2 yrs, £20. 20 April 1895

720 Burfitt, Alfred James: to William Robert Rawlings, electrical and domestic engineer, of 82 Gloster Rd, S. Kensington. 4 yrs, £25. 8 May 1895

721 Haines, Florence Amy: to Amy Dowding, dressmaker, of 46 Church St, Warminster. 2 yrs, £20. 6 June 1895

722 Griffen, Herbert Edward: to Henry Snook, tailor, of Silver St, Trowbridge. 5 yrs, £20. 26 June 1895

County apprentice.

723 Neate, Charles Edward: to Benjamin Hillier, builder, carpenter and joiner, of High St, Marlborough. 7 yrs, £20. 31 July 1895

County apprentice.

724 Bishop, Henry James: to William Griggs, chromo-lithographer, of Elm House, Hanover St, Rye Lane, Peckham, SE. 6 yrs, £20. 12 Aug. 1895

725 House, Henry John: to Messrs Benjamin Parsons and Son, carpenters and builders, of Warminster. 5½ yrs, £20. 31 Aug. 1895

County apprentice.

726 Charlton, Kate Augusta: to Ada Emily Lewthwaite, dressmaker, of Ravenswood House, Balham, London. 2 yrs, £15. 1 Oct. 1895

727 Barton, Mary: to Arthur Egerton Heathcote, dressmaker, of Fore St, Trowbridge. 2 yrs, £20. 22 Oct. 1895

728 Brown, William Charles: to Henry Robert Watts, watchmaker and jeweller, of Westbury. 5 yrs, £20. 28 Oct. 1895

County apprentice.

729 Haywood, George Ernest: to Peter Glanville Meek, engraver and lettermaker, etc, of 44, Blackfriars Rd, SE. 5 yrs, £20. 30 March 1896

730 Ranger, Edith Rose: to Elizabeth Hodges, furrier, of 14 Castle Place, Kentish Town Rd. 2 yrs, £20. 22 April 1896

731 Pollard, George: to Arthur Reynolds, upholsterer, of 43 and 44 Park Lane, Regents Park, NW. 5 yrs, £20. 28 April 1896

732 Hunt, Henry Matthew: to James Boscombe, bootmaker, of Corsham. 4 yrs, £20. 11 May 1896

County apprentice.

733 Gillman, Freelove Annie: to Miss Mary Beaven Marks, costumier, of 2 Roundstone St, Trowbridge. 2 yrs, £20. 13 May 1896

County apprentice.

734 Day, Edward George: to Joseph Gaisford, carpenter and joiner, of 39 George St, Warminster. 6½ yrs, £20. 10 June 1896

County apprentice.

735 Collett, Joseph Herbert: to Walter Isaac Hiscock, wheelwright, smith, etc, of Hilperton, Trowbridge. 5 yrs, £20. 28 July 1896

County apprentice.

736 Stevens, Herbert: to Berkley Wheeler, carpenter and joiner, of 22 Wyke Rd, Hilperton, Trowbridge. 4 yrs, £20. 28 July 1896

County apprentice.

737 Dobson, William Thomas: to Messrs Thomas and William Edward Free, cabinet makers, of St Peter's, Marlborough. 5 yrs, £20. 3 Sept. 1896

County apprentice.

738 Simmons, Harriett Fanny: to James Chopping, gold and diamond jewellery polisher, of 53 Frith St, Soho, W. 3 yrs, £20. 17 Sept. 1896

739 Whatley, Frederick John: to the West Wilts Printing Co. Ltd., printers, of Warminster. 6 yrs, £20. 12 Oct. 1896

County apprentice. Indentures cancelled 8 Nov. 1900 by order of the Committee.

740 Pannell, George Elijah Maslem: to George Joseph Inder, registered surgeon-dentist, of 141 Camberwell Rd, SE. 6 yrs, £20. 10 Oct. 1896

741 Harvey, Frank Edward, son of Walter and Esther: to Robert William Palmer, plumber and zinc worker, of 19 and 21 King St, Broadway, Deptford. 6 yrs, £20. 10 Oct. 1896

Apprentice was born at Trowbridge. Father is a cabman; his average earnings are about 4s. a day, and he has eight children, two of whom are already apprenticed by the Society.

742 Bishop, Charles Frederick: to Edwin Amery, upholsterer, of 26, Whitfield St, Tottenham Court Rd. 6 yrs, £20. 22 Feb. 1897

743 King, Walter George: to Edward Linzey, builder and carpenter, of the Halve, Trowbridge. 4 yrs, £20. 22 March 1897

County apprentice.

744 Pearce, Arthur Gerald: to Frank Curtis, carpenter and joiner, of 11 Portway, Warminster. 4 yrs, £10. 20 March 1897

County apprentice.

745 Vallis, Francis William James: to Frank Curtis, carpenter and joiner, of 11 Portway, Warminster. 7 yrs, £20. 10 May 1897

County apprentice.

746 Smith, Clement Walter: to William Gale, printer, of High St, Marlborough. 5 yrs, £20. 15 May 1897

County apprentice.

747 Dunn, Thomas Henry: to William Carson Toone, engineer, of Warminster. 7 yrs, £20. 29 May 1897

County apprentice.

748 Barton, Ann Newman: to Sarah Heathcote, dressmaker, of the Parade, Trowbridge. 2 yrs, £20. 30 June 1897

County apprentice.

749 Hull, Olive: to Madam Eva Furber, dressmaker, of 49 Emperor's Gate, SW. 2 yrs, £20. 16 July 1897

750 Taylor, Lucy Mabel: to Sarah Heathcote, dressmaker, of the Parade, Trowbridge. 2 yrs, £20. 30 July 1897

County apprentice.

751 Lippitt, Laura Gertrude: to Elizabeth Matilda Jones, dressmaker, of Bradford-on-Avon. 2 yrs, £20. 9 Sept. 1897

County apprentice.

752 Wilkins, Frederick George: to Robert Edwin Downing Rudman, contractor and builder, of Old Rd, Chippenham. 5 yrs, £20. 30 Aug. 1897

County apprentice.

753 Holloway, Gertrude Mary: to Frederick William Goodall, draper, of 33 and 34 Blue Boar Row, Salisbury. 3 yrs, £20. 2 Nov. 1897

County apprentice.

754 Bishop, Frank: to Stewart James Webb, cabinet maker, of 51 Market Place, Warminster. 5 yrs, £20. 1 Nov. 1897

County apprentice.

755 Mullings, Edith Ethel: to Messrs. Walter and Slade, dress and mantle maker, of 56 New Park St, Devizes. 3 yrs, £20. 2 Nov. 1897

County apprentice.

756 Stowe, Charles William: to Messrs Garrett Brothers, hairdressers, of Trowbridge. 4 yrs, £20. 3 Nov. 1897

County apprentice.

757 Austin, Percy Harold: to Herbert Moore and Co., electrical engineers, etc, of 3 Stratford Rd, Kensington, W. 5 yrs, £20. 9 March 1898

758 Lindsey, Jesse: to Edward Linzey, builder, of the Halve, Trowbridge. 5 yrs, £20. 12 March 1898

County apprentice.

759 Hopgood, Robert: to James Beriden, carpenter and wheelwright, of Durrington. 3 yrs, £20. 3 June 1898

760 Cane, William John, son of Edward and Eliza, of Warminster: to Frank Curtis and Son, carpenter, of 11 Portway, Warminster. 7 yrs, £20. 10 June 1898

Mother, a widow, has eleven children, five of whom are dependent upon her for support. Her husband died in June 1896, leaving her and his children totally unprovided for. Her income averages about 12s. a week, of which she gets 4s. 6d. from the guardians. The candidate earns 2s. 6d., and the balance she earns herself by washing.

761 Bush, Louis William, son of Matthew and Comfort, of Mere: to Webb and Sons, cabinet makers, of Warminster. 5 yrs, £20. 18 June 1898

Candidate was born at Warminster, and now lives at Mere. Father died three years ago, leaving a widow and two children, who earn nothing. She has to help support her father and mother, who live with her. She is a dress-maker by trade, and earns about 10s. a week. She wishes to apprentice the boy to a useful trade, but cannot do so at her own expense.

762 Cork, Harold Reinard, son of Edward Robert and Louisa, of Melksham: to Alfred Edward Cork, baker etc, of Dean Rd, St Georges, Bristol. 5 yrs, £15. 21 June 1898

Father is a compositor earning 26s. a week. He has five sons alive, two of whom are earning their own living, and three are living at home. The boy wishes to be apprenticed to Mr Arney, of Bank St, tailor.

763 Bennett, Miriam Jessica, son of William and Miriam, of Southwick, North Bradley: to Sarah Jane Lucas, dressmaker, of Bridge House, Trowbridge. 2 yrs, £20. 8 Aug. 1898

Her father is a blacksmith but is out of work. Candidate desires to be apprenticed to Miss Lucas, dressmaker, of Trowbridge, and she has been with Miss Lucas some months already. Mother does occasional charring or washing, and is caretaker of the Baptist Chapel at Southwick, and at most earns 4s. 6d. per week.

764 Barton, Thomas William, son of Thomas George and Emily Maria Lowe Barton, of Trowbridge: to John Richmond, joiner and undertaker, of 19 Newtown, Trowbridge. 5 yrs, £20. 5 Aug. 1898

He was born in London, but has spent his youth at Trowbridge, and wishes to be apprenticed to a carpenter. Father was a native of Corsham, and died in 1892 after six years of ill-health, during which all he had to support his family was the sick pay derived from his club. Mother now keeps a small shop at Trowbridge. Master bankrupt April 1901; reapprenticed to Edward Linzey.

765 Hatter, Albert, son of Albert George and Mary, of Heddington: to Bigwood and Co., builders etc, of Melksham. 4 yrs, £20. 8 Oct. 1898

Father is a labourer earning 10s. to 12s. a week, but is constantly unable to work, owing to ill-health. He has ten children, the eldest of whom is sixteen. The boy is anxious to be a carpenter. Apprenticeship cancelled after master's bankruptcy; boy reapprenticed to Edward Linzey.

766 Harvey, Walter T.: to Edwin William Hayes., zinc worker, of 82 High Road, Lee, Kent. 6 yrs, £20. 27 Oct. 1898

767 King, Ethel Sophia, daughter of George William and Julia, of Southwick near Trowbridge: to Sarah Heathcote, dressmaker, of the Parade, Trowbridge. 2 yrs, £20. 3 Nov. 1898

Father was a police constable, who died in 1883 while stationed at Southwick, where the widow still lives. She has three children, of whom the candidate is the youngest, and she wishes to apprentice the candidate to a dressmaker.

768 Thomas, William George, son of John and Emma, of Langley Burrell: to Spencer and Co. Ltd., engineers, millwrights and founders, of Melksham. 6 yrs, £20. 15 Dec. 1898

Father has been employed at Langley Burrell Brewery for 34 years and his wages have never exceeded 16s. a week. He is now in bad health. He has five children, three of whom are still dependent upon him.

769 Brown, William: to William Carson Toone, engineers and ironfounders, of Warminster. 7 yrs, £20. 20 May 1899

Transferred to Messrs Toone and Gray of the same address, 3 March 1903.

770 Haines, Edwin J.: to James Barber Greenland, sign-writer and decorator, of 18 High St, Warminster. 6 yrs, £20. 22 July 1899

771 Love, Daniel Rew, son of Daniel and Mary, of Wingfield: to Frederick Isaac White, carpenter, joiner, and undertaker, of 7a Castle St, Trowbridge. 5 yrs, £20. 24 Aug. 1899

Father was for 36 years a coachman at Wingfield, in the family of a gentleman living in that village, but broken health has compelled him to give up his situation. He has three children, all of whom are at home, and are dependent upon him. One of the children is a confirmed invalid and another is a cripple. The candidate wishes to be apprenticed to a carpenter.

772 Cole, Charles: to Richard E.D. Rudman, builder contractor, of Chippenham. 5 yrs, £20. 30 Aug. 1899

Master trading as Downing and Rudman.

773 Woods, Richard William: to T.B. Whitmee, wheelwright, of York Rd, Battersea. 7 yrs, £20. 27 Oct. 1899

Master trading as C.R. Whitmee. Indenture cancelled on account of boy stealing goods. £5 refunded to Society 14 Feb. 1900.

774 Merrett, Walter Joseph: to George Moore, builder, of Church St, Trowbridge. 5 yrs, £20. 16 Nov. 1899

775 Garlick, Ellen Maria: to Caroline Bernard, costume manufacturer, of 178 Kingsland Rd, London. 3 yrs, £20. 20 Nov. 1899

776 Hillier, Ethel Rebecca: to Mary Newbold, dressmaker, of 6 Cheverton Rd, Hornsey Lane North. 3 yrs, £20. 13 Nov. 1899

777 Barnes, Joseph: to John Austin Cole, electrical engineer, of 15 Gloucester St, West Norwood, Surrey. 5 yrs, £20. 17 Nov. 1899

778 Dickinson, Percy: to Traies and Son Ltd., contractors (carpenter), of Notting Hill, London. 7 yrs, £25. 11 April 1900

Indenture transferred to Robert Rundell, of Grove Rd, Chiswick, Jan. 1900.

779 Ford, Frederick William: to John Austin Cole, electrical engineer, of 15 Gloucester St, West Norwood, Surrey. 5 yrs, £20. 29 Jan. 1900

780 Batt, Philip Stanley: to Francis New, carpenter and wheelwright, of Chilton Foliat. 5 yrs, £20. 23 May 1900

781 Day, Charles Harold: to Ernest Frank White, whitesmith, of 86 Portway, Warminster. 6 yrs, £20. 1 June 1900

Master trading as R. White.

782 Scammell, Willie Sidney H.: to Charles George Matthews, carpenter and builder, of Hilperton, Trowbridge. 5 yrs, £20. 2 June 1900

783 Wells, Walter Henry: to William Carpenter, carpenter, joiner, and builder, of Cannon Square, Melksham. 4 yrs, £20. 13 June 1900

784 Tucker, Louis Edgar: to William Carson Toone, engineers and iron-founders, of Warminster. 7 yrs, £20. 20 June 1900

Master trading as Messrs Carson and Toone. Apprentice transferred 3 March 1903 to Messrs Turner and Gray, of the same address, Warminster, with all rights and liabilities.

785 Pollard, Florence Edith: to Susanna Haworth Bland, ladies' tailor, of 45 New Bond St, Middlesex. 3 yrs, £20. 20 June 1900

786 Woodroffe, George Howard: to Arthur William Chard, carpenters, joiners and undertakers, of Union St, Trowbridge. 5 yrs, £20. 25 June 1900

Master trading as T. Chard and Co.

787 Bishop, Henry John: to Henry John and George William Rose, printers, of Edward St, Westbury. 6 yrs, £20. 16 July 1900

Master trading as Michael and Co., West Wilts Printing Company.

788 Molden, James Richard: to David Williams, builder and shop-fitter, of 14 Queen's Crescent, Haverstock Hill, NW. 6 yrs, £20. 16 July 1900

Apprentice reapprenticed, 1 March 1901, to Harrison and Sons, St Martin's Lane, WC., printers, for 7 years £20.

789 Woodroffe, William Frank: to Michael William Hiscock, engineer, smith, and farrier, of Castle Iron Works, Castle St, Trowbridge. 5 yrs, £20. 24 July 1900

Indenture transferred to C.E. Wiggins at same address, 2 May 1903.

790 Barnett, John: to John Lewis Foreman, tailor, of 34 High St, Warminster. 5 yrs, £20. 26 July 1900

791 Sage, Eva Florence: to Mrs Sarah Heathcote, dressmaker, of the Parade, Trowbridge. 2 yrs, £20. 30 July 1900

792 Bennett, Violet Kate: to Mrs Sarah Heathcote, dressmaker, of the Parade, Trowbridge. 2 yrs, £20. 27 Aug. 1900

793 Kitley, Walter Francis: to Isaac Cordingley, general engineers, of Trowbridge. 6 yrs, £20. 8 Aug. 1900

794 Taylor, Jessica Agnes: to Mrs Heathcote, dressmaker, of the Parade, Trowbridge. 2 yrs, £20. 27 Aug. 1900

Indenture cancelled.

795 Wheeler, Lewis George, son of Charles and Eliza, of Heddington: to Isaac George Hunt and others, trading as Hunt Bros., carpenters and wheelwrights, of Heddington, Calne. 3½ yrs, £20. 23 Aug. 1900

Father is a labourer earning 13s. to 15s. a week, and his wife earns about 5s. a week by washing. He has five children, three of whom are dependent upon him. Candidate is a willing and intelligent lad, and is likely to make good use of an apprenticeship.

796 Austin, Herbert Stanley: to British Electric Transformer Manufacturing Co. Ltd., of Harrow Rd, W. 3½ yrs, £30. 23 Aug. 1900

797 Stanley, Leslie Ernest: to Foster and Nickoll, stonemasons, of Marvissa Rd, Chelsea, London, and Rugby. 5 yrs, £20. 29 Oct. 1900

798 Cane, Frank Charles: to William Carson Toone, engineers etc, of Warminster. 7 yrs, £20. 29 Dec. 1900

Master trading as Carson and Toone. Apprentice transferred March 1903 to Messrs Turner and Gray at the same address.

799 Humphries, Ernest Benjamin: to Spencer and Co. Ltd., engineers, of Melksham. 6 yrs, £20. 23 Feb. 1901

800 Francis, Edward James: to Haden and Sons, engineers and iron-founders, of Trowbridge. 7 yrs, £20. 26 March 1901

801 Ranger, Mabel Esther (Gladys): to Swan and Edgar Ltd., dress-makers, of Regent St, W. 2 yrs, £20. 30 April 1901

802 James, Algernon W.C.: to J.W. Titt, engineer and iron-founder, of Warminster. 6 yrs, £20. 11 May 1901

803 Marks, Howard John: to John. W. Hiscock, engineer, smith, and farrier, of Castle Iron Works, Trowbridge. 5 yrs, £20. 14 May 1901

804 Gibbs, Reginald F. G.: to W.H. Payne, baker and confectioner, of 9-10 George St, Warminster. 3 yrs, £15. 7 June 1901

Indenture transferred to C.E. Wiggins at same address.

805 Best, Ada: to William Welman and Son, general drapers, of 37 and 38 St John St, Devizes. 2 yrs, £20. 13 June 1901

806 Boulter, Edwin: to Ernest G. Marsh, hosier, shirt-maker etc, of Regent St, Clifton, Bristol, Glos. 3 yrs, £20. 24 June 1901

807 Haywood, Frank Harold: to Lane and Walker, carpenters and joiners. 4 yrs, £20. 20 July 1901

808 Cole, James: to G.W.R. Works, wheelwright, of Swindon. 3 yrs, £15. 18 June 1901

Amount of premium expended in the purchase of tools.

809 Hull, Ebenezer Harvey: to G.G. Wade, builder and decorator (carpentering), of 6 Arthur St, Chelsea. SW. 3 yrs, £20. 2 Aug. 1901

810 Sutton, Samuel James: to Thomas Dawkins, builder (carpentering), of Barford St Martin. 4 yrs, £15. 24 Aug. 1901

£5 allowed for tools in addition to premium.

811 Scammell, Ida Irene: to Mrs. Heathcote, dressmaker, of the Parade, Trowbridge. 2 yrs, £20. 2 Dec. 1901

812 Hall, Francis James: to Wenham and Walters Ltd., engineers, metal sash and casement makers, of Paragon Works, Vicarage Rd, Croydon, Surrey. 7 yrs, £15. 2 Dec. 1901

Till 21 years of age. Cancelled; boy dismissed.

813 Walter, Henry: to R. and J. Reeves and Son, carpenter, of Bratton Iron Works, Westbury. 6 yrs, £20. 13 May 1902

Committee sanctioned payment of £2 for tools, 26 April 1906 [*Minute Book*].

814 Laver, William Ewart: to R.D. Gilman, newspaper and letter-press printing, of Devizes. 5 yrs, £20. 8 May 1902

Master newspaper publisher and proprietor.

815   Carter, Albert Victor: to Frank Curtis, carpenter and joiner, of 11 Portway, Warminster. 7 yrs, £20. 5 May 1902

816   Ferris, Joseph: to Stewart James Webb, cabinet maker, of Warminster. 6½ yrs, £20. 10 June 1902

817   Lloyd, Alice Phebe: to William Arthur Welch, milliner, of Cavendish House, Marlborough. 3 yrs, £20. 7 June 1902

818   Smith, James Thomas: to C.E. Gilbert, carpenter and wheelwright, of Collingbourne Ducis. 5 yrs, £20. 11 June 1902

819   Smith, Joseph William A.: to S.G. King, carpenter and wheelwright, of Netheravon. 4½ yrs, £20. 24 July 1902

820   Fidler, Louis Tom: to Benjamin Hillier, carpenter, of Marlborough. 7 yrs, £20. 28 July 1902

821   Harvey, Ada Jane: to George Stroud, dressmaker, of 65-71, High St, Lewisham. S.E. 2 yrs, £20. 3 Sept. 1902

822   Hulbert, Herbert Hains: to J.W.W. Hulbert, plumber, painter, and glazier, of 19 High St, Chippenham. 4 yrs, £20. 3 Sept. 1902

823   Bishop, William Frank: to William Dodson, jeweller and goldsmith, of 223 Oxford St, W. 7 yrs, £20. 3 Sept. 1902

824   Jones, Laura Edith: to Emma Payer, milliner, of 11 Montpelier Vale, Blackheath, SE. 2 yrs, £20. 6 May 1903

825   Rose, Edith H.E.: to Mrs Heathcote, dressmaker, of the Parade, Trowbridge. 2 yrs, £20. 9 May 1903

826   Lucas, Jesse Gladstone: to George Stokes and Son, bellhanging and gas fitting etc, of Castle St, Trowbridge. 5 yrs, £20. 7 May 1903

827   Hockey, Mabel Lilian: to John Saxty, tailor, of 32 Fore St, Trowbridge. 3 yrs, £20. 28 May 1903

828 Elloway, William Charles: to Fred Futcher, portrait and landscape photographer, of 36 High St, Warminster. 4 yrs, £20. 6 June 1903

829 Barton, William Stephen: to H.W. Beaven, plumber, hot-water engineer and decorator, of Bradford on Avon. 5 yrs, £20. 31 July 1903

830 Miller, Florence Winifred: to Hobden Bros., milliner, of Silver St, Salisbury. 2 yrs, £25. 17 Aug. 1903

831 Trowbridge, Albert John: to Felix G. Alford, bootmaker, of East Knoyle. 3 yrs, £20. 13 Aug. 1903

Special allowance of £10 for tools and lodgings, in hands of Rev. T.J. Perkins of Fonthill Bishop (*Bishop's Fonthill*).

832 Beaven, Herbert John: to Jabez Chivers, carpenter and joiner, of 23 Sidmouth St, Devizes. 4 yrs, £20. 31 Oct. 1903

833 Edwards, Sidney Charles: to Henry Manning Knapp, carpenter, of North Curry near Taunton, Somerset. 5 yrs, £20. 4 Nov. 1903

834 Molden, Frederick Ernest: to Frederick William Beadle, wood carver, of 14 De Beauvoir Crescent, Whitmore Rd, Hoxton. 6 yrs, £20. 3 March 1904

Till 1 Aug. 1910, when he is 21.

835 Staples, George: to Charles Edward Neate and Sons, cabinet maker, of 24 Maryport, Devizes. 4 yrs, £20. 21 March 1904

Indenture cancelled by consent 5 March 1908.

836 Alexander, James: to George Offer, carpenter and wheelwright, of Southbroom Place, the Green, Devizes. 5 yrs, £20. 18 April 1904

Letter from Miss Milman, 13 April 1905, asking for a grant for tools; the committee sanctioned payment of £4.

837 Pullen, Florence: to Sarah Heathcote, dressmaker, of the Parade, Trowbridge. 2 yrs, £20. 29 April 1904

838 Wickham, Ulva: to Sarah Heathcote, dressmaker, of the Parade, Trowbridge. 2 yrs, £20. 29 April 1904

839 Brown, Dora May: to Sarah Heathcote, dressmaker, of the Parade, Trowbridge. 2 yrs, £20. 29 April 1904

840 Rawlings, Ellen Mary: to Mrs Powell, dressmaker, of Southwick, Trowbridge. 2 yrs, £20. 4 May 1904

See **863**.

841 Baverstock, Reginald Vere: to Edwin J. Butcher, baker and confectioner, of Silver St, Warminster. 4 yrs, £20. 4 May 1904

842 Newman, Joseph Albert: to Charles H. Woodward, printer, of St John St, Devizes. 4 yrs, £25. 10 May 1904

843 Mundy, Frederick John: to Arthur M. Walton, bootmaker, of Lavington House, Market Lavington. 4 yrs, £20. 10 May 1904

Indenture transferred 27 Nov. 1905 to Alfred Harrod, Market Lavington. The Secretary received a communication from Mr A. Harrod, 12 Nov. 1907, stating that he was giving up the business of bootmaker and proposing to hand it over to his apprentice F. Mundy. It was agreed to pay the second moiety of £2 subject to Mr Harrod agreeing not to commence business again within a radius of five miles of Market Lavington for ten years.

844 Carter, Bill Cue: to William Beazley, mason, of Wood St, Calne. 5 yrs, £20. 7 May 1904

845 Cole, Marjory Cecilia: to Lucy Persis Doswell, dressmaker, of 18 High St, Chippenham. 2 yrs, £20. 4 June 1904

846 Ludlow, Francis Harry: to Walter Rogers, carpenter, of Shaw Hill, near Melksham. 5 yrs, £20. 4 July 1904

847 Gumm, Frederick William: to William Baker Stephens, carriage builder, of Trowbridge. 6 yrs, £20. 1 May 1904

848 James, Howard Edwin Harry: to Carson and Toone, engineers, of Wiltshire Foundry, Warminster. 7 yrs, £20. 30 May 1904

849 Barnes, Thomas Loveday: to Burkin and Co., engineers, of 15 Beckenham Rd, Penge. 3 yrs, £30. 1 Dec 1904

Burkin and Co bankrupt; reapprenticed to W. Bailey. See **860**.

850 Walter, Frederick John: to John Knight, carpenter, of Trowbridge Rd, Bradford-on-Avon. 5 yrs, £20. 5 May 1905

851 Whittle, Edward Francis: to Robert Frederick Houlston, printer, of High St, Chippenham. 5 yrs, £20. 9 May 1905

852 Doel, Lillian Kezia, of Trowbridge: to Sarah Heathcote, dressmaker, of Bridge House, Trowbridge. 2 yrs, £20. 11 May 1905

853 Abbott, Elsie Ivy, of North Bradley: to Sarah Heathcote, dressmaker, of Bridge House, Trowbridge. 2 yrs, £20. 11 May 1905

854 Jeffries, William Thomas: to Michael and Co., printers, of Edward St, Westbury. 6 yrs, £20. 13 May 1905

855 Ryman, Alfred Lewis: to J.H. Wooldridge, carpenter etc, of Hungerford, Berks. 3 yrs, £20. 19 May 1905

856 Pratt, Charles Edwin, son of James Pratt: to Messrs Hames and Johnson, masonry contractors, of 58 Andalus Rd, Stockwell. 4 yrs, £20. 24 May 1905

Letter from James Pratt, father, 13 April 1908, informing of bankruptcy of W.H. Johnson, the master of his son.

857 Merrett, Victor: to Gowen and Stevens, plumber, of Roundstone St, Trowbridge. 6 yrs, £20. 29 May 1905

858 Jones, Florence Isabel: to Mrs C. Barnes, dressmaker, of 126 Coleraine Rd, East Greenwich. 2 yrs, £20. 5 June 1905

859 Kitley, Charles Richard, of Trowbridge: to Edward Linzey, builder, of Trowbridge. 5 yrs, £20. 20 July 1905

860 Barnes, Thomas Loveday: to W. Bailey, engineer, of 72 Mitcham Rd, Croydon, Surrey. 5 yrs, £30. Aug. 1905

See **849**.

861   Elloway, Henry George: to John Lewis Foreman, tailor, of Market Place, Warminster. 5 yrs, £16. 17 April 1905

862   Woodroffe, Albert Edward: to William Baker Stephens, coach builder, of Castle Carriage Works, Trowbridge. 7 yrs, £20. 17 April 1905

863   Rawlings, Ellen Mary: to Mrs F.L. Jones, dressmaker, of Crittholm, Newtown, Trowbridge. 5 yrs, £5. March 1906

864   Smith, Walter, of Southwick, Trowbridge: to George Moore, builder, of Church St, Trowbridge. 5 yrs, £20. 5 May 1906

865   Harvey, Henry Samuel: to Haycraft and Son Ltd, cycle engineers, of 199 and 201 Lewisham High Rd, SE. 6 yrs, £20. 27 April 1906

866   Amer, Harry: to I. Cordingley, general engineer, of Innox Foundry, Trowbridge. 7 yrs, £20. 24 Feb. 1906

Master bankrupt, 2 June 1908; reapprenticed 6½ yrs until 23 Aug. 1912.

867   Trubridge, Alma Rosina: to Messrs Bloom, dressmaker, of Canal, Salisbury. 3 yrs, £30. 23 June 1906

868   Edwards, Llewellyn: to Spencer and Co., fitters, of Melksham. 5 yrs 4 months, £20. 10 July 1906

869   Lewis, Herbert Daniel, of Winterbourne Bassett: to Henry Chequer and Sons, coach builders, of Wootton Bassett. 5 yrs, £20. 1 Aug. 1906

870   Edwards, Sidney Charles: to John Holmes, paperhanger and decorator, of 20 Elswick Rd, Lewisham. 2½ yrs, £12 10s. 15 Nov. 1906

871   Newman, George, of Colerne: to George Blackmore Caple, baker, confectioner, grocer etc, of High St, Box. 3 yrs, £20. 12 Jan. 1907

Master also at 11 Broad St, Bath, Somerset.

872   Naile, Arthur: to Messrs Parsons Bros., builders, contractors, and wheelwrights, of Station Rd, Westbury. 6 yrs, £20. 1 Feb. 1907

873 Gunstone, Frank Thomas: to Messrs Spencer Co. Ltd., engineers, of Melksham. 5½ yrs, £20. 9 April 1907

874 Jacobs, Irene Winifred: to Mrs Albinson and Miss Evans, dressmaker, of 18 Hyde Vale, Greenwich, SE. 2 yrs, £20. 2 May 1907

875 Beak, Evelyn Kate Mary: to Mrs F.L. Jones, dressmaker, of Lydenburg, Westbourne Gardens, Trowbridge. 2 yrs, £20. 7 May 1907

876 Pike, Freda Grace: to Messrs Heathcote and Co., dressmakers and milliners, of Trowbridge. 2 yrs, £20. 1 May 1907

877 Wilkins, Francis John: to Edward Linzey, builder etc, of the Halve, Trowbridge. 5 yrs, £20. 13 May 1907

878 Saye, Arthur Robert: to Henry James Wheeler, florist etc, of East St, Warminster. 4 yrs, £20. 22 July 1907

879 Baverstock, Alfred Egbert: to Warminster Cooperative Society Ltd., bread bakers, of Warminster. 4 yrs, £20. 3 Sept. 1907

880 Westall, Jesse: to W.J. Loveday, ironmoulder, of the Green, Aldbourne. 4 yrs, £20. 25 Nov. 1907

881 Walter, Herbert William: to H.A.D. Beard, ironmongers, of 33 Market Place, Bradford-on-Avon. 4 yrs, £30. 23 Nov. 1907

882 Lewis, Francis Edgar: to H. Chequer and Son, carpenters and wheelwrights, of Wootton Bassett. 5 yrs, £20. 25 Nov. 1907

883 Davey, William Warden: to S.G. Lonnie and Co., cabinet makers and upholsterers, of Southampton St, Camberwell, SE. 6 yrs, £40. 6 Dec. 1907

884 Culverhouse, Frederick James: to Holdaway Cockell, builders etc, of Eden Vale, Westbury. 6 yrs, £20. 17 Dec. 1907

885 Shefford, Arthur: to J. Edwards and Son, builders etc, of Inkpen, Hungerford, Berks. 5 yrs, £20. 10 Dec. 1907

886 Tidmarsh, Alfred John: to W. Tomes, stone mason etc, of G.W.R. Depot, the Grove, Hammersmith. 5 yrs, £25. 30 Dec. 1907

887 Lyddall, Audley George: to F. Davidson and Co., opticians, of 29 Great Portland St, W. 5 yrs, £40. 26 March 1908

Cancelled 2 March 1909, master retiring.

888 Richardson, George, son of B. Richardson: to Darling and Son Ltd., printers, of 34-40 Bacon St, E. 6 yrs, £20. 31 March 1908

Enlisted in the Buffs, June 1915; posted to Salonika, Sept 1916; still there in 1917.

889 Dallimore, Elsie Elizabeth: to Kate Morris, dressmaker, of the Parade, Trowbridge. 2 yrs, £20. 7 May 1908

890 Forsyth, Edwin: to Thomas Carder, carpenter and joiner, of Maiden Bradley. 6¼ yrs, £20. 9 May 1908

Master was clerk of works to the Duke of Somerset.

891 Lockey, Christina Bessie: to Madame Florence Shaw, court dressmaker, of 25 Lower Seymour St, W. 2 yrs, £25. 8 May 1908

892 Tidmarsh, Herbert George: to T.H. Lambert, stone mason etc, of 2 Kingston Villas, Box. 3 yrs, £20. 11 May 1908

893 Cray, Chrissie B.E.: to Kate Morris, dressmaker, of the Parade, Trowbridge. 2 yrs, £20. 14 May 1908

894 Bainton, Mary Ann Jane: to Heathcote and Co., dressmakers, of Bridge House, Trowbridge. 2 yrs, £20. 29 May 1908

895 Hayward, Ethel Daisy: to Mrs A.E. Thomas, dressmaker, of Ivyside, Roundstone St, Trowbridge. 2 yrs, £20. 12 June 1908

896 Hooper, Clara Emily: to Mrs K.E. Franklin, dressmaker, of 13 Union St, Trowbridge. 2 yrs, £20. 12 June 1908

897 Amer, Harry: to W.G. Parriss, ironmonger, of 19 Silver St, Trowbridge. 5 yrs, £15. 1 November 1907

898 Maskeline, Stanley W.G.: to Thomas Swayne, woodworker, of London Road, Chippenham. 5 yrs, £20. 22 June 1908

899 Bennett, Percy: to A.G. Randall, plumber and decorator, of 3 and 4 Newtown, Trowbridge. 4 yrs, £20. 10 June 1908

900 Sawkins, Olive Grace: to A. Talbot and Son, dressmakers, of Top of the Brittox, Devizes. 3 yrs, £20. 13 July 1908

901 Tilley, Frederick William: to Brown and May Ltd., engine builders, of Devizes. 3 yrs, £25. 23 July 1908

902 Weston, Ernest George: to W.C. Harper, cycle and motor engineer, of Wood St, Calne. 5 yrs, £20. 20 July 1908

903 Richardson, Benjamin: to Arnold and Sons, surgical and veterinary instrument maker, of West Smithfield. 7 yrs, £30. 10 Aug. 1908

Enlisted in R.F.A., 15 May 1915; posted to France, Oct 1915, and still serving there, C battery, 77th Army Artillery Brigade. Still serving in France, June 1918; recommended for a commission and now training in Brighton. Eldest brother (**888**) formerly apprenticed to Darling and Son; enlisted in the Buffs, June 1915, to Saloniika, Sept 1916, still there. Younger brother joined R.N., Sept. 1915, now (1917) in H.M.S. Scorpion.

904 Taylor, Arthur Henry George: to J.G. Norman, carpenter and joiner, of 63 Victoria Rd, Swindon. 5 yrs, £20. 30 Nov. 1908

905 Tucker, Arthur Percival James: to J. Wallis Titt, engineer, of Woodcock Iron Works, Warminster. 7 yrs, £20. 20 Jan. 1909

906 Jones, Gertrude Emily: to Miss A. Parsons, dressmaker, of 72 Park St, Trowbridge. 2 yrs, £20. 17 May 1909

907 Giddings, Florence Emily, of Devizes: to Miss L. Best, dressmaker, of 42 New Park St, Devizes. 3 yrs, £20. 7 May 1909

908 Brown, Frank Stanley, of Southwick, Trowbridge: to E.J. Weston, carpenter and decorator, of Southwick, Trowbridge. 4 yrs, £20. 11 May 1909

909 Townsend, Hildred Jane, of Southwick, Trowbridge: to Miss K.E. Franklin, dressmaker, of 13 Union St, Trowbridge. 2 yrs, £20. 2 June 1909

910 Lee, Kathleen Emily, of Great Bedwyn: to Miss E.M. Challis, dressmaker, of Carnarvon House, West St, Newbury, Berks. 2 yrs, £20. 22 July 1909

911 Liddall, Ellen Millicent: to George Gray, draper, of Regent St, Swindon. 3 yrs, £30. 9 Aug. 1909

912 Hobbs, Sidney Claud: to Spencer and Co. Ltd., engineers, of Melksham. 6 yrs, £30. 6 Sept. 1909

913 Doel, Percy Horace, of Southwick, Trowbridge: to B. Lansdown and Sons, printers, of Silver St, Trowbridge. 6 yrs, £20. 20 Sept. 1909

Indenture cancelled Nov. 1911.

914 Melsom, Arthur Henry: to S.W. Dowglas, motor engineer, of 96 Upper Richmond Rd, SW. 4 yrs, £50. 18 Oct. 1909

915 Emm, Thomas Charles Hillier, of Fulham: to W. Douglas and Sons Ltd., engineers, of Douglas Wharf, Putney, SW. 5 yrs, £50. 1 Nov. 1909

Enlisted in R.F.A., 3 Aug. 1914; still serving in France (1918). Mr Douglas applied for his return; he returned and finished his articles.

916 Dunford, Reginald Sidney: to J. Mills and Son, bootmakers, of 29 East St, Warminster. 5 yrs, £20. 29 Nov. 1909

Enlisted in Welsh Bantams; became sergeant of signalling in France at brigade for 3 yrs; now training in O.T.C. (1918). Became lieutenant in infantry regiment. Started on his own account after war.

917 Minty, Thomas, of Lower Edmonton: to Alfred Smellier, smith and hot-water fitter, of 11, 13, 15 Rochester Row, SW. 5 yrs, £25. 20 Sept. 1909
Enlisted on completion.

918 Newman, Alfred William Harry, of Maiden Bradley: to Mrs D.J. Warr, hairdresser, of Station Rd, Gillingham, Kent. 4 yrs, £30. 6 Dec. 1909

919 Nash, Cecil Ernest, of Battersea: to Messrs A.W. Penrose and Co., electrical engineers, of 109 Farringdon Rd, EC. 2 yrs, £50. 29 Nov. 1909

920 Grist, James, of Warminster: to Messrs Foreman and Sons, tailors and breeches makers, of Warminster. 5 yrs, £20. 16 May 1910

921 Tiley, Albert Henry: to Walter Hicks, carpenter and builder, of Colerne. 4 yrs, £20. 30 May 1910

£5 for tools.

922 Moules, Henry, of Colerne: to Weeks and Bradfield, masonry contractors, of Box Station, Box. 4 yrs, £20. 30 May 1910

923 Fear, Ernest Frank: to J.B. Titt, engineers, of Woodcock Iron Works, Warminster. 4 yrs, £20. 30 May 1910

Master trading as J.W. Titt.

924 Simper, Stanley Richard, of Codford St Mary: to O.B. Chambers, watchmakers, of 37 Market Place, Warminster. 7 yrs, £20. 30 May 1910

925 Turner, Walter Henry: to H. Curtis and Sons, carpenter, of Warminster. 5 yrs, £20. 30 May 1910

Mobilised in regiment, 4 Aug. 1914. Wounded at Ypres, 30 April 1917; now in Northumberland (Oct. 1917). Master will take him back.

926 Clack, Arthur Leonard, of Devizes: to H. Kendall and Sons, plumbers and engineers, of St John St, Devizes. 5 yrs, £20. 30 May 1910

Enlisted 7 Sept. 1914 in 4th Regiment; and to India, in hospital with ague. Now serving as orderly in Temperance Canteen Board. Has volunteered to go to the Persian Gulf; still in India (1918). Master will take him back.

927 Whitbread, Arthur, of London EC.: to Messrs Fairbrother and Co., engineers, of 86 Goswell Rd, EC. 4 yrs, £20. 20 June 1910

Completed and enlisted 1914.

928   Orchard, Frank Trevor, of Edington: to William Burridge, builder, of Steeple Ashton. 5 yrs, £20. 11 July 1910

Completed and enlisted.

929   Smith, Stephen, of London SE.: to Walter Falkner, builder etc, of 163 New Cross Rd, SE. 5 yrs, £40. 11 July 1910

Completed and enlisted, 2/20 London Regiment; sent to Palestine and then France, and now (1918) in base hospital with dysentery.

930   Horne, Stanley William: to G.R. Ede, dental mechanic, of Bromley, Kent. 4 yrs, £50. 14 Nov. 1910

Completed and enlisted.

931   Giddings, Herbert Edward, of Devizes: to Messrs Brown and May, engineers, of Devizes. 4 yrs, £25. 15 Aug. 1910

Enlisted in 2nd Regiment when foundry closed. Went to India early in the war; now (1916) lance corporal. Transferred to Machine Gun Corps, 28 Oct. 1917; now in Mesopotamia (1918).

932   Noble, Sidney Cedric Hulbert, of Chiseldon: to A.J. Colborne, builder, of County Rd, Swindon. 4 yrs, £25. 6 March 1911

933   Gray, Stanley Charles Eber, of Great Wishford: to H. Mundy, carpenter etc, of Wishford, near Salisbury. 4 yrs, £20. 22 May 1911

Enlisted 1914; mobilised with 4th Regiment; served in Egyptian Expeditionary Force; killed in action in Palestine in April 1916.

934   Budden, Ronald, of Wylye: to W. Mundy, carpenter etc, of Wishford, near Salisbury. 3 yrs, £20. 22 May 1911

935   Baverstock, Percy Stewart: to R.B. Butcher and Son, builders etc, of George St, Warminster. 5 yrs, £20. 26 June 1911

936   Greenhill, Clarence Albert Dunning, of Southwick, Trowbridge: to J. Irons and Sons Ltd., brush manufacturers, of Castle Court Factory, Trowbridge. 6 yrs, £20. 24 July 1911

Called up May 1916. Now with Royal Warwickshire Regiment in France (1918).

937 Brewer, Frederick John, of Seend: to W.M. Cook, motor engineer, of Bath Road, Devizes. 5 yrs, £30. 30 Nov. 1911

Enlisted 5 Sept. 1914; and to India, Dec. 1914; and with 4th Regiment to Mesopotamia, 6 Aug. 1916 in 2nd Wireless Signalling Squadron.

938 Boulton, William Henry, of Corsham: to Alfred Butt, tailor, of Cheviot House, Corsham. 2 yrs, £10. 20 May 1912

Parents reside at Corsham; there are nine children.

939 Kitley, Beatrice Nelly: to G.W. Usher, tailor, of 15 Church St, Trowbridge. 3 yrs, £25. 20 May 1912

Both parents born at Trowbridge. There are four children dependent upon the mother. The father is in the County Asylum.

940 Grearson, Honor Louisa, of Westbury: to Bessie Grearson, dressmaker, of Hospital Terrace, Westbury. 2 yrs, £10. 20 May 1912

Parents reside at Westbury; four children dependent on them.

941 Stowe, Ernest Robert Savage, of Trowbridge: to Oliver Hire, decorator etc, of 32 Halve, Trowbridge. 3 yrs, £20. 17 June 1912

Father, a widower, residing at Trowbridge. There are five children, three dependent upon him. Apprentice enlisted in 4th Regiment, Sept. 1914; in India. Now hospital orderly with his regiment near Poona (1918).

942 Smith, Charles Henry: to G.A. Harvey and Co., metal manufacturers, of Loampit Vale, Lewisham, SE. 7 yrs, £25. 27 July 1912

Father, a widower, was born at Bishop's Cannings, and is a tram conductor; has eleven children. Apprentice enlisted 13 May 1916 in K.R. Rifles. Passed out first as physical exercise instructor, now (1916) corporal and at Bedford. Transferred to 2/2nd London Regiment; has been wounded, shot through the leg, and now in York hospital. His brother, S. Smith, apprenticed by the Society, also enlisted. Three other brothers also enlisted; one is in Italy, one in France and one in England. All well (1918).

943 Reeves, Henry John, of Rodbourne Cheney: to Great Western Railway, Engineer of Locomotive Dept., Engineer's Office, Swindon. 5 yrs, £25. 10 June 1912

Left G.W.R. at his own request, 21 Sept. 1916, and joined Crayford Aircraft Works. Working on munitions at Stoney Stratford, Bucks. as engineering fitter (1918).

944   Rice, Osborne, of Wroughton: to Great Western Railway, Engineer of Locomotive Dept., Engineer's Office, Swindon. 5 yrs, £25. 15 Sept. 1912

Mother, a widow, resides at Wroughton, with no means whatever beyond parish relief. Apprentice called up, 30 Oct. 1916. Working at a factory in Bath (1917). Serving in Royal Air Force at Bembridge (1918).

945   Randall, Albert Victor, of Warminster: to R. Butcher and Son, carpenters etc, of George St, Warminster. 5 yrs, £20. 5 May 1913

Parents have four children. Enlisted in territorials before the war and went to India; and in Oct. 1916 to Mesopotamia, and is a signaller (1917). In 2/4th, 35th Brigade, signals, in Mesopotamia (1918).

946   Gingell, William, of Derry Hill: to C.R. Stevens and Sons, bootmakers, of Avondale Boot Works, Chippenham. 3 yrs, £20. 12 May 1913

Deaf and dumb. Articles completed; he is remaining with the firm (1918).

947   Harding, Evelyn Lily, of North Bradley: to Heathcote and Co., dressmakers, of Bridge House, Trowbridge. 2 yrs, £20. 12 May 1913

Parents have seven children.

948   Hill, John, of Calne: to Calne Gas and Coke Co. Ltd., of Horsebrook, near Calne. 5 yrs, £20. 2 June 1913

Parents have seven children. Enlisted 9 Sept. 1916; Sapper Field Co. R.E., serving in France (1918).

949   Tidmarsh, Thomas Edward: to T. Merrett and Son, carpenters, of Box. 4 yrs, £20. 11 Aug. 1913

Enlisted in R.A.M.C., 25 Nov. 1915; now in field ambulance, France (1917); gassed 30 May 1918; discharged from hospital, 5 Sept. 1918; now with London Ambulance (1918).

950   Tidmarsh, Stribley: to C.W. Courtenay, of Swan Wharf, High St, Fulham, SW. 5 yrs, £30. 18 Aug. 1913

Father, from Colerne, has seven children. Enlisted 14 Nov. 1914, without permission. Further payment not to be made. Now serving in 13th London Regiment in France (1917). In 6th Somerset Light Infantry, now in V.A.D. hospital at Ilfracombe with trench fever (1918).

951 Nash, Leslie Athelstane: to Eagle Motor Manufacturing Co. Ltd., of 1a Shepherds Bush Rd, W. 5 yrs, £50. 29 Aug. 1913

The father, a railway porter, came from Tilshead. Transferred, 4 Aug. 1914, to Messrs Lacy-Hulbert and Co., pneumatic engineers, Beddington, Surrey. Badged for munitions work, and still serving (1917); rejected for service on account of health. The firm suggests his articles be terminated, as work is too heavy (1918).

952   Moors, Ernest Collins: to F. Horsfield and Co., electrical engineers, of 16 St Anne's Court, W. 3 yrs, £25. 6 Aug. 1913

Enlisted May 1916; now 1st AM-B Flight, 100 Squadron R.F.C. in France (1916); serving in R.A.F., France (1918); now a corporal.

953   Miles, Jesse, of Devizes: to A. Smith and Son, builders etc, of 6 Cyprus Terrace, Devizes. 6½ yrs, £20. 19 Jan. 1914

Father earns £1 a week and has nine children. Enlisted 11 Oct. 1915 for 7 years in 6th Regiment. Wounded 7 July 1916; discharged 25 April 1917; still in hospital at Devizes. Right arm stiff from shrapnel going through elbow (1917). Wound healed, now going to Salisbury Infirmary for another operation (1918).

954   James, Albert Edgar, of Warminster: to Messrs Mills and Sons, bootmakers, of 29 East St, Warminster. 4 yrs, £20. 18 June 1914

Father, from Warminster, dead; two children. Class C; serving as bootmaker in R.F.C. and now at Gosport (1917). Still at Gosport as bootmaker in R.F.C. School (1918).

955   Player, Arthur William, of Warminster: to Messrs R. Butcher and Son, builders etc, of George St, Warminster. 6½ yrs, £20. 18 June 1914

Father from Warminster; three children. Joined up in Jan. 1918 and now in Suffolk (1918).

956   Newman, Henry, of Potterne: to H.L. Burden, carpenters etc, of the Butts, Potterne, Devizes. 5 yrs, £20. 19 June 1914

Father from Potterne; both parents dead; six children. Apprentice enlisted 20 April 1915, now in Delhi (1917). Wounded in April 1918, but now in Egypt (1918).

957   Feltham, Arthur Henry, of Hilperton: to C.G. Matthews, builder etc, of Hilperton, Trowbridge. 5 yrs, £20. 19 June 1914

Father from Hilperton; eight children dependent on him. Still serving, but Grade 3 and exempted until 30 Dec. (1918).

958 Wootton, William Franklin: to Uriah White and Son, farriers etc, of Weymouth St, Warminster. 4 yrs, £20. 30 June 1914

Father, a police pensioner, from Warminster; four children. Apprentice enlisted and mobilised 4 Aug. 1914; in 4th, and went to India. Still there, as a bandsman (1917). In India with band of the 4th Regiment (1918).

959 Gleed, Roland Robert, of Purton: to T. and E. Sanders, tailors, of 153-4 Victoria Rd, Swindon. 3 yrs, £25. 16 July 1914

Father from Purton. The boy, a cripple, apprenticed as a tailor. Left nearly 12 months ago on completion of articles, and is a permanent cripple.

960 Moules, Leonard Walter Roger: to Geo. Cooling and Sons, seed merchants and nurserymen, of 11 Northgate St, Bath, Somerset. 3 yrs, £20. 20 July 1914

Father from Colerne; seven children. Apprenticed as a gardener. County apprentice. Joined up May 1916, now with Royal Fusiliers in France (1917). Reported missing in April 1918 and not since heard of (1918).

961 Gardiner, Edgar Wilfred: to Messrs Foreman and Sons, tailors, of 55 Stallard St, Trowbridge. 4 yrs, £25. 21 July 1914

Deaf and dumb; still serving (1917). Articles completed but still employed (1918).

962 Penn, Wilfred Charles, of Warminster: to Messrs F. Curtis and Son, builders etc, of Warminster. 6 yrs, £20. 30 June 1914

Parents have six children. Joined Hants. Carabineers in 1917; now en route for Egypt (M.G Section) (1917).

963 Tinnams, Hedley Frederick: to R. and J. Reeves and Son Ltd., agricultural engineers and ironfounders, of Bratton Iron Works, Westbury. 6 yrs, £16. 7 July 1915

Father, from Imber, died leaving a widow and two children. £5 for tools, Dec. 1915. Still serving; not of military age (1917). Still with Reeves and Son, but has protection certificate (1918).

964 Wootton, Percy Henry: to J. Mills and Son, bootmakers, of 29 East St, Warminster. 4 yrs, £20. 7 Aug. 1915

Father, police pensioner, from Warminster; four children. Still serving (1918), unfit for military service.

965 Rice, Albert Edward: to Great Western Railway, engineers, of Engineer's Office, Locomotive Department, Swindon. 5 yrs, £25. 19 Aug. 1915

Father, from Wroughton, died leaving a widow and five children. County apprentice. Still serving (1917); holds a retention card. In Gloucester Regiment in France (1918).

966 Moules, Sidney Albert, of Colerne: to E.C. Richards, mason, of Thornwood, Box. 3 yrs, £20. 1 Aug. 1914

Father from Colerne; seven children. The apprentice's articles were not received until Oct. 1915. Employer enlisted; works closed Dec. 1915. Moules enlisted July 1916, gunner R.F.A., now on his way to Mesopotamia (1917). In R.F.A. expeditionary force (1918). Resumed apprenticeship 1 July 1920. £5 to father, July 1920, for tools.

967 Mead, Margaret: to Mrs E.G. Smith, costumiers etc, of 1 Willow Vale, Frome, Somerset. 2 yrs, £30. 7 Feb. 1916

Father, from Chapmanslade, an ex-police sergeant; eleven children. County apprentice. Making good progress (1918).

968 Horton, Arthur Thomas: to Percy Witts, bootmaker, of 35 Fleet St, Swindon. 5 yrs, £30. 27 Nov. 1915

County apprentice, deaf and dumb. Father from Stratton St Margaret; wife died 1912, leaving seven children. Still serving and going on satisfactorily (1917).

969 Taplin, Arthur Herbert: to L.J. Bigwood, ironmonger, of High St, Melksham. 3 yrs, £20. 27 April 1916

With West Somerset Yeomanry at Athlone, Ireland (1918).

970 Naish, George William: to G.N. Haden and Sons, engineers, of Trowbridge. 6 yrs, £20. 1 May 1916

Not of military age, but working on war work (1918).

971 Tanner, Edward George: to E. Linzey and Son, builders, of Trowbridge. 4 yrs, £20. 3 May 1916

Still serving, not of military age (1918).

972 Johnson, John Alfred: to J. Merritt and Son, builders, of Box. 5 yrs, £20. 12 May 1916

Indenture cancelled, April 1918.

973 Rawlings, Victor Henry Edward: to K.T.S. Piano Company, musical instrument makers, of Warminster. 2 yrs, £20. 1 July 1916

974 Burgess, Arthur John: to R. and J. Reeves and Son Ltd., ironfounders, of Westbury. 5 yrs, £16. 8 June 1917

Indenture cancelled on medical certificate before second moiety paid.

975 Pearce, Donald F.F.: to W.M. Cook, motor engineer, of Devizes. 5 yrs, £30. 1 Aug. 1917

976 Bailey, William B.: to J.J. Stevens, carpenter, of 4 Northgate St, Devizes. 4 yrs, £20. 27 April 1918

977 Chapman, William John: to R. and J. Reeves and Son Ltd., ironfounders, of Westbury. 5 yrs, £16. 14 May 1918

978 Yockney, Rhoda Louisa: to Miss E.M. Hayward, dressmaker, of Marlborough. 2 yrs, £20. 1 June 1918

979 Wills, Percival W.: to Curtis and Son, builders, of Warminster. 6 yrs, £30. 1 Aug. 1919

980 Bailey, Hubert E.: to William Mundy, carpenter and wheelwright, of Wishford. 6 yrs, £30. 1 Aug. 1919

981 Merritt, Arthur T.: to Joseph J. Stevens, builder, of 4 Northgate St, Devizes. 5 yrs, £25. 16 July 1920

Father from Nursteed, Devizes, a leather sales tradesman; three children. Granted £5 for tools.

982 Cockrell, Frederick C.: to Frederick W. Butcher, builder, of George St, Warminster. 6 yrs, £30. 10 July 1920

Father, from Warminster, a builder's labourer; three children.

983 Dew, Arthur E.: to James E. Spratt, motor engineer, of Stallard's Garage, Trowbridge. 6 yrs, £30. 10 July 1920

Father, from Trowbridge, a wheelwright, but father and mother both in ill-health and unable to work regularly; one child.

984 Pearce, Dennis Edgar: to Hancock and Roberts, founders, of Innox Foundry, Trowbridge. 6 yrs, £40. 30 April 1920

Father died before child was born and mother subsequently. Only child, brought up by grandmother.

985 Marshall, Percy James: to Edward Mills, bootmaker, of East St, Warminster. 4 yrs, £45. 13 Sept. 1920

Father from Kingston Deverill, a carter, dead; two children.

986 Yockney, Godfrey H.: to Thomas E. Leadley, builder, of 100 High St, Marlborough. 5 yrs, £30. 25 Sept. 1920

Father from Marlborough, a house-painter; ten children. £15, part of the premium, was paid to the Society by Rev W. Henderson, rector of Kingston Deverill.

987 Moon, John: to W.H. White, carpenter, of Bradford Rd, Trowbridge. 2 yrs, £30. 12 Oct. 1920

Father a telephone operator. Both parents dead; three children.

988 Gibbs, Walter: to Charles G. Matthews, builder, of Hilperton, Trowbridge. 3 yrs, £30. 1 Jan. 1921

Father from Hilperton, a shepherd; ten children.

989 Newman, William A.: to John T. Parsons. J.P., builder, of Westbury. 4 yrs, £20. 1 Jan. 1921

Father from Bratton, a blast-furnace worker; two children.

990 Yandell, Leslie J.: to E. Linzey and Son, builders, of Trowbridge. 5 yrs, £30. 24 Jan. 1921

Father, a maltster from Trowbridge, dead; only child.

991 Walker, Albert H.: to J. and E. Russell, tailors, of Marlborough. 4 yrs, £50. 1 March 1921

Father from Ogbourne St Andrew, a carter; the second of seven children. The boy has been in five hospitals and has undergone seven operations, and is not fit to work on a farm again, being a cripple.

992 Philpott, Robert H.: to William H. Huntley, carpenter, of Honeystreet (*Honey St*), Marlborough. 5 yrs, £20. 16 May 1921

993 Guy, Horace F.: to Alfred Merritt, builder, of Box. 4 yrs, £30. 1 Oct. 1921

994 Burt, Cyril E.: to F. Rendell and Sons, builders, of John St, Devizes. 5 yrs, £25. 1 Nov. 1921

995 Dance, Walter W.: to T.E. Leadley, builder, of High St, Marlborough. 5 yrs, £30. 30 Jan. 1922

996 Ham, Bertrand F.: to J.H. Hughes, clerk of works, Longleat. 6 yrs, £40. 1 June 1922

997 Bartlett, Charles G.: to F. Rendell and Sons, builders, of John St, Devizes. 5 yrs, £25. 1 July 1922

998 Plank, Lawrence S.: to W.G. Elisha, tailor, of 7 High St, Market Lavington. 4 yrs, £25. 19 June 1922

Elisha died Feb. 1924; apprentice transferred to Parson and Son, Devizes.

999 Godden, Bob: to F. Rendell and Son, builders, of John St, Devizes. 5 yrs, £25. 1 June 1922

1000 Plowman, George H.: to Wessex Motors Ltd., motor engineers, of Salisbury. 4 yrs, £31 10s. 14 Aug. 1922

1001 Webb, Reginald: to F. Curtis and Son, builders, of 11 Portway, Warminster. 6 yrs, £40. 1 June 1922

1002 Cox, Joseph H.: to Duck, Son and Pinker Ltd., piano merchants, of Swindon. 5 yrs, £25. 30 Oct. 1922
Additional £5 for tools.

1003 Allen, Charles W.: to Linzey and Son, builders, of Trowbridge. 5 yrs, £30. 17 Nov. 1922

1004 Jenkins, C. Ivor: to T.A. Bush, motor engineers, of Pulteney Mews, Bath, Somerset. 5 yrs, £30. 22 Jan. 1923

Cancelled [*no date*].

1005 Little, Gordon F.: to T.I. Stevens, carpenter, of 4 Northgate St, Devizes. 5 yrs, £25. 3 April 1923

1006 Brown, H.J. Hillier: to F. Rendell and Sons, builders, of John St, Devizes. 5 yrs, £25. 9 May 1923

EXHIBITIONERS

A1 Hale, Emily Maud, daughter of William and Emily Flora, of Devizes. 1881.

Elected to a county exhibition. Father is a gardener earning 25s. a week. She passed the sixth standard in arithmetic at St Peter's School, Devizes, and has attended the School of Science and Art at Devizes, where she has shown exceptional ability. It is intended by the candidate's parents to make designing for art manufacture her means of livelihood, for which avocation, if she is enabled to get proper instruction, she is peculiarly fitted. In May 1881 she passed Grade II Government Examination, and in April last her works, four in number, consisting amongst others, a group of models painted in sepia, were accepted by the Science and Art Department for an art teacher's Certificate. In the local competition she gained a second prize in the first class. Twenty-seven of her paintings and designs were sent to South Kensington in April for examination but the results have not yet been received. [*1882 Annual Report*]

A2 Beasant, Henry John. 1882

Obtained a certificate for wood-work at the King's College Examination, and a prize for perspective, a certificate for plane geometry and a certificate for model drawing; which entitles him to a full certificate of the Grade II Art of the Science and Art Department at South Kensington. He also obtained a certificate for elementary building construction at the same institution.

A3 Thomas, William Davis. 1882

Apprentice **509**. [*1880 Annual report:*] Candidate elected to Town Exhibition. Born 14 Dec. 1862, he was educated at Clapham Parochial School and passed sixth standard in arithmetic, June 1875. He was apprenticed in May 1878 and has been working satisfactorily. At the examinations for the Night Schools of Science and Art (Battersea) held May 1879 he obtained second class certificate for success in practical and plane geometry, and also in building construction and drawing. The candidate desires to attend the Battersea classes until May, and after attend lectures at King's College, London.

A4 Holmes, Catherine Mary. 1889

CANDIDATES WHO FAILED TO GAIN APPRENTICESHIPS

B1 Wody, Robert, son of Robert and Ann, of China Court, Lambeth. 1823

Candidate in 1823, not elected. Parents from Bradford, with four children.

B2 Bodman, Henry. 1830

Father from Bremhill. Unsuccessful.

B3 Austin, Henry. 1830

A native of Westbury. Unsuccessful.

B4 Oakey, Nathaniel. 1830

Mother from Fifield. Unsuccessful.

B5 Haynes, John Ferand. 1830

Parents from Warminster. Unsuccessful [*possibly brother to* **B13**].

B6 Gilmore, Walter. 1832

Candidate in 1832, not elected. Father from Marlborough, and mother from Swindon.

B7 Purnell, Edmund. 1832

Candidate in 1832, not elected. Mother from East Knoyle [*possibly brother of* **68** *and* **113**].

B8   Croom, John James. 1832

Candidate in 1832, not elected. Father from Melksham.

B9   Evans, William Henry. 1832

Candidate in 1832, not elected. Parents from Marlborough.

B10   Axford, James. 1835

Father from Melksham. Unsuccessful.

B11   Vezey, Henry. 1835

Father from Melksham, mother from Wolverton. Unsuccessful.

B12   Gillingham, Elizabeth. 1835

Father from Tisbury, mother from Marlborough. Unsuccessful [*possibly sister to* **93**].

B13   Haynes, Edwin Washington. 1835

Father from Warminster. Unsuccessful [*possibly brother to* **119**, **148** *and* **B5**].

B14   Moffatt, William. 1835

Father from Warminster, mother from Bratton. Unsuccessful.

B15   Spicer, Richard Thomas. 1835

Father from Preshute. Unsuccessful [*possibly brother to* **65**].

B16   Edds, John. 1836

Parents from Dilton. Unsuccessful.

B17   Roberts, Isaac. 1836

Mother from Atworth. Unsuccessful [*possibly brother to* **52**].

B18   Dare, Robert. 1839

Both parents from near Swindon. Unsuccessful [*see* **120**].

B19 Stevens, John. 1839

Mother a widow, father from Bradford. Unsuccessful.

B20 Boucher, Henry. 1839

Mother from Sutton Veny. Unsuccessful.

B21 White, George, son of George and Elizabeth. 1844

Father from Bromham, mother (formerly Elizabeth Swatton) from All Cannings. Unsuccessful. Brother of **216**.

B22 Applegate, Stephen. 1844

Applicant an orphan; parents from Westbury. Unsuccessful [*possibly brother to* **152**].

B23 Fryer, William Thomas. 1844

Father from Trowbridge. Unsuccessful.

B24 Deacon, Samuel. 1844

Father from North Bradley, mother from Trowbridge, where candidate was born. Unsuccessful.

B25 Kemp, John Rymill. 1844

Father from Melksham. Unsuccessful.

B26 Mason, John Watts. 1844

Both parents from Westbury. Unsuccessful.

B27 Hayes, Thomas Stead. 1844

Father from Malmesbury. Unsuccessful.

B28 Harding, James. 1844

Father from Hindon. Unsuccessful.

B29 Dix, John. 1844

Father from Bradford. Unsuccessful.

B30 Haines, William Frederick. 1844

Father from Warminster. Unsuccessful [*possibly brother to* **167**].

B31 Barton, Joseph. 1846

Candidate in 1846, not elected. Mother from Shrewton.

B32 Townsend, George. 1846

Candidate in 1846, not elected. Mother from Melksham [*possibly brother to* **105**].

B33 Clare, Thomas Richard. 1846
Candidate in 1846, not elected. Father from Warminster.

B34 Toop, Charles, son of Nelson and Phoebe (Martha). 1855

Parents from Westbury: mother Phoebe or Martha Ayers; father, a journeyman shoemaker, finds great difficulty in maintaining so large a family, the eldest of whom is sixteen. Nine children in family; candidate was age 14 in Aug. 1855. Unsuccessful candidate.

B35 Higgins, Edward S., son of Stephen and Jane Helen. 1855

Father, from Chippenham, is a labourer; his children are dependent on him. Candidate is the eldest and was at the parish school for four years, afterwards at a school in Bath for a twelve-month. Mother (Jane Ellen Smith) from Corsham. Five children in family; candidate was age 14 in Jan. 1856. Application not successful.

B36 Telling, Frederick, son of Jonathan and Ann. 1876

Parents are of Cricklade. Father is a labourer and has eight children; mother is dead. No application before as the candidate and his friends were ignorant of the existence of the Society.

B37 Newton, William Wilmot, son of Thomas and Maria, of South Newton, Salisbury. 1876

Candidate in 1874, not elected. The candidate is a cripple owing to a chill. Father works on the roads and has five children. This application was made in 1874, and since then the rule as to age has been modified, and comes now into operation.

B38 Griffin, Henry, son of George and Jane. 1876

Application was not successful. Mother (formerly Jane Read) of Steeple Ashton. Father was an agricultural labourer, but has for some time been incapacitated from diseased leg. He has five children.

B39 Elliott, Ada Elizabeth, daughter of George and Emma. 1876

Father, from Bradford, a carpenter now earning 36s. a week, has been in his present employ for 21 years; has a wife and three children, together with his father and his wife's mother dependent upon him. Elected for apprenticeship in April 1876, but not in register.

B40 Bray, Samuel Edward, son of William John and Sarah Ann. 1882

Mother was born at Potterne; father is a cab-driver. It is wished to apprentice the lad to an engineer, if means can be found to do so. He is at present attending Walworth Board School.

B41 Hawkins, George Henry, son of Thomas and Sarah. 1882

Father was born at Ogbourne St Andrew. Five of his eight children are dependent on him. He is employed as a carman by Messrs Perrott of Tenter St., Moorfields.

B42 Burrough, Walter John, son of Samuel James and Ellen. 1889

Father was born at Salisbury, and mother at Westbury. Father, who is a journeyman tailor, earns on an average 24s. a week. He suffers from chronic bronchitis, which at times prevents him from following his trade. They have had thirteen children, four of whom are now living; three are entirely dependent upon the father. Application unsuccessful.

B43 Smith, Alfred John, son of Joseph Matthew and Jane. 1889

Mother was born at Chisbury. Father, who is employed at the General Post Office as a carpenter, earns 27s. a week, and has eight children, six wholly and two partially dependent upon him. Not in apprentice register.

B44 Taylor, Sidney Herbert, son of Benjamin and Annie. 1898

Candidate is a brother of **B45**. Elected for apprenticeship in April 1898, but not listed in the register.

B45 Taylor, Arthur Joseph, son of Benjamin and Annie, of Trowbridge. 1898

Father is by trade a painter, with average earnings of 18s. a week. He has a family of twelve children, five of whom are dependent on him. He suffers from a weak heart and general debility, his only income now being his sick pay from a benefit society. Candidate has obtained a certificate for passing the sixth standard, and for good conduct at the Parochial School, Trowbridge. Elected for apprenticeship in April 1898, but not listed in the register.

B46 Ranger, Walter Herbert, son of Francis George and Mary Ann. 1898

Father was born at Hindon, where his family has lived for several generations. He died in July 1892, leaving a widow and five children totally unprovided for. Mother earns a little money by needlework. One of her girls is a cripple, and one of the boys is apprenticed through the Society. Elected for apprenticeship in April 1898 but not listed in the register.

B47 Pollard, Albert Edward, son of Frederick Henry and Margaret Eleanor. 1898

Father was born in Chippenham. He has been in the employment of the Great Western Railway as a labourer for twenty-four years; he has seven children, three of them being at work, and the boy is to be apprenticed to one of the Great Western carpenters without premium, the Society undertaking to find the boy tools, instead of paying a premium for him. Elected for apprenticeship in April 1898, but not listed in the register.

B48 Hodges, Mahala Mabel. 1911

Town apprentice. Not in apprentice register. Father from Highworth; three children.

B49 Clutterbuck, Sidney Herring, of London N. 1912

Father a clerk; mother born in Swindon. Town apprentice. Not in apprentice register.

B50 Fry, Henry Robert. 1912

Father a labourer; mother born at Swallowcliffe, eight children. Town apprentice. Not in apprentice register.

B51 Golledge, Francis Herbert. 1913

Father, who was from Bradford on Avon, died Jan. 1912, leaving the mother a widow with two children to support. Elected in 1913, but not in apprentice register. Brother to **B55**.

B52 Hiskett, Edwin Charles, of Warminster. 1913

Father earns 15s. a week and has six children. Elected in 1913, but not in apprentice register.

B53 Richardson, Henry. 1913

Mother from Bromham. Elected in 1913, but not in apprentice register [*possibly brother to* **B59**].

B54 Poole, Russell Lawrence, of Devizes. 1913

Mother in Asylum. Elected in 1913, but not in apprentice register.

B55 Golledge, Ida Kathleen. 1914

Father, from Bradford, died Jan. 1912, leaving a widow and two children. The other child is also an apprentice of this Society. Town apprentice. Not in apprentice register. Sister to **B51**.

B56 Smallbones, Phillis. 1914

Father, from Bedwyn, died leaving widow and four children. Town apprentice. Not in apprentice register.

B57 Gay, Herbert Arthur, of Trowbridge. 1915

Father from Trowbridge; six children. Apprentice joined R.N. Feb. 1915. County apprentice. Not in apprentice register.

B58 Gray, Ernest Albert. 1915

Father from Colerne; four children. County apprentice. Not in apprentice register.

B59 Richardson, William Charles, of Victoria Park. 1915

Mother from Bromham; four children. Town apprentice. [*Not in apprentice register; possibly brother to* **B53**]

B60 Trapp, Harold Frederick. 1915

Father from Warminster; four children. County apprentice. Not in apprentice register.

B61 Hancock, Frank. 1915

Both parents dead; father from Swindon. Town apprentice. [*enlisted*]. Not in apprentice register.

B62 Wotton, Percy Henry. 1915

Father, police pensioner, from Warminster. Four children. Elected in 1915, but not in apprentice register.

APPENDIX A RULES OF THE WILTSHIRE SOCIETY 1823

1. An Annual Subscription of One Guinea constitutes a Governor.

2. A single Subscription of Ten Guineas constitutes a Governor for life.

3. Any person presenting the Society a larger sum than Ten Guineas, in one payment, will be entitled to vote in the proportion of one vote for every ten guineas.

4. Every person who pays One Guinea a year, in addition to a Donation of Ten Guineas, will be entitled to a second vote, and so on in proportion.

5. Upon any Legacy being paid to the Treasurer, the Executors who have administered shall be made Life Governors, with one vote, calculating at the rate of £50 each; and in case the Legacy shall not amount to a sufficient sum to extend the privilege to all, preference shall be given to the person first named in the will.

6. A Donation of £210 in one payment, or paid in the course of one year, entitles the Donor either to the privilege of twenty votes, or to have one apprentice always on the Institution.

7. Any Governor whose subscription is one year in arrear shall not be entitled to a vote at any election, or sign any petition, until such arrear be paid.

8. The Society to be under the direction of a President, and a Committee of twelve gentlemen, besides a Treasurer and a Secretary, who are members of the Committee, *ex officio*.

9. The President to be elected annually at the Anniversary meeting.

10. The Treasurer and Honorary Secretary to be appointed at such Anniversary meeting.

11. Such vacancies as shall occur in the Committee to be supplied at the Anniversary Meeting next ensuing, and the Secretary to call an extra meeting of the Committee, upon the request of three of the said Committee at least, and on having reasonable notice for that purpose. Any member who neglects to attend four successive Quarterly Meetings of the Committee, thereby forfeits his seat.

12. The Committee to meet four times at least in each year, of which Committee five shall be an efficient number for the transaction of business.

13. The Committee to be empowered to appoint Agents and Receivers for the Society; to print a state of its funds at each Anniversary, with the names and number of Children apprenticed in each year; together with a list of the Governors, and such other particulars as they may think advisable.

14. The Committee to call a General Meeting of the Society, upon a requisition for that purpose being made to them through the Secretary, signed by at least ten Governors of the Society (provided such requisition sets forth the special business to be done at such meeting), and that such General Meeting be convened within 21 days after the requisition be made.

15. A General Meeting of the Society may be convened for any special purpose by the President or by the Committee.

16. A General Meeting, when necessary, is to be held on the first Tuesday in February, in each year.

17. An Anniversary Meeting to be held for managing the Business of the Society, when the members will dine together, due notice of which is to be given by the Secretary, under the directions of the Committee.

18. No Governor, whose subscription shall be in arrear, will be entitled to vote, or affix his name to any petition; and no petition to be received unless signed by the President or by two Governors.

19. No sum exceeding £25 will be given by the Society as a premium for apprenticeship.

20. The Committee for the time being to have the power of lending for four years, without interest upon proper security, sums of money not exceeding £60 each, to persons whose apprenticeship shall have expired, and whose conduct shall have been meritorious; and application for such loans, to be made in writing, to the Secretary before the 1st October in every year.

21. All petitions to be submitted to the consideration of the Committee, who are to report respecting such persons as are eligible, at the General meeting, previous to ballot.

22. All petitions to be admissible, if either the father or mother, or the object for whom the application is made, be a native of the county of Wilts., and such object not to exceed 14 years of age at the time of election. The parties interested, are to observe, that in cases where premiums are to be given, all persons entitled are to receive the same by two payments, and must make application for the first moiety of the premium, by sending one part of the indenture duly executed to the Secretary, at least one month previous to the then ensuing meeting of the Committee; and for the second moiety of the premium, by transmitting, at the expiration of half the apprenticeship, the certificate of the minister, and one of the churchwardens or overseers of the poor of the parish where the master resides, in the following form viz.

We do hereby certify that A.B apprenticed by the Wiltshire Society to C.D of the parish of , in the county of , following the trade of , in the month of in the year of, continues in the service of the said C.D. as his apprentice.

Dated:

Signed

minister of said parish

Churchwarden or Overseer.

APPENDIX B GOVERNORS OF THE WILTSHIRE SOCIETY, 1817 - 1921

The Society's annual reports include lists of those who had supported its work by donations and subscriptions, and who were thereby known as governors. The scope of these annual lists altered over time. From those reports available for inspection, it appears that until 1843 all past and present governors were included. Thereafter, until c.1873, the lists excluded the names of those whose contribution had been less than £5, and had been made more than four years previously. Then, until c.1904, all donors and subscribers since 1869 were included, but only the names of those donating £5 or more before 1869. Between 1901 and 1913 (or later) two lists appeared, one of past governors donating at least five guineas (£5 5s.), and another of current governors. Later lists include only current governors and life members (eligibility for which required a donation of at least ten guineas, £10 10s.).

This appendix aims to present as complete a list as possible of those governors who contributed at least £5 5s. during the period 1817-1921. Its bases are the lists of past and present governors and contributors printed in the 1913 report, and the list of present governors and contributors printed in the 1921 report. These lists were evidently compiled from the lists in earlier reports, and, depending on the accuracy of earlier record-keeping, should be comprehensive, apart from contributors of sums less than £5 5s., or governors who both joined and left (having not become life governors), or joined and died, between 1913 and 1921.

Information is presented in this list in the following way: name, as printed in the report; address, where given (in some cases slightly abbreviated); date(s) of contributions; total amount of contribution (insofar as this can be calculated). A date followed by an asterisk denotes that the contributor was still listed as a governor in 1921. Some small amounts (generally £1 1s.) refer not to a total contribution, but to an annual subscription.

Because a payment of £10 10s. or more in a single year entitled the contributor to life governorship, contributors continued to be listed as present governors for a long time (sometimes fifty or sixty years) after they had made their contribution. It should not be assumed, therefore, that the last dates given for contributions in the list below are either the dates of death, or of contributors ceasing to be governors of the society.

Absolom, Edward, esq; 1852-67; £15 15s.
Ailesbury, Marquis of; 1818; £10 10s.
Ailesbury, Marquis of; 1839; £10 10s.
Ailesbury, Marquis of; 1853-64; £21.
Ailesbury, Marquis of, Savernake, Marlborough; 1879; £10 10s.
Ailesbury, Marquis of, D.S.O., Savernake Forest, Marlborough; 1901*; £10 10s.
Albany, H.R.H. Duke of, K.G.; 1881; £25.
Alexander, G., esq; 1839-69; £31 10s.

Alexander, James, esq; 1817-24; £10 10s.
Alexander, James, esq, M.P.; 1825; £10 10s.
Alexander, Robert, esq; 1840-1; £15 15s.
Alford, John Lush, esq; 1843; £10 10s.
Anstie, E.L., esq, Market Place, Devizes; 1902*; £5 5s.
Antrobus, Sir Cosmo G., bart, Amesbury Abbey; 1899*; £25.
Antrobus, Sir Edmund, bart, Amesbury; 1824; £10 10s.

Antrobus, Sir Edmund, bart; 1828-32; £21.

Antrobus, Sir Edmund, bart, M.P.; 1843-74; £42.

Antrobus, Col Sir Edmund, bart, Amesbury Abbey; 1907-13 [and perhaps later: listed as governor in 1913, but not in 1921]; £13 13s.

Antrobus, Lady; 1840; £10 10s.

Archer, D., esq; 1848; £13 13s.

Arkell, Thomas, esq, Kingsdown, Swindon; 1901; £1 1s.

Arnold-Foster, Mrs, Bassett Down House; 1899*; £1 1s.

Artindale, R.H., esq, East House, Warminster; 1901*; £21.

Arundell of Wardour, Lord; 1892; £1 1s. annually.

Ashburton, Lord; 1825; £10 10s.

Ashe, Rev Robert, Langley House; 1842; £10 10s.

Ashe, Rev R.M., Langley House; 1856; £10 10s.

Ashley, Lord, M.P.; 1860-3; £6 6s.

Astley, Sir F. Dugdale, bart; 1826; £10 10s.

Astley, Rev Francis B., Manningford; 1827; £18 18s.

Astley, Sir John Dugdale, bart, M.P., Everleigh; 1819-33; £37 16s.

Aston, Thomas, jun, esq; 1819-24; £17 17s.

Atherton, Nathaniel, esq; 1823-32; £10 10s.

Attwood, Francis, esq; 1864-70; £7 7s.

Atwood, Rev G.H.S., Bishopstrow rectory; 1900-7; £4 4s.

Awdry, A.J., esq, R.A.; 1897-1909; £10 10s.

Awdry, Ambrose, esq, Seend; 1818; £12 12s.

Awdry, Mrs Ambrose, Crossways, Crowthorne, Berks; 1865*; £10 10s.

Awdry, Charles, esq, 2 Hyde Park Street, W; 1885-1912; £155 14s.

Awdry, Charles Selwyn, esq, Hitchambury, Taplow; 1894-1912; £16 16s.

Awdry, Edmund M., esq, Chippenham; 1913*; £1 1s.

Awdry, John, esq, Seend; 1820-8; £17 17s.

Awdry, Sir John Wither; 1820-39; £21.

Awdry, R.J. esq, 2 Hyde Park Street, W; 1897; £10 10s.

Awdry, Major R.W., Hawkeswell, Little Cheverell; 1898*; £10 10s.

Awdry, Rev Canon W.; 1892; £1 1s.

Banbury, Sir Frederick G., bart, M.P., Warneford Place, Highworth; 1905*; £3 3s.

Banning, John, esq; 1819-30; £11 11s.

Banning, Thomas, esq; 1819-23; £5 5s.

Bannister, Matthew, esq; 1824; £10 10s.

Baring, Alexander, esq; 1826; £10 10s.

Baring, H.B. esq, M.P.; 1834-8; £15 15s.

Baring, Thomas, esq, M.P.; 1854-61; £21.

Baron, Rev John, D.D.; 1865-85; £24 3s.

Barton, Major-General, Ramsbury; 1889-92; £5 5s.

Barton, Nathaniel, esq; 1872; £10 10s.

Baskerville, Henry, esq; 1840; £10 10s.

Bastings, Henry, esq; 1832-48; £16 16s.

Bath, Marquis of; 1819-32; £40 10s.

Bath, Marquis of; 1855-90; £36 15s.

Bath, Marquis of, K.G., Longleat; 1887*; £67 10s.

Bathurst, Charles, esq, M.P., Lydney Park; 1912-13 [and perhaps later: listed as governor in 1913, but not in 1921]; £5 5s.

Bathurst, Sir Frederick, bart; 1843-81; £81 18s.

Bathurst, Col Sir F. Harvey, bart; 1861; £10 10s.

Beach, M. Hicks, esq; 1821; £10 10s.

Beach, Sir M.H. Hicks, bart; 1849; £10 10s.

Beaufort, Duke of, Badminton; 1883*; £10 10s.

Beaufoy, Mrs; 1879; £10 10s.

Beaufoy, Mark, esq, 87 South Lambeth Road, SW8; 1880*; £26.

Bell, Lt-Colonel W.C. Heward, D.S.O., M.P., Cleeve House, Seend; 1920*; £1 1s.

Bell, W. Heward, esq, Cleeve House, Seend; 1907*; £46 4s.

Benet-Stanford, Vere Fane, esq, Pyt House; 1859-84; £37 16s.

Benet-Stanford, John, esq, Pyt House; 1896-9; £8 3s.

Benett, John, esq, Pyt House; 1818; £70 7s.

Benett-Stanford, Major J., Hatch House; 1896*; £6 10s. 6d.

Bennett, James, esq; 1849-58; £10 10s.

Bernard, Rev Canon, High Hall, Wimborne; 1901-8; £8 8s.

Bertodano, B. de, esq, Cowbridge House, Malmesbury; 1906; £10 10s.

Bevir, Harry, esq, The Lime Kiln, Wootton Bassett; 1887-1906; £12 12s.

Biggs, George, esq; 1823; £10 10s.

Blackman, Dr, Ramsbury; 1822-36; £14 14s.

Blackmore, Dr Humphrey Purnell, St Ann's Street, Salisbury; 1871*; £10 10s.

Blackmore, William, esq; 1864; £10 10s.

Bladworth, Thomas, esq; 1902*; £1 1s.

Blagg, Thomas Ward, esq; 1831-66; £13 13s.

Blathwayt, G.W.W., esq, Porlock Weir; 1908*; £3 1s.

Bleaden, Charles, esq; 1819; £32 12.

Bledisloe, Lord, Lydney Park; 1912*; £7 7s.

Bleeck, Charles, Warminster; 1850-77; £27 6s.

Bleeck, Charles Albert, esq, Kingmead, Pyrford, Woking; 1865*; £10 10s.

Boldero, Colonel, M.P.; 1831; £10 10s.

Bolton, Mrs; 1842-55; £15 15s.

Bolton, W.G., esq; 1839; £10 10s.

Bourne, Rev R.B.; 1869-77; £8 8s.

Bouverie, Hon Rev Canon B. Pleydell, Pewsey; 1880-8*; £9 9s.

Bouverie, Walter P., Lavington; 1880-8; £16 16s.

Bowles, Charles, esq; 1818-24; £7 7s.

Bowles, Rev W.R.; 1819-41; £23 2s.

Bowley, Edward, esq, Cirencester; 1848; £32 11s.

Brabant, W. Hughes, esq; 1835; £10 10s.

Bracher, George, esq; 1829-36; £7 7s.

Bradford, J.E. Goddard, esq; 1886-1912; £21.

Bradford, James, esq; 1824-35; £23 2s.

Brettell, Thomas, esq; 1851-9; £16 16s.

Brewer, John Hibberd, esq; 1843; £10 10s.

Briscoe, J.J., esq; 1838; £10 10s.

Britton, John, esq; 1817-36; £21.

Brodie, Dr; 1879; £5 5s.

Brodie, Peter, esq; 1817-28; £12 12s.

Brodie, W.B. esq, M.P., Sarum; 1822-48; £37 16s.

Brooke, S.B., esq; 1817-51; £142 16s.

Brooks, Thomas, esq; 1823; £5 5s.

Broughton, Lord; 1822-34; £21.

Brown, Henry, esq; 1820; £5 5s.

Brown, Henry, Blacklands; 1879-1906; £10 10s.

Brown, John, esq, Chisledon; 1833-40; £7 7s.

Brown, John, esq, Marlborough; 1822-32; £11 11s.

Brown, John, esq, Marlborough; 1833-40; £16 16s.

Brown, Sir Roger, Trowbridge; 1855-97; £22 1s.

Brown, Stephen, Marlborough; 1833; £10 10s.

Brown, Stephen, Wantage; 1860-1908; £10 10s.

Brown, T. Pearce, esq, Baydon; 1857; £10 10s.

Brown, Thomas, esq, Burderop; 1831; £14 14s.

Brown, W.R., esq, Broad Hinton; 1833; £10 10s.

Brown, Mrs W.R., Broad Hinton; 1841; £10 10s.

Brown, Wade, esq; 1840-6; £21.

Brown, William, esq, Broad Hinton; 1846-55; £21.

Browne, Rt Rev Bishop Forest (formerly bishop of Bristol), Campden House Road, Kensington W8; 1903-11*; £13 13s.

Bruce, Lord Charles Brudenell; 1867; £10 10s.

Bruce, Lord Ernest, M.P.; 1835-7; £15 15s.

Bruce, Lord Frederick Brudenell, 11 Gloucester Terrace, Regent's Park, NW; 1893-1911; £25 15s.

Bruce, George Brudenell, esq; 1863; £10 10s.

Bruce, Lord Robert Brudenell; 1879-1911; £13 13s.

Bruges, Thomas, esq, Seend; 1823; £10 10s.

Bruges, W.H. Ludlow, esq, M.P., Seend; 1830-9; £21.

Buckerfield, W.H. esq; 1823; £10 10s.

Buckler, John Russell, Warminster; 1901-4; £36 5s.

Buckley, A., esq, New Hall; 1854; £10 10s.

Buckley, Colonel E.D.H., O.B.E., New Hall; 1917*; £10 10s.

Buckley, General E.P., New Hall; 1844; £10 10s.

Buckton, George, esq; 1825; £10 10s.

Budd, G.O., esq; 1867-76; £10 10s.

Budd, T.H., esq; 1821; £10 10s.

Burbidge, Richard, esq, 51 Hans Mansions, SW; 1902-7; £14 14s.

Burdett, Sir Francis, bart, M.P., Ramsbury; 1822; £10 10s.

Burdett, Sir Francis, bart; 1887-90; £5 5s.

Burne, Henry Holland, esq; 1895-1912; £33 12s.

Burrough, the Hon Sir James, Laverstock; 1825; £10 10s.

Burrows, Dr; 1819-23; £5 5s.

Burt, H.P., esq; 1851-9; £29 8s.

Burt, Joseph, esq, Devizes; 1852-67; £16 16s.

Burton, L.A., esq; 1840; £10 10s.

Bury, Lindsay, esq, Stanford Wood, Bradfield, Berks; 1908*; £13 13s.

Bush, F. Whittaker, esq, K.C.; 1869-1903; £42.

Bush, John, esq; 1824; £10 10s.

Butcher, H., jun, esq; 1845; £10 10s.

Butler, Kennett, esq; 1825-30; £6 6s.

Buxton, Major Gerald J., Tockenham Manor; 1913★; £8 8s.

Buxton, Sir John Jacob, bart, Tockenham; 1833; £10 10s.

Bythesea, Rev George; 1839; £10 10s.

Bythesea, J., jun, esq; 1828-35; £8 8s.

Bythesea, S.W., esq; 1838-59; £11 11s.

Cafe, Henry Smith, esq; 1834-48; £15 15s.

Caillard, His Honour Judge, 1877-92; £12 12s.

Calley, Major; 1873; £10 10s.

Calley, John James, esq, Burderop; 1837-43; £14 14s.

Calley, Maj-General T.C.P., C.B., C.B.E, M.V.O., Burderop Park; 1881-1911★; £37 16s.

Calley, Thomas, esq, M.P.; 1817-22; £15 15s.

Campbell, John H., esq, M.P.; 1844; £10 10s.

Candy, Mr, Chicklade; 1833-48; £16 16s.

Canning, Davis, esq, Ogbourne; 1832-7; £6 6s.

Canning, Samuel, esq, Ogbourne; 1820; £10 10s.

Canning, Sir Samuel; 1867-1908; £14 14s.

Capel, John, esq; 1819; £10 10s.

Cardwell, T.H., esq, Newton House, Tetbury; 1891-1901; £11 11s.

Carey, Rev Tupper, Fifield; 1870-88; £25 4s.

Carnarvon, Earl of; 1826; £10 10s.

Carpenter, Joseph, esq, Manor House, Stratford-sub-Castle; 1902-11; £10 9s.

Cary, John, esq, Steeple Ashton; 1891-4; £5 5s.

Caswell, Alfred, esq; 1848-54; £7 7s.

Chaloner, Colonel Richard, Gisborough Hall, Yorks.; 1904; £5 5s.

Chamberlain, Mr William, 1838; £6 6s.

Chamberlaine, Rev E.; 1901★; £1 1s.

Chandler, Richard, esq, Pewsey; 1864-9; £5 5s.

Chandler, Stephen, esq; 1821-4; £14 14s.

Chapman, Miss E., Sambourne House, Warminster; 1907★; £5 5s.

Chapman, John, esq; 1861-5; £17 17s.

Chapman, W. esq, Warminster; 1875-1906; £33 12s.

Chubb, C.F., esq; 1848-54; £7 7s.

Chubb, Thomas Norwood, esq, Sarum; 1819; £10 10s.

Chubb, William, esq; 1872; £10 10s.

Churchward, G.J., esq, Newburn, Swindon;

1918★; £10 10s.

Clarendon, Earl of; 1825-37; £48 6s.

Clark, Major, Trowbridge; 1874-6; £11 11s.

Clark, John, esq, Trowbridge; 1825; £10 10s.

Clark, John, esq; 1833-41; £9 9s.

Clarkson, E.T., esq, Calne; 1842; £10 10s.

Clutterbuck, D. Hugh, esq, Corsham; 1896-1907; £11 11s.

Clutterbuck, Daniel, esq; 1817-21; £14 14s.

Clutterbuck, E.H., esq, Hardenhuish; 1888-99; £12 12s.

Clutterbuck, Thomas, esq, Harnish; 1826; £10 10s.

Coates, Henry, esq; 1827-37; £21.

Cohen, Isaac, esq; 1822; £10 10s.

Coles, Cary, esq, Manor House, Winterbourne Stoke; 1905-9; £2 2s.

Collett, Mr M.B.; 1841-51; £12 12s.

Collins, Rev J.F., Charlton; 1895-1910; £15 15s.

Colston, C. Edward, esq, Roundway Park; 1881-1913 [and perhaps later: listed as governor in 1913, but not in 1921]; £47 5s.

Colston, Edward Francis, esq, Roundway; 1843; £10 10s.

Cooke, Miss F., 20 Long Street, Devizes; 1908; £1 1s.

Cookson, H. Theodore, esq, Sturford Mead, Warminster; 1896; £10 10s.

Cooper, Henry, esq; 1829; £10 10s.

Coote, Sir Eyre, West Park, Damerham; 1905-12★; £22 17s.

Cosway, Rev S., Chute; 1874-82; £9 9s.

Cousins, J. Ratcliffe, esq, 10 King's Bench Walk, Temple, EC4; 1910★; £1 1s.

Cowley, Earl; 1888-94; £6 6s.

Coxe, the Ven Archdeacon, Bemerton; 1819-28; £10 10s.

Crewe, the right Hon Lord, 1888-92; £10 10s.

Cripps, William, esq, Wootton Bassett; 1827-37; £13 13s.

Croft, Sir Herbert Denman, bart; 1867-77; £11 11s.

Crowdy, A.S., esq; 1859; £10 10s.

Crowdy, Charles, esq; 1820-40; £22 1s.

Crowdy, Miss E.F., 100 Beaufort St, Chelsea SW3; 1893★; £10 10s.

Crowdy, Francis, esq; 1825-30; £7 7s.

Crowdy, James, esq; 1824-32; £9 9s.

Crowdy, James, esq; 1862; £11 11s.

Crowdy, James, esq; 1878-1909; £10 10s.

Crowdy, James F., esq, Rockcliffe Park, Ottawa, Canada; 1892*; £10 10s.
Crowdy, William, esq; 1822; £10 10s.
Crowdy, William Morse, esq; 1826; £10 10s.
Cubitt, Thomas, esq; 1820-5; £6 6s.
Cunnington, Captain B. Howard, F.S.A.(Scot), Devizes; 1914*; £1 1s.
Curtis, Sir William, bart, Bedwyn; 1837; £10 10s.
Curtoys, Charles, esq; 1820-36; £17 17s.

Davis, John, esq; 1826; £10 10s.
Davis, John, esq; 1849-76; £29 8s.
Davis, Thomas, esq; 1822-57; £40 19s.
Davis, Thomas, Warminster; 1830-9; £10 10s.
Davis, Thomas M., esq; 1825-36; £12 12s.
Dean, Mrs Adbury, Windlesham, Surrey; 1866*; £10 10s.
Deramore, the right Hon Lord; 1865-85; £19 19s.
Devenish, M.H.W., Durnford; 1900-13; £16 16s.
Dickson, Major-General J.B.B., C.B., C.M.G, Keevil Manor; 1913*; £1 1s.
Divett, Thomas, esq, M.P.; 1823-7; £9 9s.
Dixon, H.P., esq, Marlborough; 1880-4; £5 5s.
Dixon, Stephen Brown, esq, Pewsey; 1862; £10 10s.
Doling, Mr John; 1837; £10 10s.
Donaldson, John, esq; 1821-6; £6 6s.
Dowding, William, Salisbury; 1823-6; £6 6s.
Dowding, William Drummond; 1879-94; £15 10s.
Dundas, the Hon Mrs; 1837; £5 5s.
Dundas, Admiral Sir James, K.C.B., Kintbury; 1836; £10 10s.
Dunne, A.M., esq, K.C., Highlands, Calne; 1920*; £2 2s.
Dyer, Capt Stewart, D.S.O., Milford Grove, Salisbury; 1912; £1 1s.

Earlsman, R. esq; 1832; £90 (legacy, less duty).
Ebsworth, Mrs; 1822-9; £8 8s.
Ebsworth, Thomas, esq; 1820; £10 10s.
Eden, Thomas Duncombe, esq; 1888-96; £8 8s.
Edmeades, Rev M.R., Great Bedwyn; 1885-1904; £27 6s.
Edmonds, Ezechiel, esq, Bradford; 1854; £10 10s.
Edmonds, John, esq; 1839-40; £11 11s.

Edmonds, William Mills, esq; 1852; £10 10s.
Edwards, J. Passmore, esq, M.P., Sarum; 1885; £10 10s.
Ellis, Sir J. Whittaker, bart; 1899; £21.
Ellis, Lady Whittaker; 1882; £10 10s.
Errington, Sir George, bart, Ramsfort, Gorey, Ireland; 1885; £10 10s.
Esmeade, G.M. Moore, esq; 1851; £10 10s.
Estcourt, Lord, Estcourt, Tetbury; 1864-95; £22 1s.
Estcourt, General Bucknall; 1849; £10 10s.
Estcourt, Edward D. Bucknall, esq; 1859; £10 10s.
Estcourt, T. Grimston Bucknall, esq, M.P.; 1818-23; £21.
Estcourt, Right Hon T.H. Sotheron, M.P.; 1833-8; £21.
Estcourt, Mrs Sotheron; 1844; £10 10s.
Everett, Charles W., esq, Sarum; 1825-40; £26 5s.
Everett, Edward, esq, Sarum; 1857; £7 7s.
Everett, Henry, esq, Andover; 1875-83; £9 9s.
Everett, John Gale, esq, Heytesbury; 1818; £10 10s.
Everett, Joseph H., esq, Heytesbury; 1824; £10 10s.
Exmouth, Viscount; 1817; £10 10s.
Eyles, Edward, esq; 1829-47; £12 12s.
Eyles, Capt. James (H.E.I.C.S.); 1833-63; £16 14s.
Eyles, R.S., esq; 1819-67; £48 6s.
Eyles, R.W., esq; 1820-41; £25 4s.
Eyre, C.L.P., esq; 1844-1902; £12 12s.
Eyre, G.E., esq; 1840-79; £91 7s.
Eyre, G.E. Briscoe, esq; 1867*; £10 10s.
Eyre, H.S.P., esq; 1847-54; £8 8s.
Eyre, Henry, esq; 1863; £10 10s.

Fairthorne, Thomas, esq; 1819-24; £6 6s.
Fane, Rev Prebendary; 1855-72; £21.
Farmer, S.W., esq, Little Bedwyn; 1908-10*; £3 3s.
Farmer, William, esq, Swindon; 1820-46; £28 7s.
Fellowes, T. Abdy, esq; 1839-40; £11 11s.
Fellowes, W. Gordon, esq, 17 Onslow Gardens, SW7; 1909-10*; £18 18s.
Fennell, Isaac, esq; 1825; £10 10s.
Festing, H.B., esq, Maiden Bradley; 1864-80; £17 17s.
Festing, Michael J., esq, Maiden Bradley; 1831; £10 10s.
Few, R., esq; 1832-42; £26 5s.

Finch, Charles H.M., esq; 1832-7; £16 16s.

Fisher, A.B., esq, Potterne; 1888-1900; £18 18s.

Fisher, Money C., esq; 1875-98; £37 16s.

FitzGerald, Gerald A.R., esq, K.C., 9 Park Town, Oxford; 1903-20*; £26 5s.

Fitzmaurice of Leigh, the Right Hon Lord, Leigh, Bradford on Avon; 1873*; £89 17s.

Fletcher, Mrs, 5 Stanford Rd, Kensington, W8; 1871*; £10 10s.

Fletcher, Hamilton, esq, Leweston Manor, Sherborne; 1902*; £16 16s.

Flooks, Mr John Harris; 1830-1; £12 12s.

Forbes, Sir Charles, bart, M.P.; 1829; £10 10s.

Forge, Mr R.A., 1827-38; £12 12s.

Fort, Capt G.H., Alderbury House; 1905-7; £3 3s.

Fowle, Rev G.F., esq; 1857-62; £6 6s.

Fowle, Rev H., Chute; 1857-62; £6 6s.

Fowle, Thomas E., esq, Chute; 1863-77; £14 14s.

Fowle, W.H., esq, Chute; 1878-90; £13 13s.

Fowler, Sir Robert N., bart, M.P., Corsham; 1870-87; £26 5s.

Fowler, Sir Thomas, bart, Gastard; 1890-1902; £15 15s.

Fowler, William, esq; 1872; £10 10s.

Frampton, James Alexander, esq; 1825; £10 10s.

Freke, A.D. Hussey, esq, Hannington Hall; 1866-89; £25 4s.

Frowd, Edward, esq; 1817; £10 10s.

Fry, F.M., esq, 34 Russell Square, WC1 (executor of Miss Ellen Pressly); 1913*.

Fulford, Rev F., 1838-43; £6 6s.

Fuller, George Pargiter, esq, Neston Park; 1874-98*; £11 11s.

Fuller, J.B., esq; 1852; £10 10s.

Fuller, John, esq, Neston Park; 1819-26; £15 10s.

Fuller, Rt Hon Sir John M.F., bart, Cottles, Melksham; 1891-1909; £30 9s.

Fuller, Major Robert F., Great Chalfield; 1912*; £10 10s.

Furness, Lord; 1909-12; £10 10s.

Furness, Sir Christopher, M.P.; 1899; £5 5s.

Gaby, Edward, esq; 1852; £10 10s.

Gaisford, Thomas, esq; 1888; £5 5s.

Gale, John, esq; 1821; £10 10s.

Gandell, Edward, esq; 1833; £10 10s.

Gardener, John, esq, Marlborough; 1850-4; £5 5s.

Gardiner, John, esq; 1820; £10 10s.

Gardner, Charles, esq, 80 Cheapside, EC2 (executor of Miss Ellen Pressly); 1913*.

Garton, Major James W., Lilliput House, Parkstone; 1905*; £10 10s.

Gibbes, Charles, esq; 1820; £10 10s.

Gibbes, Thomas, esq; 1820; £10 10s.

Gibson, Rev Herbert F., The Gaer, St Giles Hill, Winchester; 1886-1904*; £18 18s.

Giffard, Francis, esq; 1829-35; £7 7s.

Giffard, Francis, esq, Upavon; 1820-3; £15 15s.

Gilbert, Henry, esq; 1834; £10 10s.

Gilbert, Thomas W., esq; 1823-35; £23 2s.

Gisborough, Lord, Gisborough Hall, Yorks; 1904*; £5 5s.

Gladstone, John E., esq, Bowden Park; 1895-7*; £17 17s.

Gladstone, Capt. John Neilson, R.N., Bowden; 1854; £10 10s.

Glenconner, Lord, Wilsford House; 1901-12; £39 18s.

Goddard, Ambrose, esq, M.P., Swindon; 1817-20; £12 12s.

Goddard, Ambrose Lethbridge, M.P.; 1849-97; £28 7s.

Goddard, Rev Edward, Clyffe; 1828-35; £18 18s.

Goddard, Major F.P., The Lawn, Swindon; 1888-1906*; £40 10s.

Goddard, Rev George, Clyffe; 1846-8; £12 12s.

Goddard, H. Nelson, esq, Clyffe; 1839-1900; £10 10s.

Goddard, Robert, esq; 1821; £10 10s.

Goldney, Frederick H., esq, Beachfield, Corsham; 1885-1908*; £22 1s.

Goldney, Sir Gabriel, bart, Chippenham; 1840-95; £15 15s.

Goldney, Sir John T., Monks Park, Corsham; 1901-13 [and perhaps later: listed as governor in 1913, but not in 1921]; £21 17s.

Goldney, Sir Prior, Bt., C.B., C.V.O., Derriads, Chippenham; 1864-1906*; £31 3s.

Gooch, Sir Daniel, bart; 1866; £12 12s.

Gooch, Sir Henry D., bart; 1873; £10 10s.

Gordon, Sir Robert, bart; 1817-29; £24 3s.

Gore, F.W.G. esq, The Orchard, Cromer; 1885*; £10 10s.

Gore, Montague, esq, M.P.; 1832; £10 10s.

Gosling, John, esq, Marlborough; 1817-23; £19 19s.

Gough, Henry, esq, Highbury, Mortimer, Berks; 1902-3★; £13 13s.

Goulding, Rt Hon Sir E.A., bart, M.P., Wargrave Hall, Berks; 1901★; £1 1s.

Graham, Captain Henry; 1881-8; £8 8s.

Gramshaw, W.H., esq; 1888-95; £12 12s.

Grant-Meek, A., esq, Hillworth, Devizes; 1875-97; £12 12s.

Gray, George, esq; 1852; £10 10s.

Greenwood, George, esq; 1817-23; £7 7s.

Gregory, H., esq; 1831-56; £12 12s.

Greville, Hon Louis, Heale House, Woodford; 1896-1920★; £50.

Griffith, C. Darby, esq, M.P.; 1857-68; £13 13s.

Grissell, H., esq; 1845; £12 10s.

Grissell, Martin D.; 1845-1906; £12 10s.

Grosett, J.R., esq, M.P.; 1820; £10 10s.

Grove, Miss Julia T. Chafyn; 1871; £10 10s.

Grove, Sir Thomas Fraser, bart, M.P., Ferne, 1854-68; £21.

Grove, William, esq, Netherhampton House, 1843; £10 10s.

Grubbe, Capt. H.J. Hunt, Eastwell, Potterne; 1888-92; £9 9s.

Gumersall, F.B., esq; 1833; £10 10s.

Gwatkin, R. Gascoigne, esq, Manor House, Potterne; 1890★; £25.

Gye, Frederick, esq, M.P.; 1827; £10 10s.

Hadow, Rev George R., Hillside, Warminster; 1903; £10 10s.

Halcomb, John, esq; 1820-2; £13 13s.

Halcomb, Mr Serjeant; 1828; £10 10s.

Hale, Edmund, esq; 1817; £10 10s.

Hale, R.H.B., esq; 1836; £10 10s.

Hale, Samuel, esq; 1818; £10 10s.

Hall, Marshall, esq; 1859; £10 10s.

Hall, W.R., esq, Hungerford; 1829-37; £9 9s.

Halliday, John, esq, Chicklade House; 1903-13 [and perhaps later: listed as governor in 1913, but not in 1921]; £23 18s.

Hamilton, Edward, esq, M.P.; 1866; £10.

Hanbury, Edgar, esq, Paxton Hill House, St Neots; 1863; £10 10s.

Hancock, James Lyne, esq; 1861-3; £13.

Hancock, Thomas Lyne, esq; 1860-3; £24.

Hanham, Sir John, bart, Wimborne; 1883-99; £16 16s.

Harding, Major; 1817-24; £8 8s.

Harding, James, esq; 1817-27; £11 11s.

Harding, William, esq; 1820; £10 10s.

Harris, C. and T., and Co. Ltd, Calne; 1880; £1 1s.

Harris, George, esq, Calne; 1867; £10 10s.

Harris, Thomas, esq, Calne; 1879-91; £14 14s.

Hartley, Rev A.O., Steeple Ashton; 1877-88; £11 11s.

Hassell, George, esq; 1821; £10 10s.

Hatzfeldt, Prince, Draycot; 1898; £5 5s.

Hawkshaw, Sir John, bart; 1864; £10 10s.

Hayter, Lady; 1836; £10 10s.

Hayter, Thomas, esq; 1823; £10 10s.

Hayter, Right Hon Sir W.G., bart, Q.C.; 1817-27; £22 1s.

Hayward, J. esq, Devizes; 1830; £10 10s.

Hayward, Thomas. esq; 1835-42; £15 15s.

Haywood, Charles Burt, esq, Salisbury House, London Wall, EC2; 1881★; £10 10s.

Haywood, Thomas Burt, esq; 1855-88; £33 12s.

Haywood, Thomas Scott, esq; 1871; £10 10s.

Helme, Captain Burchall; 1878-92; £21.

Helme, Col Sir George, C.B., C.M.G., Rowden Lodge, Chippenham; 1898-1905★; £7 7s.

Heneage, Major G., 61 Grosvenor Street, W1; 1907★; £15 15s.

Heneage, G.H.W., esq, M.P.; 1831-42; £33 12s.

Henly, Edward R., esq; 1888-97; £10 10s.

Herbert, Lord, of Lea; 1833-60; £79 16s.

Herbert, Thomas, esq; 1832-6; £5 5s.

Hetley, Richard, esq; 1821; £10 10s.

Hewett, Dr Grailey; 1873-84; £12 12s.

Heytesbury, Lord; 1863; £10 10s.

Hickman, Rev W., The Poplars, Maidenhead Thicket, Maidenhead; 1873-1905; £24 3s.

Hill, J. Ledger, esq, Bradford; 1890-1911; £52 10s.

Hillhouse, Charles, esq; 1854-5; £10.

Hillier, E., esq; 1819-31; £25 4s.

Hillier, E.F., esq; 1833; £10 10s.

Hitchcock, Mr J; 1825-39; £15 15s.

Hoare, Sir H. A., bart; 1858-98; £43 1s.

Hoare, Henry, esq, Stourhead; 1819; £11 11s.

Hoare, Sir Hugh Richard, bart; 1844; £10 10s.

Hoare, Peter R., esq; 1826-37; £35 14s.

Hoare, Sir Richard Colt, bart; 1820; £12 12s.

Hobbs, Mr; 1847-61; £16 16s.

Hobhouse, Sir Benjamin, bart, Whitton Park; 1817-31; £69 8s.

Hobhouse, H.W., esq; 1819-38; £31 10s.

Hobhouse, Sir J.C., bart; 1823-35; £21.

Hobhouse, Thomas B., esq; 1835; £10 10s.

Hodding, Matthew T., esq, Sarum; 1824-63; £66 3s.

Hodgson, Rev Canon; 1892; £5 5s.

Holford, R.S., esq, Dorchester House; 1837; £10 10s.

Holloway, Thomas, esq, 19 Cedars Road, Clapham Common, SW, and Manor House, West Lavington; 1908-13 [and perhaps later: listed as governor in 1913, but not in 1921]; £6 6s.

Hooper, G.D., esq, Wootton Bassett; 1847; £10 10s.

House, Mr William; 1833-7; £5 5s.

Houseman, John, esq; 1831-43; £13 13s.

Howse, Thomas, esq; 1838-53; £27 6s.

Hughes, Robert, esq; 1819-34; £24 3s.

Hughes, William, esq; 1819; £10 10s.

Hulbert, Charles A., esq; 1848-60; £16 16s.

Hulbert, H.V., esq; 1838-51; £14 14s.

Hulbert, Henry, esq; 1838; £10 10s.

Hulbert, Mrs J.; 1848-64; £29 8s.

Hulbert, John, esq; 1838-51; £21.

Hulse, Charles F., esq; 1850; £10 10s.

Hulse, Sir Edward, bart, Breamore; 1843-66; £36 15s.

Hulse, Sir Edward, bart, Breamore; 1880-1903; £20 15s.

Hurd, Philip, esq; 1817; £10 10s.

Hurd, Philip, esq; 1832; £10 10s.

Hurle, Henry, esq, Ramsbury; 1820; £10 10s.

Hussey, Ambrose, esq, Sarum; 1841-9; £15 15s.

Hussey, Ambrose D., esq; 1860-4; £5 5s.

Hutton, Rev R.R.; 1864; £10 10s.

Ingledew, Thomas, esq; 1820-37; £32 11s.

Ingram, Rev Dr; 1849; £21.

Ingram, Christopher, esq; 1826; £10 10s.

Ingram, J.A., esq, Wily; 1849; £10 10s.

Ingram, John, esq, Wilton; 1830-55; £26 5s.

Ings, Edward, esq, Devizes; 1823; £10 10s.

Ings, Edward jun; 1829-36; £8 8s.

Isaacs, Mrs K.L. (nee Merriman), 16 Leskinnick Terrace, Penzance; 1881-93*; £23 2s.

Isherwood, Robert, esq; 1819-36; £28 7s.

Islington, Rt Hon Lord, G.C.M.G., D.S.O., Hartham Park, Corsham; 1888-1913*; £26.

Iveson, John, esq; 1830-40; £13 13s.

Jackson, A., esq, Salisbury; 1856-66; £11 11s.

Jackson, Thomas, esq, Marlborough; 1895-1910; £14 3s.

Jacob, J.H., Sarum; 1879-1905; £18 18s.

Jeans, Gerald M., esq, 50 Bedford Row, WC1; 1913*; £2 2s.

Jeans, Mark, esq, King Hall, Milton, Marlborough; 1902*; £4 4s.

Jenkinson, Sir George, bart; 1869; £10 10s.

Jenkyns, John, esq; 1817-59; £44 2s.

Jervoise, F.J.E., esq, Herriard; 1868; £10 10s.

Jervoise, G. Purefoy, esq, Herriard; 1823-43; £31 10s.

Jesse, Thomas, esq; 1820-38; £18 18s.

Jones, G.D., esq; 1860-7; £8 8s.

Jones, Hy. Parr, esq; 1865-1909; £12 12s.

Jones, J.O., esq; 1846-50; £5 5s.

Jones, R.H., esq; 1821-36; £11 11s.

Jones, W.S., esq, Malmesbury; 1883-98; £17 17s.

Joy, Henry Hall, esq, Q.C.; 1826; £10 10s.

Joy, Michael Hall, esq, Hartham Park; 1818; £10 10s.

Jukes, Thomas, esq, Tisbury; 1856-65; £12 12s.

Kaye, Daniel, esq; 1817-21; £5 5s.

Kaye, John, esq; 1817-51; £39 15s.

Kelk, Sir John E., Letton Hall, Thetford; 1892-3*; £31 10s.

Kemble, Miss; 1821-6; £6 6s.

Kemble, Mrs C.A.; 1846; £10 10s.

Kemble, Rev Charles; 1846; £10 10s.

Kemble, Charles Adams, esq, Montvale House, Hallatrow, Bristol; 1858*; £10 10s.

Kemble, Ed. B., esq; 1818-50; £82 19s.

Kemble, Mrs E.B.; 1835; £10 10s.

Kemble, Mrs E.B.; 1849; £10 10s.

Kemble, Edward, esq, M.P.; 1820-44; £31 10s.

Kemble, H., esq, M.P.; 1821-44; £21.

Kemble, Mrs Henry; 1836-82; £86 2s.

Kemble, Mrs Henry; 1858; £10 10s.

Kemble, Horatio, esq; 1833; £10 10s.

Kemble, Samuel Brooke, esq; 1850; £10 10s.

Kemble, Thomas, esq; 1820-1; £12 12s.

Kemble, Thomas N., esq; 1820-33; £23 2s.

Kemble, Rev William; 1826; £10 10s.

Kemble, Mrs William; 1836; £10 10s.

Kemm, James, esq; 1845-60; £17 17s.

Kemm, Thomas, esq, Avebury; 1847-56; £8 8s.

Kennard, Coleridge, esq, M.P.; 1880-7; £8 8s.

Kerry, Earl of, M.P.; 1833; £10 10s.

Kerry, Earl of, D.S.O., 16 Gloucester Place, Portman Square, W1; 1907-13*; £12 12s.

King, W.E., esq, Donhead Lodge; 1903*; £4.

Kingsbury, Rev Canon, Coombe Bissett; 1871-89; £14 14s.

Kinnier, H., esq, Redville, Swindon; 1873*; £10 10s.

Knowles, G. esq, Stockton House, Codford St Mary; 1898*; £21.

Lacy, James, esq, Sarum; 1826-37; £14 14s.

Lakin, Mrs; 1866-75; £10 10s.

Lambert, Sir John, K.C.B.; 1860-83; £23 13s.

Lampson, G. Locker, esq, M.P., Rowfont, Sussex; 1913*; £1 1s.

Lansdowne, Marquess of; 1819-62; £100 16s.

Lansdowne, Marquess of; 1836-63; £21 16s.

Lansdowne, Marquis of; 1870-95*; £156 10s.

Large, Miss; 1880-9; £10 10s.

Laverton, Abraham, esq, M.P., Westbury; 1870-5; £15 15s.

Laverton, W.H., esq, Leighton, Westbury; 1887*; £39 18s.

Lawes, Mrs, Marlborough; 1842-59; £18 18s.

Lawes, Rev J. Townsend, Marlborough; 1822-8; £7 7s.

Lawes, Thornton, esq, Ennox Lodge, Hinton Charterhouse; 1900-15*; £18 18s.

Lawes, Mrs Thornton, esq, Ennox Lodge, Hinton Charterhouse; 1910-15*; £6 6s.

Lawrence, Sir Thomas, P.R.A.; 1820-31; £36 15s.

Lawrence, William Frederick, esq, Cowesfield House, Whiteparish; 1883-1905*; £37 10s.

Leaf, Herbert, esq, The Green, Marlborough; 1910*; £15 15s.

Leake, William, esq; 1823; £10 10s.

Lee, Rev Harry, B.D.; 1862; £10 10s.

Lee, Thomas, esq; 1845-65; £43 1s.

Lee, William B., esq, Chantry, Frome; 1892; £1 1s.

Leveson, E.J., esq; 1867; £10 10s.

Lewis, T. N., esq; 1830-6; £6 6s.

Lewis, William, esq; 1819-50; £37 16s.

Lewis, Mrs William; 1836-40; £10 10s.

Liefchild, W.G., esq; 1838-49; £12 12s.

Locke, F.A.S., esq; 1839; £10 10s.

Locke, Wadham, esq; 1818; £10 10s.

Loder, Giles, esq; 1857; £10 10s.

Loder, Robert, esq; 1872; £10 10s.

London Tavern Company; 1867-95; £35 14s.

Long, D.J., esq; 1818; £10 10s.

Long, Richard, Rood Ashton; 1817-20; £14 14s.

Long, Richard P., esq, M.P.; 1855-66; £30 9s.

Long, Walter, esq, M.P.; 1836; £31 10s.

Long of Wraxall, Rt Hon Viscount, Rood Ashton; 1878-92*; £52 8s.

Lopes, Lady; 1836; £10 10s.

Lopes, G. Ludlow, esq; 1887-1909; £24 3s.

Lopes, Sir Massey, bart; 1860-1908; £10 10s.

Lopes, R.K., esq; 1881-7; £7 7s.

Lopes, R.L., esq; 1881-96; £16.

Lopes, Sir Ralph, bart, M.P.; 1834; £11 11s.

Lovell, Capt Audley, Cole Park; 1852; £10 10s.

Lovibond, J.W., esq, The Pleasaunce, Lake; 1901-9; £14 14s.

Lowndes, Mrs; 1840; £10 10s.

Lowndes, E.C., esq, Castle Combe; 1874-1909; £12 12s.

Loyd, Lt-Col Arthur P.; 1901*; £1 1s.

Lubbock, Geoffrey, esq, Greenhill, Sutton Veny; 1913*; £1 1s.

Lucas, Charles R., esq; 1856-70; £30 9s.

Luce, Col C.R., Halcombe, Malmesbury; 1877*; £12 12s.

Luce, Thomas, esq, Malmesbury; 1840-66; £25 4s.

Ludlow, Lord, Heywood; 1885-97; £15 10s.

Ludlow, Mrs; 1871; £5 5s.

Ludlow, H.G.G., esq, Heywood; 1823-50; £28 7s.

Ludlow of Heywood, Lord, 27 Portland Place, Piccadilly, W1; 1897-1901*; £5 5s.

Lush, J.A., esq, M.D., M.P., Sarum; 1872; £10 10s.

Lush, the Hon Sir Robert; 1866; £14 14s.

Lushington, Sir Godfrey, K.C.B., Bedwyn; 1901; £10 10s.

Lyall, J., esq; 1871-3; £15 10s.

Lyne, Edmund Ormond, esq, Malmesbury; 1842; £10 10s.

Macdonald, Rev Canon, Great Wishford Rectory; 1902*; £21.

Macdonald, Fitzherbert, esq, Sarum; 1883-96; £12 12s.

Mackay, Alexander, esq, Trowbridge; 1887-95; £52 10s.

Mackay, George E., esq, Kington Langley; 1894*; £10 10s.

Mackay, J., esq, Seend Manor; 1888; £10 10s.

Mackrell, John, esq; 1857-1910; £73 10s.

Madden, W.H., esq, Paignton, Devon; 1893*; £13 13s.

Malet, Sir Alex., bart, K.C.B., Wilbury; 1824-86; £116 6s.

Malet, Rt Hon Sir Edward, bart, G.C.B.; 1871-1908; £62 5s.

Malet, Lt-Col Sir Harry, bart, D.S.O., O.B.E., Wilbury; 1907*; £22 10s.

Malet, Sir Henry, bart; 1888-1903; £21 16s.

Mallinson, Edward, esq; Bradford; 1902-13; £12 2s.

Malmesbury, Earl of; 1826; £10 10s.

Mann, Major W. Horace, M.C., Brooklyn, Semington; 1903*; £11 11s.

Mann, W.J., esq, Highfield, Trowbridge; 1886*; £12 12s.

Marsh, John, esq, Devizes; 1878-86; £9 9s.

Marsh, M.H., esq, M.P., Wilbury; 1857; £10.

Martin, Charles, esq; 1820; £10 10s.

Martin, Charles, esq; 1821-8; £18 18s.

Martin, Charles, esq; 1840; £10 10s.

Martin, J. Kemble, esq; 1841; £10 10s.

Maskelyne, Nevil Story, F.R.S., Bassett Down; 1879-1911; £27 6s.

Maton, Dr; 1817-34; £18 18s.

Maton, Fred. S., esq, High Trees, Clapham Common, SW4; 1918*; £1 1s.

Maton, Leonard, esq, 21 Cannon Street, EC4; 1910*; £14 14s.

Matthews, J., esq; 1859; £10 10s.

Matthews, John, esq; 1856-9; £21.

Matthews, R., esq; 1859; £10 10s.

Maudslay, Charles E., esq, North Coker House, Yeovil; 1902*; £10 10s.

Maurice, Dr J.B., Marlborough; 1901-12; £12 12s.

Mayne, John Thomas; 1818; £11 11s.

Meade, the Hon and Rev Canon Sidney, Frankleigh House, Bradford; 1882-1911; £13 10s.

Meares, John, esq; 1833-9; £7 7s.

Medlicott, H.E., esq, Potterne; 1875-90; £26 5s.

Meek, Alexander, esq, Devizes; 1845; £10 10s.

Meek, H. Edgar, esq; 1901-9; £8 8s.

Mercers' Company, the; 1819-39; £84.

Meredith-Brown, M., esq, Nonsuch House, Chippenham; 1890-1913 [and perhaps later: listed as governor in 1913, but not in 1921]; £124 2s.

Merewether, Mrs H.; 1845; £10 10s.

Merewether, H.A., esq, Q.C.; 1837; £22 1s.

Merewether, H.A.F., esq; 1848-64; £17 17s.

Merewether, Herbert, esq, c/o Mrs Dean, Adbury, Windlesham, Surrey; 1869*; £10 10s.

Merewether, Miss Jessie, 32 Rosetti Gardens Mansions, Chelsea, SW1; 1867*; £10 10s.

Merewether, Mr Serjeant; 1820; £14 14s.

Merewether, Mrs Serjeant; 1867; £10 10s.

Merewether, W. Lockyer, esq; 1864-1912; £10 10s.

Merewether, Lieut-Col Sir William; 1849; £10 10s.

Merewether, Rev Canon Wyndham A., Langton House, Salisbury; 1868*; £10 10s.

Merrick, William, esq, jun, Broad Street Avenue, EC2; 1904*; £2 2s.

Merriman, Dr; 1821; £10 10s.

Merriman, Mrs; 1837; £10 10s.

Merriman, Miss E.F.; 1893*; £10 10s.

Merriman, Miss E.H.; 1861-81; £22 1s.

Merriman, Edward B., esq, 9 Hyde Park Gardens, W; 1875-1911; £29 8s.

Merriman, G., esq, 96 Finchley Road, NW; 1907; £3 3s.

Merriman, J.; 1830; £17 17s.

Merriman, Dr James N.; 1845; £10 10s.

Merriman, M.M., 3 Mitre Court, Temple, EC4; 1895*; £14 14s.

Merriman, Miss Mary de Berdt, 47 Lee Terrace, Blackheath, SE; 1868; £1 1s.

Merriman, Nathaniel, esq; 1821; £10 10s.

Merriman, Robert W., esq, Sempringham, Marlborough; 1864*; £15 15s.

Merriman, S.B., esq; 1839; £10 10s.

Merriman, Mrs S.B.; 1842-79; £32 11s.

Merriman, T.B., esq; 1829; £10 10s.

Merriman, T. Mark, esq, 3 Mitre Court, Fleet Street, EC4; 1872*; £28 7s.

Merriman, Thomas, esq; 1821; £10 10s.

Merriman, Thomas Hardwick; 1832; £10 10s.

Merriman, W.R.H., esq, Sempringham, Marlborough; 1895; £10 10s.

Merriman, Dr William; 1843-8; £6 6s.

Merriman, William Clark, esq; 1829; £10 10s.

Merriman, William Heath, 6 Hartington Rd, Chiswick, W4; 1887*; £10 10s.

Methuen, Lord; 1817-30; £23 10s.

Methuen, Lord; 1839-87; £41 10s.

Methuen, Field-Marshall Lord, G.C.B., G.C.M.G., G.C.V.O., Corsham Court; 1863-95*; £38 17s.

Methuen, Paul Mildmay, esq; 1833; £10 10s.

Meux, Sir Henry Bruce, bart; 1883; £10 10s.

Miles, Col C. Napier, C.B., M.V.O., Inglebourne Manor, Malmesbury; 1891-1911; £6 4s.

Miller, T. Butt, esq, Manor House, Cricklade; 1909-11; £3 3s.

Mills, P.M., esq; 1819-25; £6 6s.

Mills, Stephen, esq; 1831; £10 10s.

Mitchell, Arthur C., esq, Highgrove, Tetbury; 1888-1905; £2 2s.

Money-Kyrle, Major A.; 1908; £2 2s.

Montagu, Edward, esq; 1822-8; £8 8s.

Montagu, Captain George; 1827-33; £6 6s.

Morgan, W.F., esq, Warminster; 1889-1907; £10 10s.

Morland, Mrs C.; 1842-52; £11 11s.

Morley, Charles, esq, Shockerwick House, Bath; 1908; £10 10s.

Mornington, Earl of; 1819; £10 10s.

Morrice, Rev Canon; 1869; £10 10s.

Morrice, Rev Canon John David, Monkton Farleigh Rectory; 1887*; £10 10s.

Morrison, Alex, esq, Fonthill; 1835; £10 10s.

Morrison, Mrs Alfred, Shawford Place, Winchester; 1871*; £10 10s.

Morrison, George, esq, Hampworth; 1880-4; £9 4s.

Morrison, Hugh, esq, Fonthill; 1892-1904*; £66 4s.

Morrison, Major J.A., Basildon Park, Reading; 1901-3*; £11 11s.

Morrison, James, esq, Fonthill; 1835; £10 10s.

Morrison, James, esq, Ardle Bank, Marlborough; 1890*; £10 10s.

Morse, David, esq; 1857-63; £7 7s.

Morse, L.L., Swindon; 1902-13; £18 18s.

Mortimer, J.L., esq; 1824-37; £13 13s.

Moulton, John, esq, The Hall, Bradford; 1901*; £46 4s.

Mullings, Joseph R., esq, M.P., Eastcourt House; 1843-59; £46 4s.

Mullings, Richard, esq, Stratton; 1847-72; £40 16s.

Mullins, G., esq; 1834-40; £7 7s.

Nash, William, esq; 1828-35; £17 17s.

Neate, Francis Webb, esq; 1843; £10 10s.

Neate, Stephen, esq; 1817; £10 10s.

Neate, Stephen, esq; 1819; £14 14s.

Neeld, Lady; 1859; £10 10s.

Neeld, Mrs; 1836; £10 10s.

Neeld, Sir Algernon W., bart; 1867-94; £12 12s.

Neeld, Lt-Col Sir Audley D., bart, C.B., M.V.O., Grittleton; 1892-1904*; £57 8s.

Neeld, Elliot A., esq; 1895; £10 10s.

Neeld, Sir John, bart; 1831-41; £21.

Neeld, Joseph, esq, M.P., Grittleton; 1829-45; £62 4s.

Neeld, Lt-Col Mortimer, Langley Burrell; 1893*; £10 10s.

Neeld, Rear-Admiral R.R., R.N., Twatley, Malmesbury; 1893*; £10 10s.

Neeld, William, esq; 1831; £10 10s.

Nelson, Earl; 1850-1913; £27 2s.

Newman, Edmund L., esq; 1834-8; £5 5s.

Nicholas, Charles, esq; 1820; £5 5s.

Nicholas, Edward, esq; 1821; £10 10s.

Nicholas, G., esq; 1873-8; £6 6s.

Nickisson, Major J.L., Little Hinton Manor; 1913*; £1 1s.

Nisbet, Mrs Parry; 1849; £10 10s.

Nisbet, R.P., esq, Southbroom House; 1840-74; £49 10s.

Noad, Richard, esq; 1820-50; £32 11s.

Normanton, Earl of; 1872; £10 10s.

Olivier, Rev Dacres; 1882-8; £7 7s.

Olivier, Lieut-Colonel Henry Stephen; 1833; £10 10s.

Osborne, Henry, esq; 1817-22; £6 6s.

Page, Colonel; 1830; £10 10s.

Page, Frederick, esq; 1831; £5 5s.

Pain, George, esq, Sarum; 1826-54; £30 9s.

Pain, Thomas, esq, Sarum; 1854-64; £11 11s.

Palmer, Brig-General G.Ll., C.B., M.P., The Prospect, Trowbridge; 1892-1904*; £57 16s.

Palmer, Michael, esq, Bradford; 1883-5; £10 10s.

Palmer, Sir Walter, bart, M.P., Sarum; 1901-10; £11 11s.

Parker, F.C. Shirecliffe, esq, Green End, Northwood, Middlesex; 1903*; £3 3s.

Parker, William, esq; 1817; £5 5s.

Parr, T.H., esq, 3 Elm Court, Temple EC4; 1910*; £12 12s.

Pater, William, esq; 1820-40; £22 1s.

Patient, John, esq; 1819-27; £19 19s.

Pavy, Fred, esq, M.D., F.R.S.; 1867-73; £7 7s.

Pavy, Philip, esq; 1867-73; £7 7s.

Peachy, Major-General; 1821; £10 10s.

Pearse, Brice, esq; 1838; £10 10s.

Pearse, Brice, esq; 1846; £14 14s.

Pearse, Christopher; 1838; £10 10s.

Pearse, John, esq, M.P., Chilton; 1818-19; £21.

Pelly, Sir Harold, bart, Thorngrove, Gillingham, Dorset; 1902*; £1 1s.

Pembroke, Earl of; 1819-25; £40.

Pembroke, Earl of; 1881-9; £13 13s.

Pembroke, Earl of; 1878-1913; £58 16s.

Peniston, Mr; 1825-38; £14 14s.

Penruddocke, Charles, esq; 1826-35; £10 10s.

Penruddocke, Charles, esq, Compton Park; 1901-13*; £17 17s.

Peplar, George, esq; 1817; £7 7s.

Perkins, John, esq; 1835; £10 10s.

Perkins, Tom, esq, Salisbury; 1909*; £1 1s.

Perrior, Mrs; 1848-64; £17 17s.

Perrior, Mr John, Wylie; 1828-38; £19 19s.

Phelps, Stephen F., esq, Warminster; 1823; £10 10s.

Phillips, Edward, esq, Melksham; 1820-30; £11 11s.

Phillips, Jacob, esq; 1866; £10 10s.

Phillips, John L., esq; 1841-53; £13 13s.

Philpot, John, esq; 1849-62; £25 4s.

Phipps, A. Constantine, esq; 1845-51; £5 5s.

Phipps, C. Lewis, esq, Wans House; 1820; £10 10s.

Phipps, C.N.P., esq, Chalcot; £28 7s.

Phipps, Charles Paul, esq, Chalcot; 1847-77; £26.

Phipps, John Lewis, esq, Leighton House; 1847-50; £12 12s.

Phipps, R.L. Hothersal, esq, Leighton House; 1870; £10 10s.

Phipps, T.H. Hele, esq, Leighton House; 1835; £10 10s.

Pinckney, Erlysman, Highbury, Warminster; 1866; £10 10s.

Pinckney, Captain Erlysman Charles, Duckmead, Bradford; 1887*; £10 10s.

Pinckney, John Robert Hugh, esq, Woodspeen Lodge, Newbury; 1901*; £10 10s.

Pinckney, W., esq, Sarum; 1871-1908; £16 16s.

Pinckney, William, esq, Everley; 1826-32; £12 12s.

Pinniger, W.H., esq, Westbury; 1884-96; £13 13s.

Pitt, Joseph, esq, M.P., Eastcourt House; 1817-28; £32 11s.

Pitt, Joseph, esq, jun; 1819-28; £21.

Pocock, T.P., esq, Chippenham; 1869; £10 10s.

Pollen, Sir R.H., bart, Rodbourne, Malmesbury; 1877-1902; £26 5s.

Ponting, Thomas, esq, Warminster; 1865-88; £25 4s.

Poore, Sir Edward, bart, Rushall; 1826; £10 10s.

Poore, R.A., esq, D.S.O., Cavalry Club, Piccadilly; 1913 [and perhaps later: listed as governor in 1913, but not in 1921]; £1 1s.

Poore, Admiral Sir Richard, bart, K.C.B., C.V.O., Winsley Corner, Bradford; 1906-14*; £29 8s.

Poore, Robert Montagu, esq; 1826-33; £12 12s.

Popham, General, Littlecott; 1842; £10 10s.

Powell, Alexander, esq, Hurdcott; 1825; £10 10s.

Powell, Alexander Francis, esq; 1883; £10 10s.

Powell, James, esq; 1826-37; £27 6s.

Poynder, T.H.A., esq, Hartham Park; 1841-71; £28 15s.

Poynder, Thomas, esq; 1818; £10 10s.

Poynder, Thomas, esq, jun; 1821; £10 10s.

Poynder, William H., esq, Pew Hill; 1860-79; £210 10s.

Prangley, Mr, Sarum; 1828-33; £6 6s.

Pratt, William, esq; 1820; £10 10s.

Pressly, Sir Charles, K.C.B.; 1859-69; £21.

Pressly, Miss Ellen; 1912 (legacy); £300.

Price, R.E., esq; 1866; £10 10s.

Prince, Rev John; 1819-35; £15 15s.

Pritchett, H., esq; 1823; £12 12s.

Prower, Capt, Purton; 1847; £10 10s.

Prower, Rev J. Mervin, Purton; 1847-66; £21.

Prower, Thomas, esq, Purton; 1820-4; £5 5s.

Prowse, Capt G.J.W.; 1888; £10 10s.

Pugh, William, esq; 1822; £5 5s.

Pullen, Joseph, esq; 1817-36; £21.

Radcliffe, His Honour Judge, K.C., The Rise, Headington Hill, Oxford; 1880-1900*; £18 18s.

Radcliffe, Alex. N., esq, 28 Old Queen Street, Westminster, SW1; 1882-1900*; £10 10s.

Radcliffe, Rev Arthur, Thelbridge, Keswick Road, Bournemouth; 1883*; £10 10s.

Radcliffe, Charles H., esq, Sarum; 1856; £10 10s.

Radcliffe, John Alexander, esq; 1852; £10 10s.

Radcliffe, Rev Norman C., D.D., Walmer

Vicarage, Kent; 1890★; £10 10s.

Radnor, countess of; 1914★; £2 2s.

Radnor, Earl of; 1817-27; £29 8s.

Radnor, Earl of; 1874-99; £27 6s.

Radnor, Earl of; 1879-88; £58 16s.

Radnor, Earl of, Longford Castle; 1894★; £100 17s.

Randolph, J.R., His Honour Judge, K.C., Eastcourt, Malmesbury; 1905★; £4 4s.

Ravenhill, Colonel, R.E., C.B.; 1876-88; £13 13s.

Ravenhill, Major-General, R.A.; 1881-99; £16 16s.

Ravenhill, John, esq; 1828; £10 10s.

Ravenhill, John R., esq; 1863; £10 10s.

Ravenhill, William Waldon, esq; 1863-81; £25 4s.

Ravenshaw, Rev T.F.; 1864; £10 10s.

Rawlinson, General Lord, G.C.B., G.C.V.O., Cholderton; 1913★; £2 2s.

Reed, Charles, esq, Marlborough; 1880-5; £6 6s.

Reed, George, esq; 1817-28; £14 14s.

Reeve, Mr Jonah, Marlborough; 1838-63; £27 6s.

Reeves, Capt. E., R.N., Brookheath, Fordingbridge; 1912★; £6 4s.

Richards, Henry, esq; 1845-63; £19 19s.

Richardson, H., esq, Sigglesthorne, Marlborough; 1891; £1 1s.

Richardson, James, esq; 1817; £10 10s.

Richardson, John, esq; 1823-9; £7 7s.

Richardson, Richard, esq; 1828-36; £9 9s.

Ring, John, esq; 1817-29; £15 15s.

Roberts, Thomas, esq; 1817; £10 10s.

Roberts, Very Rev William Page, Highlands, Shanklin; 1912★; £1 1s.

Robinson, Octavius, esq, Redlynch; 1901-4; £11 11s.

Robinson, Mrs Octavius, Combe Head House, Chard; 1904-14★; £11 11s.

Rogers, Rev Dr, Rainscombe; 1817-31; £15 15s.

Rogers, F.N., esq, Rainscombe; 1902-13★; £22 1s.

Rogers, F. Newman, esq, Q.C., Rainscombe; 1817-52; £36 15s.

Rogers, William, esq; 1827-37; £11 11s.

Rooke, Mortimer, esq, The Ivy, Chippenham; 1892★; £29 1s.

Roundway, Rt Hon Lord, Roundway Park; 1881-1908★; £55 13s.

Rowland, W.H., esq, Ramsbury; 1866; £11 11s.

Rowland, William, esq, Ramsbury; 1826-65; £42.

Russell, F. Martin, esq, Marlborough; 1826-37; £12 12s.

Russell, George, esq; 1826-34; £9 9s.

Russell, J., esq, Ramsbury; 1819-33; £27 6s.

Russell, James W., esq, Marlborough; 1834-48; £15 15s.

Russell, John, esq; 1826-34; £9 9s.

Ryder, Granville R., esq; 1875-88; £14 14s.

Sainsbury, Dr, Corsham; 1829-40; £11 11s.

Sainsbury, Mr James; 1833-5; £12 12s.

Sainsbury, Thomas Popham, esq, 30 Savile Row, W; 1913 [and perhaps later: listed as governor in 1913, but not in 1921] (executor of Miss Ellen Pressly).

St Aldwyns, the Viscount, Colne St Aldwyns, Fairford; 1861-70; £21.

Salisbury, the Lord Bishop of, the Rt Rev Dr Burgess; 1821; £10 10s.

Salisbury, the Lord Bishop of, the Rt Rev Dr Denison; 1840; £10 10s.

Salisbury, the Lord Bishop of, the Rt Rev Dr Hamilton; 1856; £10 10s.

Salisbury, the Lord Bishop of, the Rt Rev Dr Moberley; 1881; £10.

Salisbury, the Lord Bishop of, the Rt Rev Dr Wordsworth; 1886-1911; £57.

Salisbury, the Dean of, the Very Rev G.D. Boyle; 1882-1901; £21.

Salisbury, the Dean of, the Very Rev H.P. Hamilton; 1871; £10 10s.

Salisbury, the Dean of, the Very Rev William Page-Roberts; 1912; £1 1s.

Salmon, F., esq; 1840-2; £10 10s.

Salmon, W., esq, Southbroom House; 1818; £10 10s.

Salmon, W.W., esq, Southbroom House; 1818-46; £21.

Sandeman, G.G., esq; 1875-83; £10 10s.

Saunders, Henry, esq, Devizes; 1831-4; £14 14s.

Saunders, John, esq; 1822-3; £15 15s.

Saunders, T. B., esq; 1838; £18 18s.

Saunders, Thomas H., esq, Bradford; 1823; £15 15s.

Saunders, William, esq; 1826-31; £6 6s.

Saunders, William, esq; 1855-63; £9 9s.

Scammell, J.B., esq; 1869-75; £7 7s.

Schomberg, E.C., esq, Seend House; 1888-1902★; £40 19s.

Schomberg, Miss Louisa, Seend; 1902-11★; £10 10s.

Scott, John, esq, Warminster; 1874-85; £12 12s.

Seton, R.G., esq, 3 Dr Johnson's Buildings, Temple, EC4; 1910-14★; £5 5s.

Seymour, Alfred, esq, Knoyle; 1864-81; £30 9s.

Seymour, Henry, esq, Knoyle; 1833-47; £25 10s.

Seymour, Henry Danby, esq, M.P.; 1854; £10 10s.

Shaw-Stewart, Sir Michael, bart, Fonthill; 1883-1903; £15 10s.

Shaw-Stewart, Walter R., esq, Hindon; 1888-1900; £12 12s.

Shephard, J., esq; 1838-42; £21.

Sheppard, J.H., esq; 1823; £5 5s.

Short, Robert, esq; 1826-34; £9 9s.

Slade, John, esq; 1829-34; £6 6s.

Slater, Alvara, esq; 1824; £10 10s.

Slater, Rev F., Shaw; 1888-97; £10 10s.

Sloper, G.E., esq, Etchilhampton; 1823; £10 10s.

Smith, Charles Robert, esq; 1858; £10 10s.

Smith, H. Herbert, esq, Calne; 1888-1913; £29 8s.

Smith, H.J., esq; 1843-68; £27 6s.

Smith, Samuel; 1821; £10 10s.

Smith, Stephen, esq, Durnford; 1843-67; £26 5s.

Smith, T. Chaloner, esq; 1851-6; £15 15s.

Smith-Barry, J.H., esq, 33 Gloucester Square, W2; 1902★; £1 1s.

Smyth, Sir Hugh, bart; 1821; £10 10s.

Soames, Rev Charles, Mildenhall; 1867-93; £27 6s.

Soames, Charles E., esq, 12 Coleman St, EC2; 1888★; £25.

Soames, Rev Gordon, Mildenhall; 1895-1902★; £8 8s.

Somerset, Duke of; 1817-55; £63.

Somerset, Duke of, Maiden Bradley; 1897-9★; £26 5s.

Somerset, Lord Arthur; 1882; £10 10s.

Southwark, the Lord Bishop of, Dr Yeatman; 1899; £5 5s.

Spark, William T., esq, Abbotstone, Whiteparish; 1905★; £2 2s.

Spencer, Rev John; 1848; £10 10s.

Spicer, Captain, Spye Park; 1891★; £16 16s.

Spicer, J.W. Gooch, esq, Spye; 1867; £10 10s.

Squarey, A.T., esq; 1865-97; £12 12s.

Squarey, E.P., esq, Downton; 1903-11; £5 5s.

Stancomb, John F., esq, Shaw House, Melksham; 1888-94; £17 17s.

Stancomb, William, esq, Blount's Court, Potterne; 1878-1911★; £21.

Stanton, the Ven Archdeacon; 1865; £10 10s.

Staples, Messrs; 1843-67; £52 10s.

Staples, John, esq; 1843-9; £11 11s.

Staples, T.H., esq, Sarum; 1871-85; £15 15s.

Starky, Rev Dr, Spye; 1820; £10 10s.

Starky, Rev J.E. Andrew, Spye; 1821-5; £15 15s.

Staunton, Sir G., bart; 1817; £10 10s.

Stephens, Edward, esq, Sarum; 1821-34; £15 15s.

Stephens, Henry C., esq, Cholderton; 1898-1909; £21.

Sterne, Capt, R.N., Devizes; 1871-98; £28 7s.

Stoddart, Sir John; 1820-37; £18 18s.

Stothert, Sir Percy K., K.B.E., Lansdowne Place West, Bath; 1903★; £12 12s.

Strange, John, esq; 1820-35; £21.

Strange, John, esq; 1837; £10 10s.

Strange, Thomas, esq; 1838; £10 10s.

Strange, William, esq; 1820; £10 10s.

Stratton, C. Harris, esq, 48 St George's Court, South Kensington, SW7; 1896★; £10 10s.

Studd, Edward, esq; 1872; £10 10s.

Suffolk, Earl of; 1820; £10 10s.

Suffolk, Earl of; 1826; £10 10s.

Suffolk, Earl of; 1879-97; £15 10s.

Suffolk and Berkshire, Earl of, Charlton Park; 1913 [and perhaps later: listed as governor in 1913, but not in 1921]; £2 2s.

Sutherland, Charles, esq, Amesbury; 1829-36; £6 6s.

Sutton, Mrs Elizabeth, Rowde; 1821; £10 10s.

Sutton, George, esq; 1837-44; £7 7s.

Sutton, James, esq; 1821-42; £17 5s.

Sutton, John, esq, Rowde; 1821; £10 10s.

Sutton, Robert, esq; 1817-46; £60 18s.

Sutton, Robert, esq, jun; 1821-2; £23 18s.

Sutton, Mrs Sarah, Rowde; 1821; £10 10s.

Swaby, James, esq; 1830; £5 5s.

Swayne, H.J.F., esq, Wilton; 1842; £10 10s.

Swayne, J., esq, Wilton; 1820-40; £21.

Swayne, Thomas, esq; 1829; £10 10s.

Tanner, William, esq, Lockeridge; 1823; £10 10s.

Tatham, John, esq; 1821-30; £10 10s.

Temple, William, esq, Bishopstrow; 1824; £10 10s.

Terrell, George, esq, M.P., 45 Wilton Crescent, SW1; 1920*; £1 1s.

Thomas, Rev J.S., Marlborough; 1891-8; £8 8s.

Thornton, Captain Cyril M.; 1898-1909; £11 11s.

Thring, John Tivitoe, esq, Warminster; 1821-5; £14 14s.

Thring, R.S., esq; 1875; £5 5s.

Tilby, James, esq, Devizes; 1817-21; £15 15s.

Timbrell, Charles, esq; 1831-5; £6 6s.

Timbrell, Thomas, esq; 1827; £10 10s.

Tinker, William, esq, Devizes; 1833; £10 10s.

Tinney, W.H., esq; 1817-36; £16 16s.

Torrance, John, esq; 1870-8' £9 9s.

Townsend, George Barnard, esq, Sarum; 1843-68; £27 6s.

Townsend, George Eyre, esq, R.A., Sarum; 1864-73; £10 10s.

Trafalgar, Viscount; 1888-1905; £17 17s.

Trenchard, Rev J.A., LL.D, Stanton; 1819; £10 10s.

Trinder, H., esq; 1848-54; £8 8s.

Troyte-Chafyn-Grove, G., esq; 1892-1913; £16 16s.

Truebridge, Thomas, esq, Wishford; 1828-40; £13 13s.

Tucker, Henry, esq; 1872; £10 10s.

Tuckey, Mr Richard; 1826-33; £8 8s.

Tuckey, Thomas, esq, Haydon; 1846-52; £7 7s.

Tugwell, William Edmund, esq; 1832; £10 10s.

Turnor, Col W.W., Pinkney Park, Sherston; 1898-1905*; £8 8s.

Tylee, Charles, esq, Seend; 1818; £10 10s.

Tylee, Edward, esq; 1838-85; £49 7s.

Tylee, John, esq, Devizes; 1818; £10 10s.

Tylee, Thomas, esq, Devizes; 1818; £10 10s.

Upcott, Lewis E., esq, Babbacombe, Torquay; 1900-14*; £4 4s.

Vaux, Joseph, esq; 1817; £10 10s.

Vilett, Lieut-Colonel; 1837; £10 10s.

Vincent, Rev E., Rowde; 1820; £10 10s.

Vincent, John, esq; 1844-94; £56 14s.

Vincent, Thomas, esq; 1818; £17 17s.

Wackerbarth, G., esq; 1821-8; £18 18s.

Wakeman, Herbert J., Warminster; 1865-96; £32 11s.

Walker, William, esq, Longfield House, Trowbridge; 1892*; £10 10s.

Wall, William, esq; 1829-36; £8 8s.

Wallington, Sir John, K.C.B., Keevil; 1888-1910; £24 3s.

Walmesley, Richard, esq, Lackham; 1876-7; £21.

Walrond, John, esq; 1827-36; £10 10s.

Walsh, Joseph, esq; 1821-34; £14 14s.

Walter, Richard, esq; 1822-48; £22 1s.

Wansey, Henry, esq, Warminster; 1820-36; £17 17s.

Wansey, Henry, esq; 1874-9; £13 13s.

Wansey, William, esq; 1856-68; £13 13s.

Ward, Rev John, Great Bedwyn; 1829; £10 10s.

Ward, John, esq, Marlborough; 1821-9; £9 9s.

Ward, Col Michael Foster, Upton Park, Slough; 1854; £10 10s.

Ward, Thomas Rowdon, esq; 1821; £10 10s.

Warneford, Lady, Wetherell; 1860; £10 10s.

Warre, Rev Canon, Bemerton; 1901; £10 10s.

Warriner, Ernle, esq; 1819; £10 10s.

Warrington, Rt Hon Lord Justice, Clyffe Hall, Market Lavington; 1904*; £35 14s.

Warry, Thomas, esq; 1817-40; £25 4s.

Washbourne, Mrs Thomas; 1830-9; £10 10s.

Waters, Edward, esq, Heathfield, Milford Hill, Salisbury; 1903*; £19 19s.

Waters, T., esq; 1849-52; £15 15s.

Watson-Taylor, Simon, esq, Erlestoke; 1845-1902; £21.

Wayet, Mrs, Pinchbeck Vicarage, Spalding; 1870*; £10 10s.

Webb, Charles, esq; 1826; £10 10s.

Webb, Francis, esq; 1851-65; £25 4s.

Webb, Frederick, esq; 1823; £10.

Webb, Henry Parker, esq, Trowbridge; 1868-85; £18 18s.

Webb, John, esq; 1825; £10 10s.

Webb, Richard, esq; 1829-36; £18 18s.

Weeks, Thomas, esq; 1839-41; £5 5s.

Welford, Richard, esq; 1823-5; £13 13s.

Wellesley, the Hon W.P.T.L., Draycott; 1819-20; £12 12s.

Westall, Dr Edward; 1845; £10 10s.
Westall, R., esq; 1848; £10 10s.
Wheeler, Miss; 1870-1909; £41.
Wheeler, J.C., esq, Sarum; 1848-69; £22 1s.
Whitaker, E.T., esq; 1846-76; £31 10s.
White, Richard, esq; 1826; £10 10s.
Whitmarsh, F., esq; 1821-35; £15 15s.
Whitmarsh, Henry, esq; 1824-35; £12 12s.
Whitmarsh, Thomas, esq; 1837-42; £6 6s.
Whitmarsh, Thomas Webb, esq; 1822-35; £14 14s.
Wild, George, esq; 1852; £10 10s.
Williams, Dr; 1832-41; £10 10s.
Williams, Rev Sir Erasmus G., bart; 1846; £10 10s.
Willis and Son; 1881-4; £21.
Willis, J. Deane-, esq, Bapton Manor; 1901*; £11 11s.
Wilson, Sir Henry and Lady Frances Wright; 1824; £10 10s.
Wilson, J., esq; 1876-85; £10 10s.
Wilson, J., esq [the same]; 1885; £90 legacy, less duty.
Wilson, R.A., esq, Salisbury; 1884; £10 10s.
Wilts and Gloucester Standard, Cirencester; 1870; £1 1s.
Wood, Charles Paul, esq; 1853-61; £11 11s.
Wood, J. Crewe, esq, Swindon; 1906*; £1 1s.

Woodley, Thomas, esq; 1869-79; £11 11s.
Woodman, J., esq, Marlborough; 1820-5; £16 16s.
Wordsworth, Rev Canon Christopher, St Nicholas Hospital, Salisbury; 1899-1901; £11 11s.
Wray, Robert, esq; 1817-23; £7 7s.
Wroughton, Lieut-Colonel, Wilcot; 1826-33; £18 18s.
Wyatt, Alfred, esq; 1821; £10 10s.
Wyatt, Matthew, esq; 1821-5; £6 6s.
Wyndham, Charles, esq, Wans House; 1875-96; £14 14s.
Wyndham, J.H. Campbell, Sarum; 1844; £10 10s.
Wyndham, Hon Percy Scawen, Clouds; 1896-1910; £32 16s.
Wyndham, Wadham, esq, Sarum; 1826; £10 10s.
Wyndham, William, esq, M.P., Dinton; 1854; £10 10s.

Yatman, W. Hamilton, esq; 1888-99; £12 12s.
Yeatman-Biggs, Rt Rev Lord Bishop of Coventry, D.D., Bishop's House, Coventry; 1899*; £13 8s.
Young, Walter C., esq, Stratford-sub-Castle; 1911; £1 1s.

APPENDIX C PAST PRESIDENTS OF THE WILTSHIRE SOCIETY

Ailesbury, Marquis of, 1864
Ailesbury, Marquis of, 1880
Albany, H.R.H. Duke of, KG, 1881
Antrobus, Sir E., bart, 1874
Antrobus, Col Sir Edmund, bart, 1907
Astley, Sir John Dugdale, bart, M.P., 1823

Baring, Thomas, esq, M.P., 1861
Bath, Marquess of, 1855
Bath, Marquis of, 1890
Bath, Marquis of, 1896-7
Bathurst, Col Hervey, M.P., 1862
Beach, Sir M.H. Hicks, bart, 1852
Bell, W. Heward, esq, J.P., 1922
Benett, John, esq, M.P., 1822
Brewer, John Hibberd, esq,, 1872
Browne, Wade, esq, (High Sheriff), 1846
Bruce, Earl, 1854
Bruce, Lord Charles, M.P., 1867
Bruce, Lord Ernest, M.P., 1856
Bruges, W.H. Ludlow, esq, M.P., 1839
Burdett, Sir Francis, bart M.P., 1824

Calley, Col. T.C.P., C.B., M.V.O., 1911
Calley, Thomas, esq, M.P., 1832
Carnarvon, Earl of, 1826
Clarendon, Earl of, 1827
Colston, Edward, esq,, 1908
Coote, Sir Eyre, 1912

Dickson-Poynder, Sir John, bart, 1891

Estcourt, G.B.Sotheron, esq, M.P., 1877
Estcourt, T.G.B., esq, M.P., 1820
Estcourt, T.H.S.B., esq, M.P., 1837
Eyre, George Edward, esq, (High Sheriff), 1844

Fitzmaurice, Lord Edmond, 1889
Folkestone, Viscount, 1875
Folkestone, Viscount, M.P., 1894
Fowler, R.N., esq, M.P., 1885
Fuller, John M., esq, M.P., 1898

Goddard, Ambrose L., esq, M.P., 1865
Goddard, F.P., esq, 1906

Gordon, Robert, esq, M.P., 1829
Grove, Thomas Fraser, esq, M.P., 1868

Heneage, G.H .Walker, esq, M.P., 1842
Herbert, Hon Sidney, M.P., 1835
Herbert, Hon Sidney, M.P., 1878
Heytesbury, Lord, 1863
Hobhouse, Sir Benjamin, bart, 1817
Hobhouse, Sir John, bart, M.P., 1834
Hussey, Ambrose, esq, M.P., 1843

Kerry, Earl of, M.P., D.S.O., 1913

Lansdowne, Marquis of, 1819
Lansdowne, Marquis of, 1870
Lansdowne, Marquis of, K.G., 1895
Lawrence, W.F., esq, M.P., 1905
Long, Richard Penruddocke, esq, M.P., 1866
Long, Walter, esq, M.P., 1838
Long, Walter H., esq, M.P., 1892
Long, Walter Hume, esq, M.P., 1883

Malet, Sir Alexander, K.C.B., 1871
Marsh, M.H., esq, M.P., 1858
Merewether, Henry Alworth, esq, Q.C., 1859
Merewether, Mr Serjeant, 1847
Methuen, Lord, 1887
Methuen, Hon Frederick H. Paul, 1848
Methuen, Paul, esq, M.P., 1818
Methuen, Col. Hon Paul, C.B., C.M.G., 1886
Morrison, Hugh, esq,, 1903

Neeld, Sir Algernon W., 1893
Neeld, Lt-Col Sir Audley D., bart, C.B., M.V.O., 1904
Neeld, John, esq, M.P., 1841
Neeld, Joseph, esq, M.P., 1836
Nelson, Earl, 1851
Nisbet, R. Parry, esq, (High Sheriff), 1849
Normanton, Earl of, 1873

Pearse, John, esq, M.P., 1830
Pembroke, Earl of, 1882
Pembroke, Earl of, 1900-1
Pembroke, Earl of, M.V.O., 1914-20
Phipps, C.N.P., esq, (High Sheriff), 1888

Pitt, Joseph, esq, M.P., 1831
Pressly, Sir Charles, K.C.B., 1869

Radnor, Earl of, C.I.E., C.B.E., 1921

Salisbury, Bishop of, 1845
Salisbury, Bishop of, 1857
Seymour, Alfred, esq,, 1876
Shelburne, Earl of, M.P., 1840
Somerset, Duke of, 1821
Somerset, Duke of, 1833
Somerset, Duke of, 1899

Stanford, Vere Benett, esq, 1884
Suffolk, Earl of, 1828
Suffolk, Earl of, 1853
Suffolk and Berkshire, Earl of, 1879

Taylor, George Watson, esq, M.P., 1825
Taylor, Simon Watson, esq,, 1850
Tennant, Sir Edward, bart M.P., 1909-10
Thynne, Lord Henry, M.P., 1860

Wyndham, Hon. Percy Scawen, 1902

INDEX OF PERSONS, PLACES, AND COMPANIES

Places are in Wiltshire unless otherwise stated. All places within the administrative county of London formed in 1889 are indexed alphabetically under London. Companies are indexed after individuals. Unless prefixed by p., references are to entries, not page numbers.

INDEX OF OCCUPATIONS

This index includes occupations of masters, parents, and apprentices, and retains, in most cases, the original terminology. Synonymous occupations are separately indexed, and cross-referenced. References are to entries, not page numbers.

WILTSHIRE RECORD SOCIETY
(As at November 1996)

President: PROF. C.R. ELRINGTON, F.S.A.
General Editor: DR JOHN CHANDLER
Honorary Treasurer: MICHAEL J. LANSDOWN
Honorary Secretary: JOHN N. D'ARCY

Committee:
MRS J.A. COLE
DR D.A. CROWLEY
S.D. HOBBS
M.J. MARSHMAN
P.M.A. NOKES
I. M. SLOCOMBE
K.H. ROGERS, F.S.A., representing the Wiltshire Archaeological and Natural History
Society

Honorary Auditor: J.D. FOY
Correspondent for the U.S.A.: CHARLES P. GOULD

PRIVATE MEMBERS

ANDERSON, MR D M, 1 St Margaret's Hill, Bradford on Avon BA15 1DP

APPLEGATE, MISS J M, 55 Holbrook Lane, Trowbridge BA14 0PS

ASAJI, MR K 1-2-401 gakuen-higahi, Nishi, Kobe 651-21 Japan

AVERY, MRS S c/o 4 Shady Bower Close, Salisbury SP1 2RQ

BADENI, COUNTESS JUNE, Norton Manor, Norton, Malmesbury SN16 0JN

BAINES, MRS B M, 32 Tybenham Road, Merton Park, London SW19 3LA

BAINES, MR R T, The Woodhouse, 52 St Mary Street, Chippenham SN15 3JW

BALL, MR S T, 19 The Mall, Swindon SN1 4JA

BARNETT, MR B A, 17 Alexandra Road, Coalpit Heath, Bristol BS17 2PY

BATHE, MR G, Byeley in Densome, Woodgreen, Fordingbridge, Hants SP6 2QU

BAYLIFFE, MR B G, 3 Green Street, Brockworth, Glos GL3 4LT

BEARD, MRS P S, The Anchorage, Port-e-Vullen, Maughold, Isle of Man

BERRETT, MR A M, 10 Primrose Hill Road, London NW3 3AD

BERRY, MR C, 9 Haven Rd, Crackington Haven, Bude, Cornwall EX23 0PD

BLAKE, MR P A, 18 Rosevine Road, London SW20 8RB

BLAKE, MR T N, Glebe Farm, Tilshead, Salisbury SP3 4RZ

BOX, MR S D, 73 Silverdale Road, Earley, Reading RG6 2NF

BRAND, DR P A, 155 Kennington Road, London SE11 6SF

BROOKE-LITTLE, MR J P, College of Arms, Queen Victoria Street, London EC4V 4BT

BRYANT, MRS D, 1 St John's Court, Devizes SN10 1BU

BUCKERIDGE, MR J M, 147 Herrick Road, Loughborough, Leics LE11 2BS

BURGESS, MR I D, 29 Brackley Avenue, Fair Oak, Eastleigh, Hants SO5 7FL

BURGESS, MR J M, Tolcarne, Wartha Mill, Porkellis, Helston, Cornwall TR13 0HX

BURNETT-BROWN, MISS J M, Lacock Abbey, Lacock, Chippenham SN15 2LG

CALLEY, SIR HENRY, Overtown House, Wroughton, Swindon SN4 0SH

CARDIGAN, RT HON EARL OF, Savernake Estate Office, Marlborough SN8 1PA

CAREW HUNT, MISS P H, Cowleaze, Edington, Westbury BA13 4PJ

CARR, PROF D R, Dept. of History, 140 7th Ave South, St Petersburg, Florida 33701 USA

CARTER, DR B J, 28 Okus Road, Swindon SN1 4JQ

CAWTHORNE, MRS N, Dawn, 47 London Road, Camberley, Surrey GU15 3UG

CHANDLER, DR J H, Jupe's School, The Street, East Knoyle, Salisbury SP3 6AJ

CHAVE, MR R A, 39 Church Street, Westbury BA13 3BZ

CHURCH, MR T S, Mannering House, Bethersden, Ashford, Kent TN26 3DJ

CHURN, MR R H, 5 Veritys, Hatfield, Herts AL10 8HH

CLARK, MR A G, Highlands, 51a Brook Drive, Corsham SN13 9AX

CLARK, MRS V, 29 The Green, Marlborough SN8 1AW

COLE, MRS J A, 113 Groundwell Road, Swindon SN1 2NA

COLEMAN, MISS J, 16 Den Road, Bromley BR2 0NH

COLLINS, MR A T, 11 Lemon Grove, Whitehill, Bordon, Hants GU35 9BD

CONGLETON, LORD, West End Farm, Ebbesbourne Wake, Salisbury SP5 5JW

COOMBES-LEWIS, MR R J, 45 Oakwood Park Road, Southgate, London N14 6QP

CORAM, MRS J E, London House, 51 The Street, Hullavington, Chippenham SN14 6DP

COULSTOCK, MISS P H, 15 Pennington Crescent, West Moors, Wimborne, Dorset BH22 0JH

COVEY, MR R V, Lower Hunts Mill, Wootton Bassett, Swindon SN4 7QL

COWAN, COL M, 24 Lower Street, Harnham, Salisbury SP3 8EY

CRITTALL, MISS E, 3 Freshwell Gardens, Saffron Walden, Essex CB10 1BZ

CROWLEY, DR D A, 2 Manor Court, Greater Lane, Edington, Westbury BA13 4QP

D'ARCY, MR J N, The Old Vicarage, Edington, Westbury

DIBBEN, MR A A, 18 Clare Road, Lewes, East Sussex BN7 1PN

EDE, DR M E, 12 Springfield Place, Lansdown, Bath BA1 5RA

EDWARDS, MR P C, 33 Longcroft Road, Devizes SN10 3AT

ELRINGTON, PROF C R, 34 Lloyd Baker Street, London WC1X 9AB

FAY, MRS M, 29 Denison Rise, Bishopsdown, Salisbury SP1 3EW

FLOWER-ELLIS, DR J G, Swedish Univ of Agric Sciences, PO Box 7072 S-750 07, Uppsala, Sweden 1972

FORBES, MISS K G, Bury House, Codford, Warminster

FOSTER, MR R E, The New House, St Giles Close, Gt Maplestead, Halstead, Essex CO9 2RW

FOY, MR J D, 28 Penn Lea Road, Bath BA1 3RA

FREEMAN, DR J, Institute of Historical Research, Senate House, London WC1E 7HU

FROST, MR B C, Red Tiles, Cadley, Collingbourne Ducis, Marlborough SN8 3EA

FULLER, MRS B, 65 New Park Street, Devizes SN10 1DR

FULLER, MAJOR SIR JOHN, Neston Park, Corsham SN13 9TG

GHEY, MR J G, 18 Bassett Row, Bassett, Southampton SO1 7FS

GIBBS, MRS E, Sheldon Manor, Chippenham SN14 0RG

GODDARD, MR R E H, Sinton Meadow, Stokes Lane, Leigh Sinton, Malvern, Worcs WR13 5DY

GOODBODY, MR E A, 12 Clifton Road, Chesham Bois, Amersham, Bucks HP6 5PU

GOUGH, MISS P M, 39 Whitford Road, Bromsgrove, Worcs B61 7ED

GOULD, MR C P, 1200 Old Mill Road, San Marino, California 91108 USA

GOULD, Mr L K, 263 Rosemount, Pasadena, California 91103 USA

GRIFFITHS, MR T J, 29 Saxon Street, Chippenham SN15

GRUBER VON ARNI, COL E E, 11 Park Lane, Swindon SN1 5HG

GUNSTONE, MR L, 47 St Michaels Road, Bath BA2 1PZ

HAMILTON, CAPTAIN R, West Dean, Salisbury SP5 1JL

HARE, DR J N, 7 Owens Road, Winchester, Hants SO22 6RU

HARTCHER, REV DR G N, PO Box 104, Arncliffe, NSW 2205, Australia

HATCHWELL, MR R C, The Old Rectory, Little Somerford, Chippenham SN15 5JW

HAWKINS, MR M J, 121 High Street, Lewes, East Sussex BN7 1XJ

HAYWARD, MISS J E, Pleasant Cottage, Crockerton, Warminster BA12 8AJ

HELMHOLZ, PROF R W, Law School, 1111 East 60th Street, Chicago, Illinois 60637 USA

HENLEY, MR R G, 33 West View Crescent, Devizes SN10 5HE

HENLY, MR H R, 99 Moredon Road, Swindon SN2 2JG

HERRON, MRS PAMELA M, 25 Anvil Crescent, Broadstone, Dorset BH18 9DY

HICKMAN, MR M R, 184 Surrenden Road, Brighton BN1 6NN

HILLMAN, MR R B, 18 Carnarvon Close, Chippenham SN14 0PN

HINTON, MR A E, Glenside Cottage, Glendene Avenue, East Horsley, Surrey KT24 5AY

HOBBS, MR S, 63 West End, Westbury BA13 3JQ

HOLLEY, MR R J, 120 London Road, Calne SN11 0AH

HORNBY, MISS E, 41 Silverwood Drive, Laverstock, Salisbury SP1 1SH

HORTON, MR P.R.G, OBE, Hedge End, West Grimstead, Salisbury SP5 3RF

HOWELLS, MS JANE, 7 St Mark's Rd, Salisbury SP1 3AY

HUGHES, PROF C J, Old House, Tisbury, Salisbury SP3 6PS

HUGHES, MR R G, 60 Hurst Park Road, Twyford, Reading RG10 0EY

HULL, MR J L F, Unit 2, 67 Barrack Street West, Hobart, Tasmania 7000, Australia

HUMPHRIES, MR A G, Rustics, Blacksmith's Lane, Harmston, Lincoln LN5 9SW

INGRAM, DR M J, Brasenose College, Oxford OX1 4AJ

JACKSON, MR D, 2 Byways Close, Salisbury SP1 2QS

JAMES, MR J F, 3 Sylvan Close, Hordle, Lymington, Hants SO41 0HJ

JEACOCK, MR D, 16 Church Street, Wootton Bassett, Swindon

JELLICOE, RT HON EARL, Tidcombe Manor, Tidcombe, Marlborough SN8 3SL

JOHNSTON, MRS J M, Greystone House, 3 Trowbridge Road, Bradford on Avon BA15 1EE

KAY, MR A H, 15 Napier Crescent, Laverstock, Salisbury SP1 1PJ

KENT, MR T A, Rose Cottage, Isington, Alton, Hants GU34 4PN

KIRBY, MR J L, 209 Covington Way, Streatham, London SW16 3BY

KNEEBONE, MR W J R, 20 Blind Lane, Southwick, Trowbridge BA14 9PG

KOMATSU, PROF Y, c/o Yushodo Co, 29 San-ei-cho, Shinjuku-Ku, Tokyo 160 Japan

KUNIKATA, MR K, Dept of Economics, 1-4-12, Kojirakawa-machi, Yamagata-shi 990, Japan

LAMPARD, MRS M L, The School House, Crockerton, Warminster BA12 8AD

LANSDOWN, MR M J, 53 Clarendon Road, Trowbridge BA14 7BS

LAURENCE, MISS A, c/o Arts Faculty, Open University, Milton Keynes MK7 6AA

LAURENCE, MR G F, St Cuthberts, 20 Church Street, Bathford, Bath BA1 7TU

LODGE, MR O R W, Southridge House, Hindon, Salisbury SP3 6ER

LONDON, MISS V C M, 55 Churchill Road, Church Stretton, Salop SY6 6EP

LONG, MR S H, 12 Goulton Close, Yarm, Stockton on Tees, Cleveland TS15 9RY

LUSH, DR G J, 5 Braeside Court, West Moors, Ferndown, Dorset BH22 0JS

MARSH, REV R, Peterhouse, 128 Ifield Road, West Green, Crawley, West Sussex RH11 7BW

MARSHMAN, MR M J, 13 Regents Place, Bradford on Avon BA15 1ED

MARTIN, MS JEAN, 21 Ashfield Road, Chippenham SN15 1QQ

MASLEN, MR A, 8 Alder Walk, Frome, Som BA11 2SN

MATHEWS, MR R, P O Box R72, Royal Exchange, NSW 2000, Australia

MATTHEWS, CANON W A, Holy Trinity Vicarage, 18a Woolley St, Bradford on Avon BA15 1AF

MERRYWEATHER, MR A, 60 Trafalgar Road, Cirencester, Glos GL7 2EL

MOLES, MRS M I, 40 Wyke Road, Trowbridge BA14 7NP

MONTAGUE, MR M D, 115 Stuarts Road, Katoomba, NSW 2780, Australia

MOODY, MR R F, Harptree House, East Harptree, Bristol BS18 6AA

MORIOKA, PROF K 3-12, 4-chome, Sanno, Ota-ku, Tokyo, Japan

MORLAND, MR T E, 47 Shaftesbury Road, Wilton, Salisbury SP2 0DU

MORRISON, MRS J, Priory Cottage, Bratton, Westbury BA13

MOULTON, DR A E, The Hall, Bradford on Avon BA15

NEWBURY, MR C COLES, 6 Leighton Green, Westbury BA13 3PN

NEWMAN, MRS R, Tanglewood, Laverstock Park, Salisbury SP1 1QJ

NOKES, MR P A, Wards Farm, Ditcheat, Shepton Mallet, Somerset BA4 6PR

O'DONNELL, MISS S J, 42 Wessington Park, Calne SN11 0AU

OGBOURNE, MR J M V,14 Earnshaw Way, Beaumont Park, Whitley Bay, Tyne and Wear NE25 9UN

OGBURN, CHIEF JUDGE ROBERT W, 317 First Avenue, Monte Vista, CO 81144, USA

OSBORNE, COL R, Unwins House, 15 Waterbeach Road, Landbeach, Cambridge CB4 4EA

PARKER, DR P F, 45 Chitterne Road, Codford St Mary, Warminster BA12 0PG

PATRICK, DR S, The Thatchings, Charlton All Saints, Salisbury SP5 4HQ

PAVELEY, MR A W, 135 Lower Camden, Chislehurst, Kent BR7 5JD

PERRY, MR S H, Priory Cottage, Broad Street, Bampton, Oxon

PLATT, MR A J, Daubeneys, Colerne, Chippenham SN14 8DB

POWELL, MRS N, 4 Verwood Drive, Bitton, Bristol BS15 6JP

RADNOR, EARL OF, Longford Castle, Salisbury SP5 4EF

RATHBONE, MR M G, Craigleith, 368 Snarlton Lane, Melksham SN12 7QW

RAYBOULD, MISS F, 20 Radnor Road, Salisbury SP1 3PL

REEVES, DR M E, 38 Norham Road, Oxford OX2 6SQ

ROGERS, MR K H, Silverthorne House, East Town, West Ashton, Trowbridge

ROOKE, MISS S F, The Old Rectory, Little Langford, Salisbury SP3 4NU

SAWYER, MR L F T, 51 Sandridge Road, Melksham SN12 7BJ

SHEDDAN, MISS J A, 8 Sefton Avenue, Auckland 2, New Zealand

SHELBURNE, EARL OF, Bowood House, Calne SN11 0LZ

SHELDRAKE, MR B, 28 Belgrave Street, Swindon SN1 3HR

SHEWRING, MR P, 73 Woodland Road, Beddau, Pontypridd, Mid-Glamorgan CF38 2SE

SHORE, MR B W, The Breck, 25 Westerham Road, Oxted, Surrey RH8 0EP

SIMS-NEIGHBOUR, MR A K, 2 Hesketh Crescent, Swindon SN3 1RY

SLOCOMBE, MR I, 11 Belcombe Place, Bradford on Avon BA15 1NA

SMITH, MR P J, 6 Nuthatch, Longfield, Kent DA3 7NS

SOPP, MR G A, 23952 Nomar Street, Woodland Hills, California 91367, USA

SPAETH, DR D A, School of History and Archaeology, 1 University Gardens, University of Glasgow G12 8QQ

STEELE, MRS N D, 4 Shady Bower Close, Salisbury SP1 2RQ

STERRY, MS K, 8 Watercrook Mews, Westlea, Swindon SN5 7AS

STEVENAGE, MR M R, 49 Centre Drive, Epping, Essex CM16 4JF

STEVENS, MISS M L E, 11 Kingshill Close, Malvern, Worcs WR14 2BP

STEVENSON, MISS J H, Inst of Historical Research, Senate House, London WC1E 7HU

STEWARD, DR H J, Graduate School of Geography, 950 Main Street, Worcester, Mass 01610-1477, USA

STEWART, MISS K P, 6 Beatrice Road, Salisbury SP1 3PN

STOKES, MR M E J, 40 New Zealand Avenue, Salisbury SP2 7JX

STRATTON, MR M J, Manor Farm, Stockton, Warminster BA12 0SQ

SYKES, MR B H C, Conock Manor, Devizes SN10 3QQ

SYLVESTER, MR D G H, Almondsbury Field, Tockington Lane, Almondsbury, Bristol BS12 4EB

TAYLOR, MR C C, 13 West End, Whittlesford, Cambridge CB2 4LR

THOMPSON, MRS A M, 18 Burnaston Road, Hall Green, Birmingham B28 8DJ

THOMPSON, MR & MRS J B, 1 Bedwyn Common, Great Bedwyn, Marlborough SN8 3HZ

THOMSON, MRS SALLY M, Shirley House, High St, Codford, Warminster BA12 0NB

TIGHE, MR M F, Strath Colin, Pettridge Lane, Mere, Warminster BA12 6DG

TSUSHIMA, MRS J, Malmaison, Church Street, Great Bedwyn, Marlborough SN8 3PE

TURNER, MR I D, Warrendene, 222 Nottingham Road, Mansfield, Notts NG18 4AB

VINCENT, MS M A, 28 Rochester Road, Lodge Moor, Sheffield S10 4JQ

WAITE, MR R E, 18a Lower Road, Chinnor, Oxford OX9 4DT

WALKER, MR J K, 82 Wainsford Road, Everton, Lymington, Hants SO41 0UD

WARNEFORD, MR F E, New Inn Farm, West End Lane, Henfield, West Sussex BN5 9RF

WARREN, MR P, 6 The Meadows, Milford Hill Road, Salisbury SP1 2RT

WEINSTOCK, BARON, Bowden Park, Lacock, Chippenham

WELLER, MR R B, 9a Bower Gardens, Salisbury SP1 2RL

WHORLEY, MR E E, 190 Stockbridge Road, Winchester, Hants SO22 6RW

WORDSWORTH, MRS G, Quince Cottage, Longbridge Deverill, Warminster BA12 7DS

WRIGHT, MR D P, Haileybury, Hertford SG13 7NU

YOUNG, MRS D L, 25 Staveley Road, Chiswick, London W4 3HU

YOUNGER, MR C, 8 Ailesbury Way, Burbage, Marlborough SN8 3TD

UNITED KINGDOM INSTITUTIONS

Aberystwyth
  National Library of Wales
  University College of Wales
Bath. Reference Library
Birmingham
  Central Library
  University Library
Brighton. University of Sussex Library
Bristol
  Central Library
  University Library
Cambridge. University Library
Chippenham. Technical College
Coventry. University of Warwick Library

Devizes. Wiltshire Archaeological and Natural History Society
Dorchester. Dorset County Library
Durham. University Library
Edinburgh
  National Library of Scotland
  University Library
Exeter. University Library
Glasgow. University Library
Gloucester. Bristol and Gloucestershire Archaeological Society
Leeds. University Library
Leicester. University Library
Liverpool. University Library

London
  British Library
  College of Arms
  Guildhall Library
  Inner Temple Library
  Institute of Historical Research
  London Library
  Public Record Office
  Royal Historical Society
  Society of Antiquaries
  Society of Genealogists
  University of London Library
Manchester. John Rylands Library
Marlborough
  Memorial Library, Marlborough College
  Merchant's House Trust
Norwich. University of East Anglia Library
Nottingham. University Library
Oxford
  Bodleian Library
  Exeter College Library
  New College Library
Poole. Bournemouth University
Reading

  Central Library
  University Library
St Andrews. University Library
Salisbury
  Bourne Valley Historical Society
  Cathedral Library
  Salisbury and South Wilts Museum
Sheffield. University Library
Southampton. University Library
Swansea. University College Library
Swindon
  Royal Commission on the Historical
    Monuments of England
  Thamesdown Borough Council
  Wiltshire Family History Society
Taunton. Somerset Archaeological and
  Natural History Society
Trowbridge
  Wiltshire County Council, Library and
    Museum Service
  Wiltshire Record Office
Wetherby. British Library Document Supply
  Centre
York. University Library

INSTITUTIONS OVERSEAS

AUSTRALIA

Adelaide. Barr Smith Library, Adelaide
  University
Canberra. National Library of Australia
Kensington. Law Library, University of New
  South Wales
Melbourne
    Baillieu Library, University of
  Melbourne
    Victoria State Library
Nedlands. Reid Library, University of
  Western Australia
Sydney. Fisher Library, University of Sydney

CANADA

Halifax, Nova Scotia. Dalhousie University
  Library
London, Ont. D.B.Weldon Library,
  University of Western Ontario
Montreal, Que. Sir George Williams
  University
Ottawa, Ont. Carleton University Library
St John's, Newf. Memorial University of
  Newfoundland Library

Toronto, Ont
    Pontifical Inst of Medieval Studies
    University of Toronto Library
Victoria, B.C. McPherson Library, University
  of Victoria

DENMARK

Copenhagen. Royal Library

EIRE

Dublin. Trinity College Library

GERMANY

Gottingen. University Library

JAPAN

Osaka. Institute of Economic History, Kansai
  University
Sendai. Institute of Economic History,
  Tohoku University

NEW ZEALAND

Wellington. National Library of New
  Zealand

SWEDEN
Uppsala. Royal University Library

UNITED STATES OF AMERICA
Ann Arbor, Mich. Hatcher Library, University of Michigan
Athens, Ga. University of Georgia Libraries
Atlanta, Ga. The Robert W Woodruff Library, Emory University
Baltimore, Md. George Peabody Library, Johns Hopkins University
Binghamton, NY. State University of New York
Bloomington, Ind. Indiana University Library
Boston, Mass.
       Boston Public Library
       New England Historic and Genealogical Society
Boulder, Colo. University of Colorado Library
Cambridge, Mass.
       Harvard College Library
       Harvard Law School Library
Charlottesville, Va. Alderman Library, University of Virginia
Chicago.
       Newberry Library
       University of Chicago Library
Dallas, Texas. Public Library
Davis, Calif. University Library
East Lansing, Mich. Michigan State University Library
Eugene, Ore. University of Oregon Library
Evanston, Ill. United Libraries, Garrett/Evangelical, Seabury
Fort Wayne, Ind. Allen County Public Library
Haverford, Pa. Magill Library, Haverford College

Houston, Texas. M.D. Anderson Library, University of Houston
Iowa City, Iowa. University of Iowa Libraries
Ithaca, NY. Cornell University Library
Las Cruces, N.M. New Mexico State University Library
Los Angeles.
       Public Library
       University Research Library, University of California
Minneapolis, Minn. Wilson Library, University of Minnesota
New Haven, Conn. Yale University Library
New York.
       Columbia University of the City of New York
       Public Library
Notre Dame, Ind. Memorial Library, University of Notre Dame
Piscataway, N.J. Rutgers University Libraries
Princeton, N.J. Princeton University Libraries
Salt Lake City, Utah. Family History Library
San Marino, Calif. Henry E. Huntington Library
Santa Barbara, Calif. University of California Library
South Hadley, Mass. Williston Memorial Library, Mount Holyoke College
Stanford, Calif. Green Library, Stanford University
Tucson, Ariz. University of Arizona Library
Urbana, Ill. University of Illinois Library
Washington. The Folger Shakespeare Library
Winston-Salem, N.C. Z.Smith Reynolds Library, Wake Forest University

LIST OF PUBLICATIONS

The Wiltshire Record Society was founded in 1937, as the Records Branch of the Wiltshire Archaeological and Natural History Society, to promote the publication of the documentary sources for the history of Wiltshire. The annual subscription is £15 for private and institutional members. In return, a member receives a volume each year. Prospective members should apply to the Hon. Secretary, c/o Wiltshire Record Office, County Hall, Trowbridge, Wilts BA14 8JG. Many more members are needed.

The following volumes have been published. Price to members £15, and to non-members £20, postage extra. Available from the Hon. Treasurer, Mr M.J. Lansdown, 53 Clarendon Road, Trowbridge, Wilts BA14 7BS.

1. *Abstracts of feet of fines relating to Wiltshire for the reigns of Edward I and Edward II,* edited by R.B. Pugh, 1939
2. *Accounts of the parliamentary garrisons of Great Chalfield and Malmesbury, 1645-1646,* edited by J.H.P. Pafford, 1940
3. *Calendar of Antrobus deeds before 1625,* edited by R.B. Pugh, 1947
4. *Wiltshire county records: minutes of proceedings in sessions, 1563 and 1574 to 1592,* edited by H.C. Johnson, 1949
5. *List of Wiltshire boroughs records earlier in date than 1836,* edited by M.G. Rathbone, 1951
6. *The Trowbridge woollen industry as illustrated by the stock books of John and Thomas Clark, 1804-1824,* edited by R.P. Beckinsale, 1951
7. *Guild stewards' book of the borough of Calne, 1561-1688,* edited by A.W. Mabbs, 1953
8. *Andrews' and Dury's map of Wiltshire, 1773: a reduced facsimile,* edited by Elizabeth Crittall, 1952
9. *Surveys of the manors of Philip, earl of Pembroke and Montgomery, 1631-2,* edited by E. Kerridge, 1953
10. *Two sixteenth century taxations lists, 1545 and 1576,* edited by G.D. Ramsay, 1954
11. *Wiltshire quarter sessions and assizes, 1736,* edited by J.P.M. Fowle, 1955
12. *Collectanea,* edited by N.J. Williams, 1956
13. *Progress notes of Warden Woodward for the Wiltshire estates of New College, Oxford, 1659-1675,* edited by R.L. Rickard, 1957
14. *Accounts and surveys of the Wiltshire lands of Adam de Stratton,* edited by M.W. Farr, 1959
15. *Tradesmen in early-Stuart Wiltshire: a miscellany,* edited by N.J. Williams, 1960
16. *Crown pleas of the Wiltshire eyre, 1249,* edited by C.A.F. Meekings, 1961
17. *Wiltshire apprentices and their masters, 1710-1760,* edited by Christabel Dale, 1961
18. *Hemingby's register,* edited by Helena M. Chew, 1963
19. *Documents illustrating the Wiltshire textile trades in the eighteenth century,* edited by Julia de L. Mann, 1964
20. *The diary of Thomas Naish,* edited by Doreen Slatter, 1965
21-2. *The rolls of Highworth hundred, 1275-1287, 2 parts,* edited by Brenda Farr, 1966, 1968
23. *The earl of Hertford's lieutenancy papers, 1603-1612,* edited by W.P.D. Murphy, 1969
24. *Court rolls of the Wiltshire manors of Adam de Stratton,* edited by R.B. Pugh, 1970
25. *Abstracts of Wiltshire inclosure awards and agreements,* edited by R.E. Sandell, 1971
26. *Civil pleas of the Wiltshire eyre, 1249,* edited by M.T. Clanchy, 1971
27. *Wiltshire returns to the bishop's visitation queries, 1783,* edited by Mary Ransome, 1972
28. *Wiltshire extents for debts, Edward I - Elizabeth I,* edited by Angela Conyers, 1973

29. *Abstracts of feet of fines relating to Wiltshire for the reign of Edward III,* edited by C.R. Elrington, 1974

30. *Abstracts of Wiltshire tithe apportionments,* edited by R.E. Sandell, 1975

31. *Poverty in early-Stuart Salisbury,* edited by Paul Slack, 1975

32. *The subscription book of Bishops Tounson and Davenant, 1620-40,* edited by B. Williams, 1977

33. *Wiltshire gaol delivery and trailbaston trials, 1275-1306,* edited by R.B. Pugh, 1978

34. *Lacock abbey charters,* edited by K.H. Rogers, 1979

35. *The cartulary of Bradenstoke priory,* edited by Vera C.M. London, 1979

36. *Wiltshire coroners' bills, 1752-1796,* edited by R.F. Hunnisett, 1981

37. *The justicing notebook of William Hunt, 1744-1749,* edited by Elizabeth Crittall, 1982

38. *Two Elizabethan women: correspondence of Joan and Maria Thynne, 1575-1611,* edited by Alison D. Wall, 1983

39. *The register of John Chandler, dean of Salisbury, 1404-17,* edited by T.C.B. Timmins, 1984

40. *Wiltshire dissenters' meeting house certificates and registrations, 1689-1852,* edited by J.H. Chandler, 1985

41. *Abstracts of feet of fines relating to Wiltshire, 1377-1509,* edited by J.L. Kirby, 1986

42. *The Edington cartulary,* edited by Janet H. Stevenson, 1987

43. *The commonplace book of Sir Edward Bayntun of Bromham,* edited by Jane Freeman, 1988

44. *The diaries of Jeffery Whitaker, schoolmaster of Bratton, 1739-1741,* edited by Marjorie Reeves and Jean Morrison, 1989

45. *The Wiltshire tax list of 1332,* edited by D.A. Crowley, 1989

46. *Calendar of Bradford-on-Avon settlement examinations and removal orders, 1725-98,* edited by Phyllis Hembry, 1990

47. *Early trade directories of Wiltshire,* edited by K.H. Rogers and indexed by J.H. Chandler, 1992

48. *Star chamber suits of John and Thomas Warneford,* edited by F.E. Warneford, 1993

49. *The Hungerford cartulary: a calendar of the earl of Radnor's cartulary of the Hungerford family,* edited by J.L. Kirby, 1994

50. *The Letters of John Peniston, Salisbury architect, Catholic, and Yeomanry Officer, 1823-1830,* edited by M. Cowan, 1996

VOLUMES IN PREPARATION

Crown pleas of the Wiltshire eyre, 1268, edited by Brenda Farr; *Wiltshire papist returns and estate enrolments, 1705-87,* edited by J.A. Williams; *Salisbury city ledger A,* edited by D.R. Carr; *Wiltshire visitation returns, 1864,* edited by D.A. Crowley and Jane Freeman; *Wiltshire glebe terriers,* edited by S.D. Hobbs and Susan Avery; *The Hungerford cartulary, vol.2: the Hobhouse cartulary,* edited by J.L. Kirby; *The Parish registers of Thomas Crockford, 1613-29,* edited by C.C. Newbury; *Marlborough probate inventories,* edited by Lorelei Williams. The volumes will not necessarily appear in this order.

A leaflet giving full details may be obtained from the Hon. Secretary, c/o Wiltshire Record Office, County Hall, Trowbridge, Wilts. BA14 8JG.±